Charles Soule
Writer-In-Chief

Alberto J. Alburquerque
Executive Artist

Dan Jackson
Executive Colorist

Shawn DePasquale
Chief of Letters

Guy Major
Executive Colorist

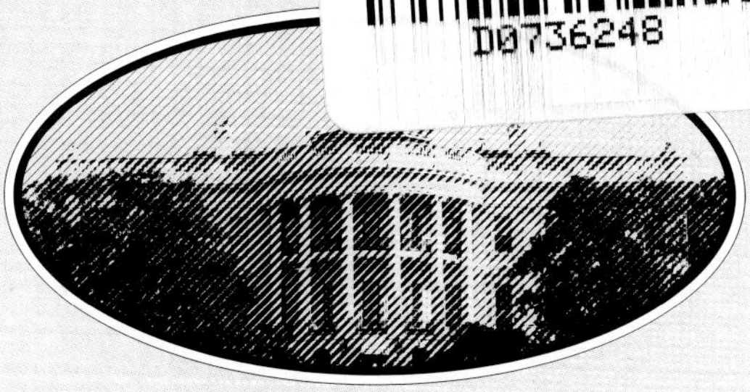

THE WHITE HOUSE

1600 PENNSYLVANIA AVE NW, WASHINGTON, DC 20500

FROM THE DESK OF THE 44TH PRESIDENT, STEPHEN HENRY BLADES

TO THE MEN AND WOMEN OF THE CLARKE:

I have never met you[redacted]er will. Even now, as my administration has only just begun, I am certain that this fact will remain, to me, one of the great tragedies of my Presidency. The service you have offered this nation-[redacted]is, quite simply and with no hyperbole intended, unparalleled in human history.

All of you chose to leave everything familiar behind, to voyage out [redacted]. Your rewards are uncertain at best-knowledge, certainly, but there will most likely be no [redacted]. But I will use every power of my office to make certain that your sacrifice is not forgotten. In time, your names will be included amongst the other great explorers of human history.

We do not know the intentions [redacted] at the end of your journey. You will be tasked with making [redacted]I envy you the opportunity. For thousands of years, humankind has looked up and wondered about the possibility [redacted]. You will be the very first to know the truth.

It may seem that you are alone-cut off from the rest of the human race, [redacted] from home, your mission secret. Nothing could be further from the truth. You are not alone. You are never far from my mind. This offer may seem hollow, but if there is anything I can do for you, for your families and friends [redacted], you have but to ask.

Be safe, and discover wonders.

Stephen Henry Blades
44th President of the United States of America

LETTER 44 VOLUME I: ESCAPE VELOCITY

WRITTEN BY
CHARLES SOULE

ILLUSTRATED BY
ALBERTO JIMÉNEZ ALBURQUERQUE

CHAPTERS 1-3 COLORED BY
GUY MAJOR

CHAPTERS 4-6 COLORED BY
DAN JACKSON

LETTERED BY
SHAWN DEPASQUALE

DESIGNED BY
JASON STOREY

ORIGINAL SERIES EDITED BY
JILL BEATON

COLLECTION EDITED BY
ROBIN HERRERA

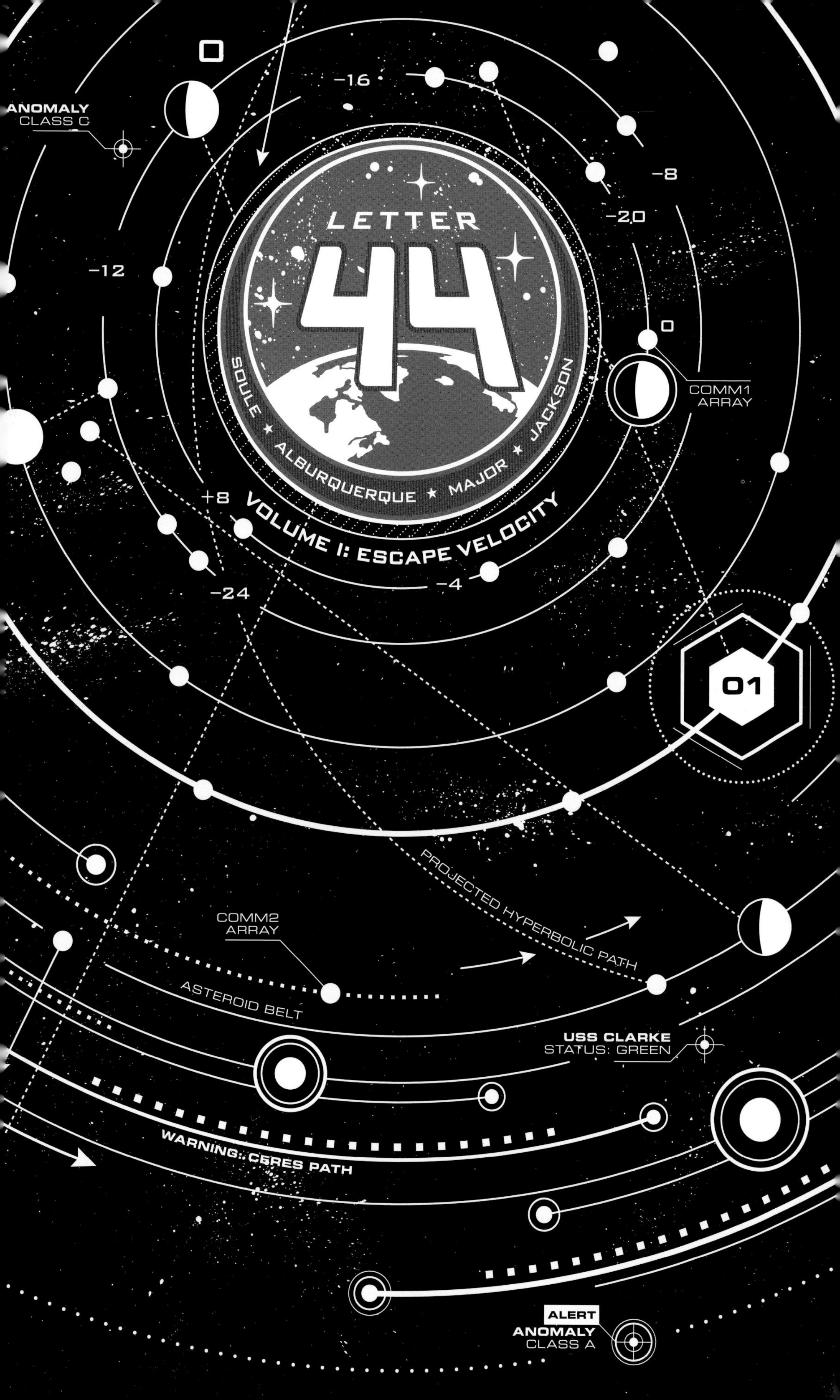

ANOMALY
CLASS C
-16
-8
-20
-12
LETTER
44
SOULE ★ ALBURQUERQUE ★ MAJOR ★ JACKSON
VOLUME I: ESCAPE VELOCITY
0
0
COMM1
ARRAY
+8
-4
-24
01
PROJECTED HYPERBOLIC PATH
COMM2
ARRAY
ASTEROID BELT
USS CLARKE
STATUS: GREEN
WARNING: CERES PATH
ALERT
ANOMALY
CLASS A

LETTER 44

THIS VOLUME COLLECTS ISSUES 1-6 OF THE ONI PRESS SERIES *LETTER 44*

Oni Press, Inc.

Publisher /// **Joe Nozemack**
Editor In Chief /// **James Lucas Jones**
Director of Sales /// **Cheyenne Allott**
Director of Publicity /// **John Schork**
Editor /// **Charlie Chu**
Associate Editor /// **Robin Herrera**
Production Manager /// **Troy Look**
Senior Designer /// **Jason Storey**
Inventory Coordinator /// **Brad Rooks**
Administrative Assistant /// **Ari Yarwood**
Office Assistant /// **Jung Lee**
Production Assistant /// **Jared Jones**

1305 SE Martin Luther King Jr. Blvd.
Suite A
Portland, OR 97214

onipress.com
facebook.com/onipress | twitter.com/onipress | onipress.tumblr.com

charlessoule.com | @charlessoule
ajaalbertojimenezalburquerque.blogspot.com

FIRST EDITION: JULY 2014

ISBN: 978-1-62010-133-9 | eISBN: 978-1-62010-134-6

Library of Congress Control Number: 2014931101

10 9 8 7 6 5 4 3 2 1

Printed in China

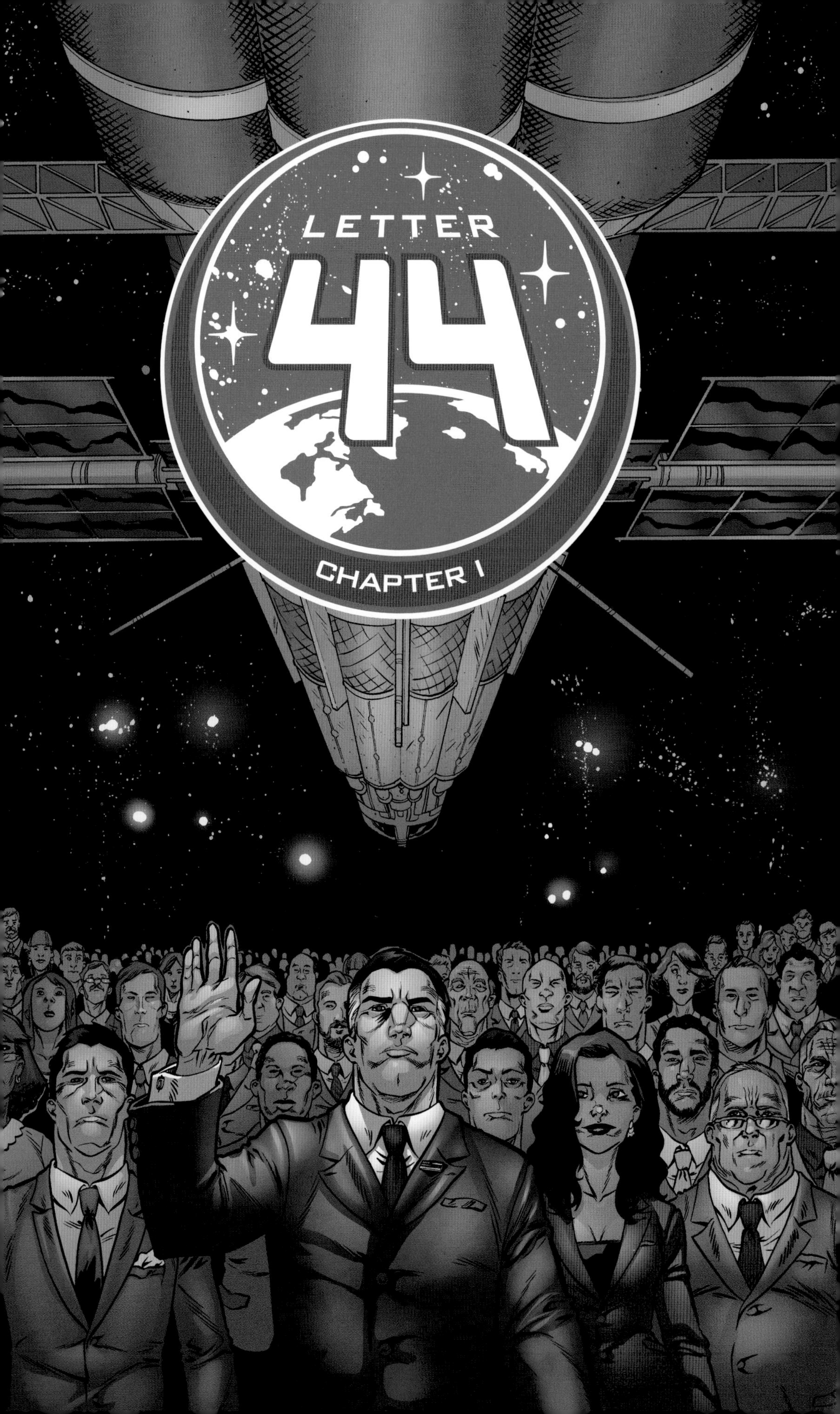
LETTER
44
CHAPTER I

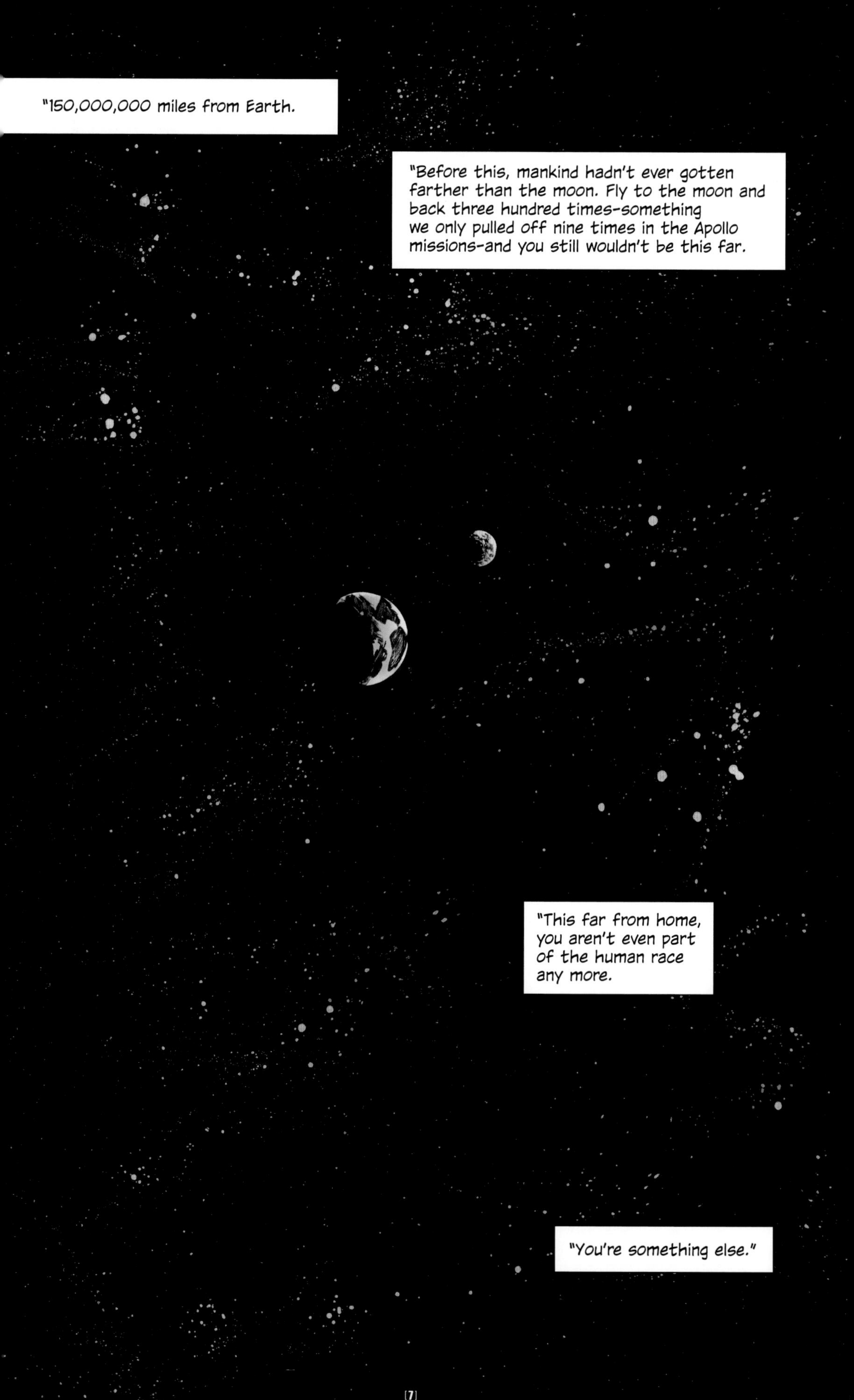
"150,000,000 miles from Earth.
"Before this, mankind hadn't ever gotten farther than the moon. Fly to the moon and back three hundred times-something we only pulled off nine times in the Apollo missions-and you still wouldn't be this far.
"This far from home, you aren't even part of the human race any more.
"You're something else."

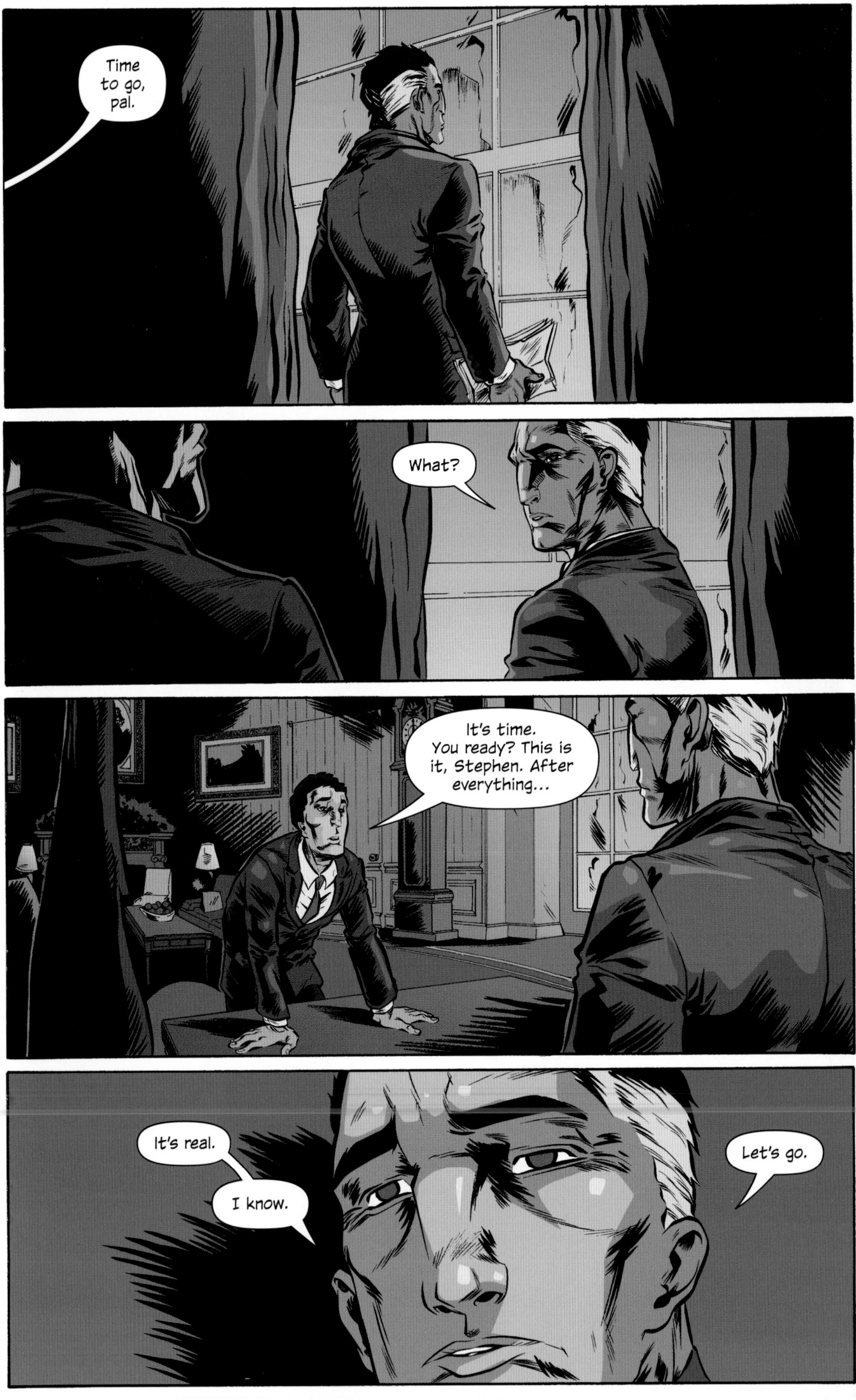
Time to go, pal.
What?
It's time. You ready? This is it, Stephen. After everything...
It's real.
I know.
Let's go.

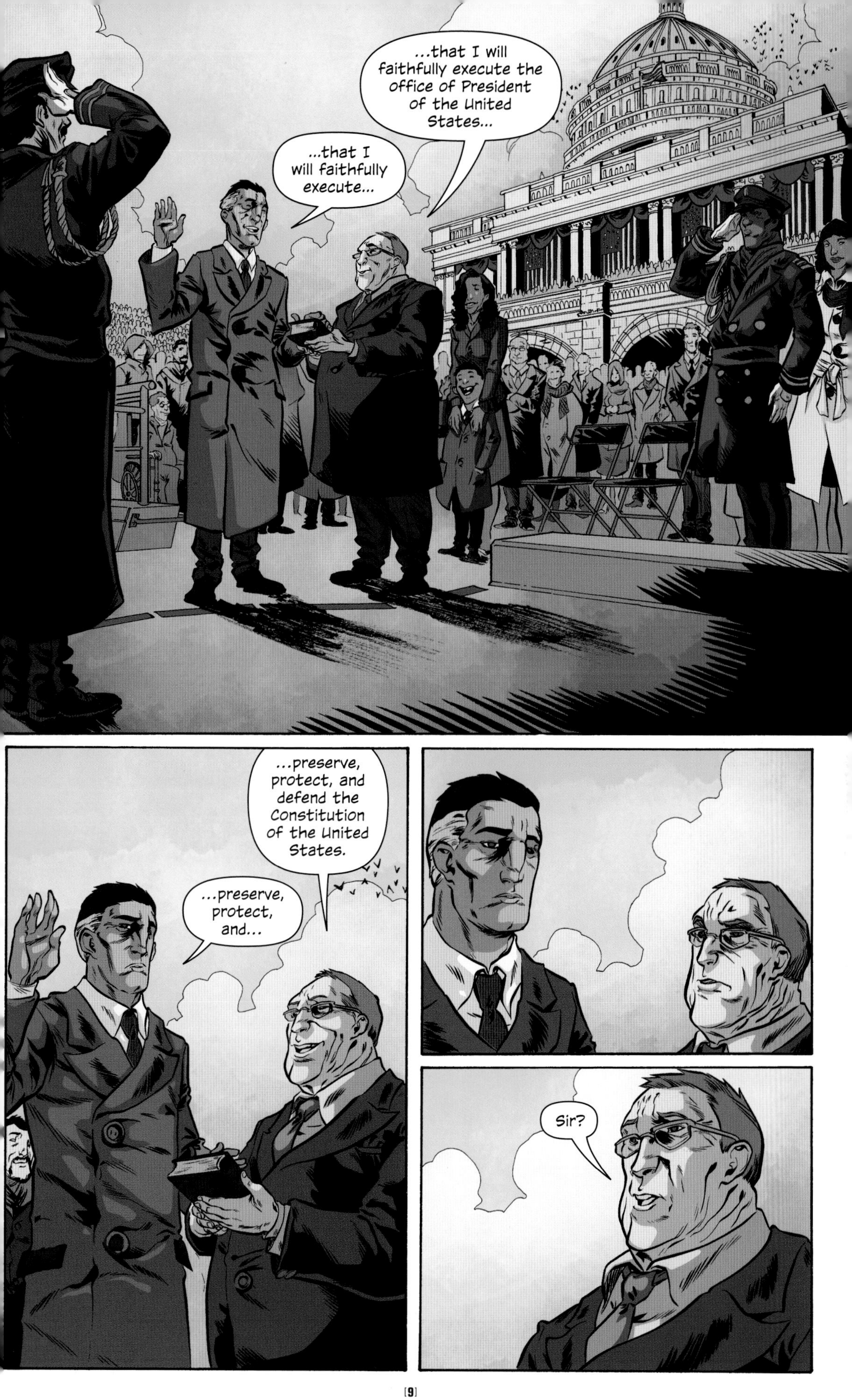
...that I will faithfully execute...
...that I will faithfully execute the office of President of the United States...
...preserve, protect, and...
...preserve, protect, and defend the Constitution of the United States.
Sir?

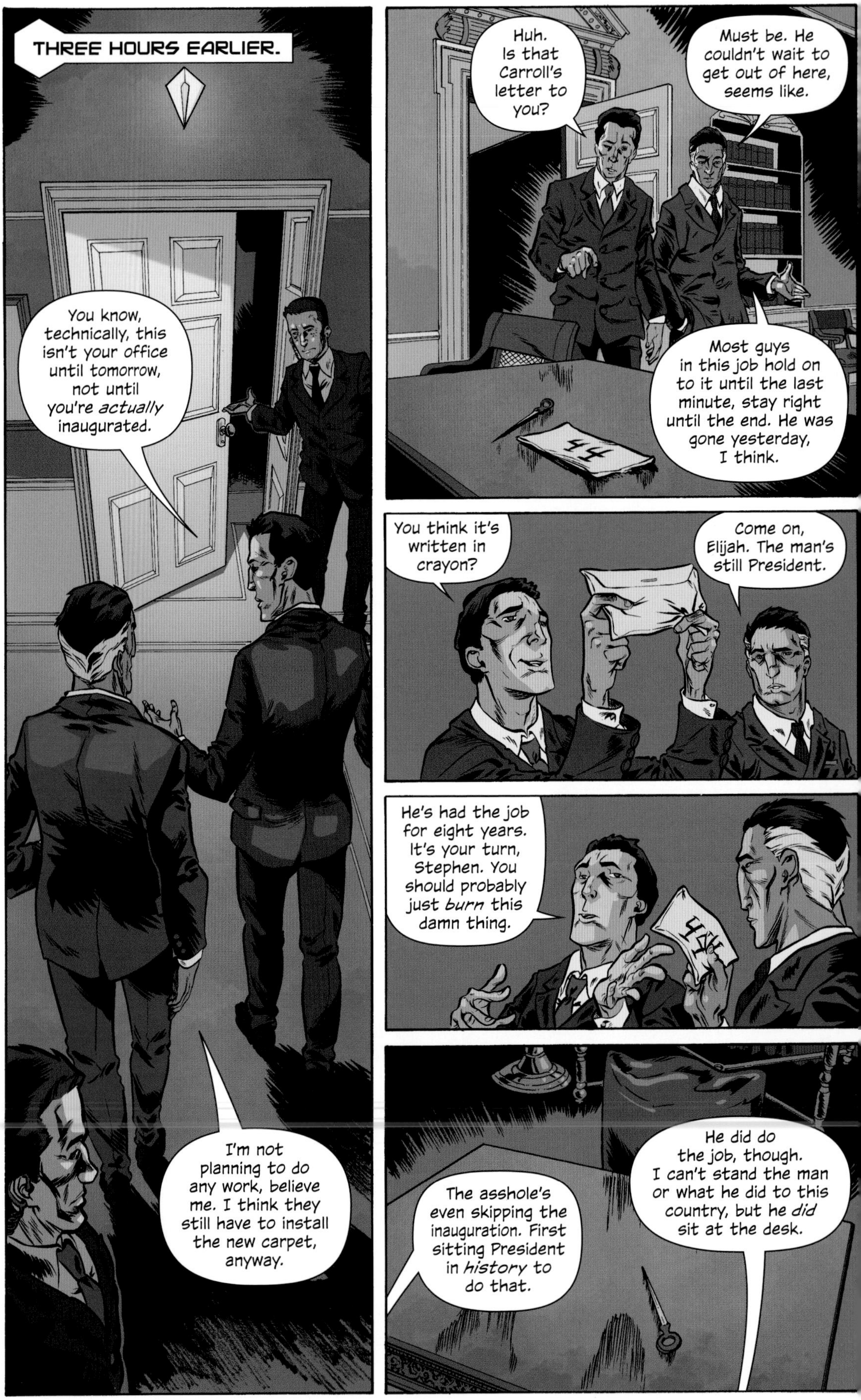
THREE HOURS EARLIER.
You know, technically, this isn't your office until tomorrow, not until you're *actually* inaugurated.
I'm not planning to do any work, believe me. I think they still have to install the new carpet, anyway.
Huh. Is that Carroll's letter to you?
Must be. He couldn't wait to get out of here, seems like.
Most guys in this job hold on to it until the last minute, stay right until the end. He was gone yesterday, I think.
44
You think it's written in crayon?
Come on, Elijah. The man's still President.
He's had the job for eight years. It's your turn, Stephen. You should probably just *burn* this damn thing.
44
The asshole's even skipping the inauguration. First sitting President in *history* to do that.
He did do the job, though. I can't stand the man or what he did to this country, but he *did* sit at the desk.

All right. I have some details to run down. You okay for a few minutes?

You've got like fifteen until we have to get to the Capitol Building.

Absolutely.

Go get everyone ready to make me President of the United States.

With the greatest of pleasure, sir.

Welcome to the job, son.

So you know, the next few days will be rough. Couple weeks of transition training doesn't really prepare you for being the Big Man in Charge — but you'll get through it.

We all do.

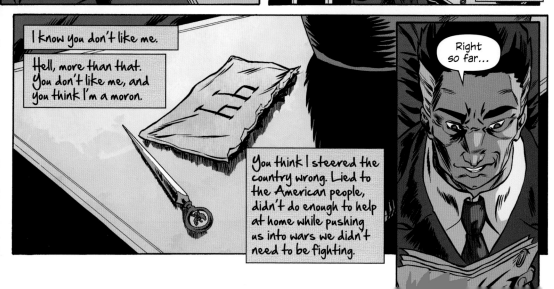

I know you don't like me.

Hell, more than that. You don't like me, and you think I'm a moron.

Right so far...

You think I steered the country wrong. Lied to the American people, didn't do enough to help at home while pushing us into wars we didn't need to be fighting.

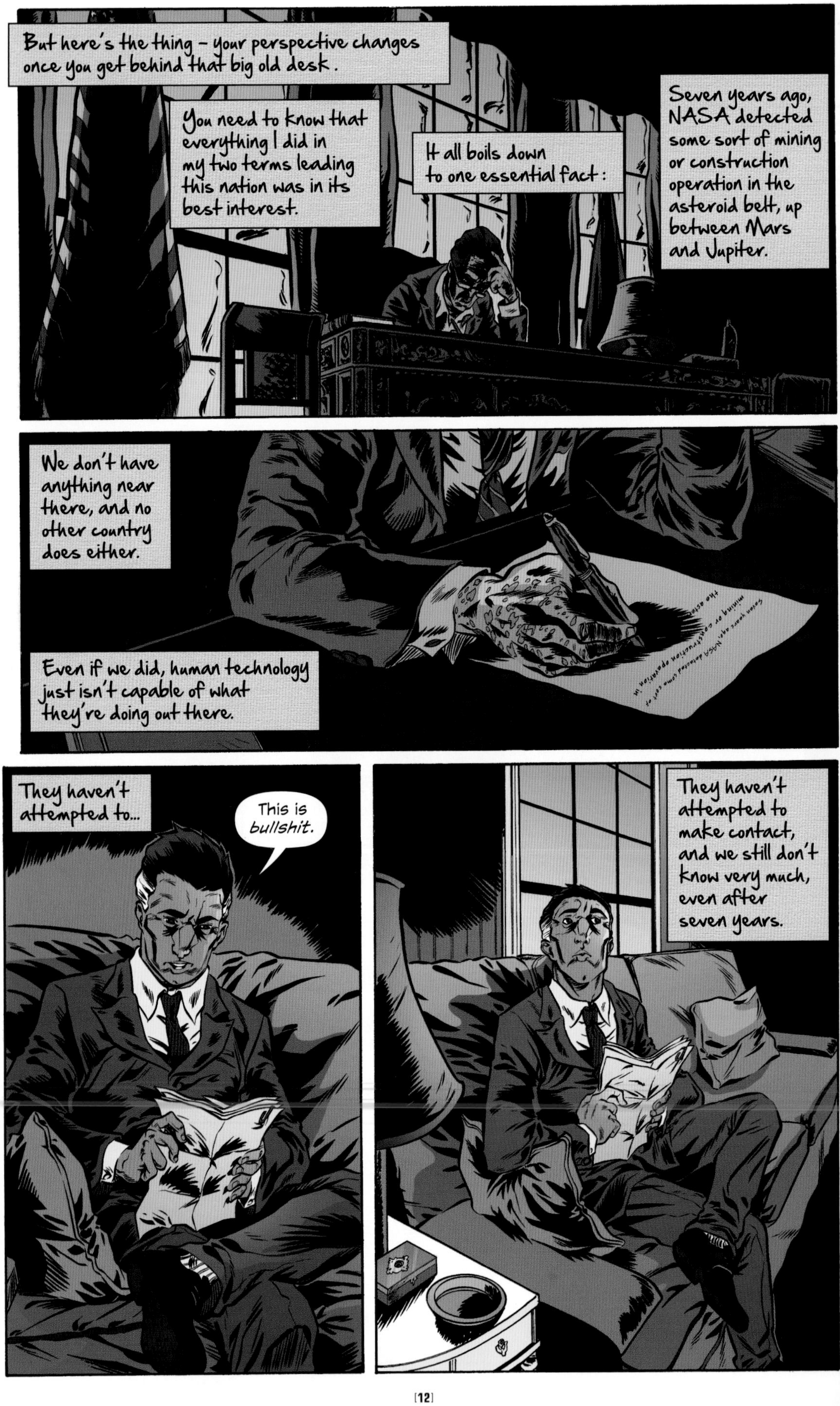
But here's the thing – your perspective changes once you get behind that big old desk.
You need to know that everything I did in my two terms leading this nation was in its best interest.
It all boils down to one essential fact:
Seven years ago, NASA detected some sort of mining or construction operation in the asteroid belt, up between Mars and Jupiter.
We don't have anything near there, and no other country does either.
Even if we did, human technology just isn't capable of what they're doing out there.
They haven't attempted to...
This is *bullshit.*
They haven't attempted to make contact, and we still don't know very much, even after seven years.

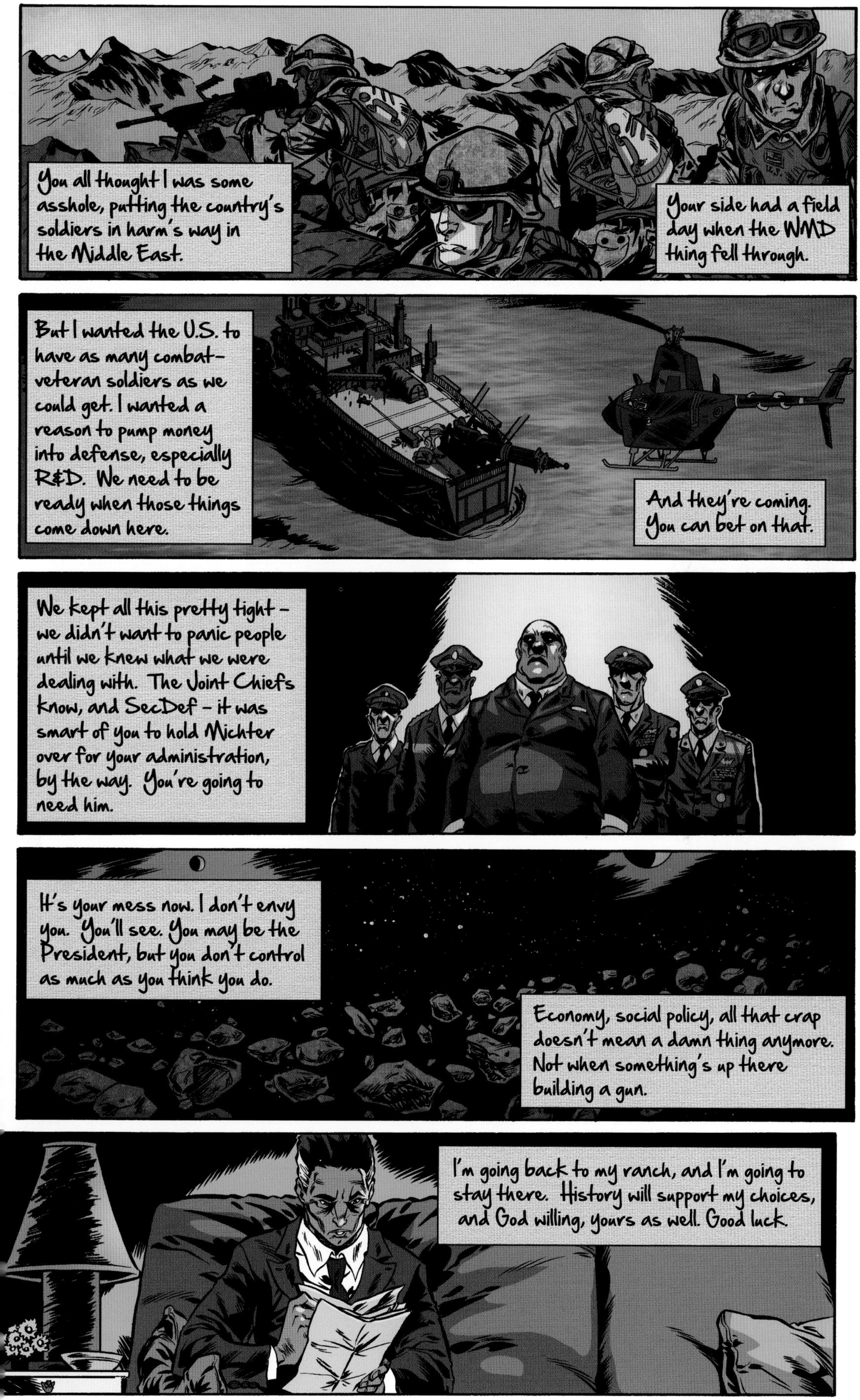
You all thought I was some asshole, putting the country's soldiers in harm's way in the Middle East.
Your side had a field day when the WMD thing fell through.
But I wanted the U.S. to have as many combat-veteran soldiers as we could get. I wanted a reason to pump money into defense, especially R&D. We need to be ready when those things come down here.
And they're coming. You can bet on that.
We kept all this pretty tight - we didn't want to panic people until we knew what we were dealing with. The Joint Chiefs know, and SecDef - it was smart of you to hold Michter over for your administration, by the way. You're going to need him.
It's your mess now. I don't envy you. You'll see. You may be the President, but you don't control as much as you think you do.
Economy, social policy, all that crap doesn't mean a damn thing anymore. Not when something's up there building a gun.
I'm going back to my ranch, and I'm going to stay there. History will support my choices, and God willing, yours as well. Good luck.

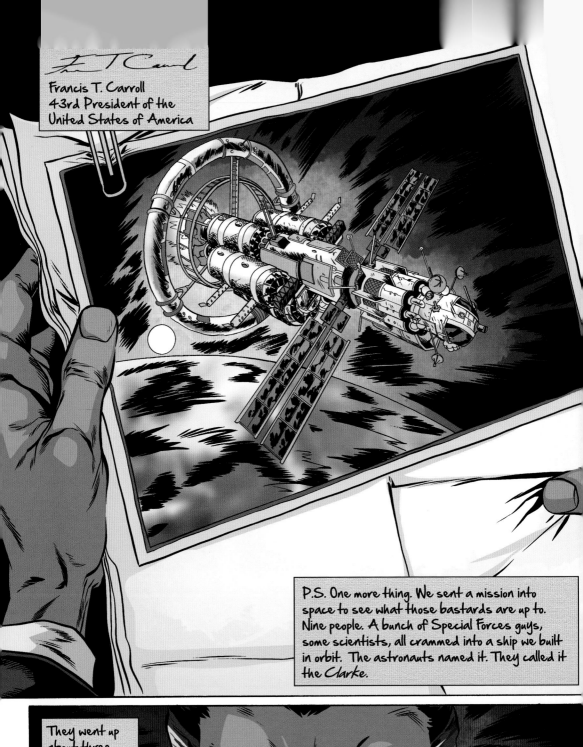

Francis T. Carroll
43rd President of the
United States of America

P.S. One more thing. We sent a mission into space to see what those bastards are up to. Nine people. A bunch of Special Forces guys, some scientists, all crammed into a ship we built in orbit. The astronauts named it. They called it the *Clarke*.

They went up about three years ago, and they're getting close. Heroes, every one.

Try to take care of them.

SOUTHERN INAUGURAL BALL.

NATIONAL GUARD ARMORY. 9:30 PM

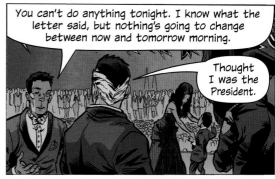

You can't do anything tonight. I know what the letter said, but nothing's going to change between now and tomorrow morning.

Thought I was the President.

You *are*, but the people who paid for you to become President need you to show up at their parties, especially if you want them to do it *again* for your second term.

Not even a day in office and we're already talking about the next election?

Phenomenal, Elijah. Fine. Tomorrow, though. First thing.

Where are you?

I'm here, Isobel. It's just been a... strange day.

I bet.

[15]

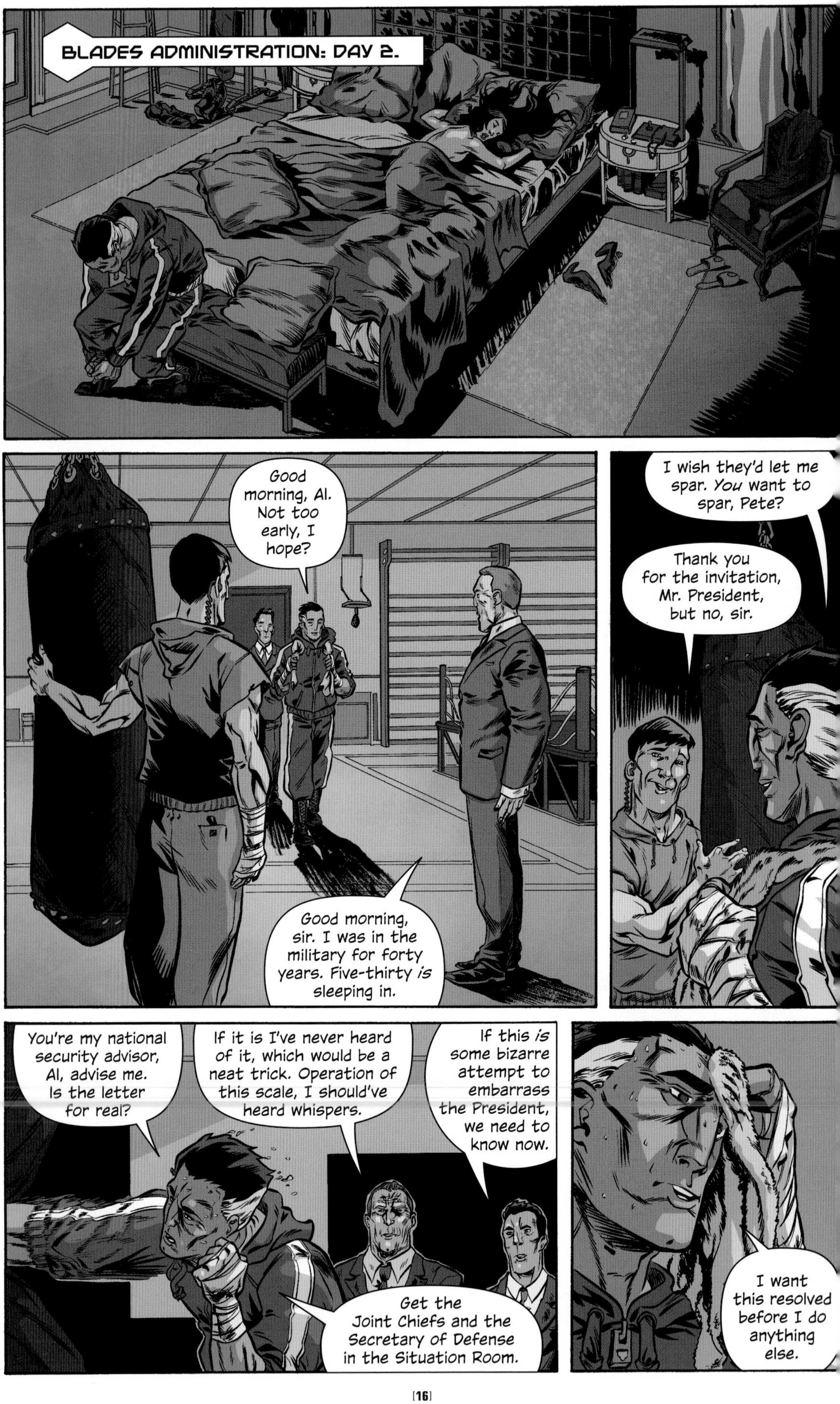
BLADES ADMINISTRATION: DAY 2.
Good morning, Al. Not too early, I hope?
Good morning, sir. I was in the military for forty years. Five-thirty *is* sleeping in.
I wish they'd let me spar. *You* want to spar, Pete?
Thank you for the invitation, Mr. President, but no, sir.
You're my national security advisor, Al, advise me. Is the letter for real?
If it is I've never heard of it, which would be a neat trick. Operation of this scale, I should've heard whispers.
If this *is* some bizarre attempt to embarrass the President, we need to know now.
Get the Joint Chiefs and the Secretary of Defense in the Situation Room.
I want this resolved before I do anything else.

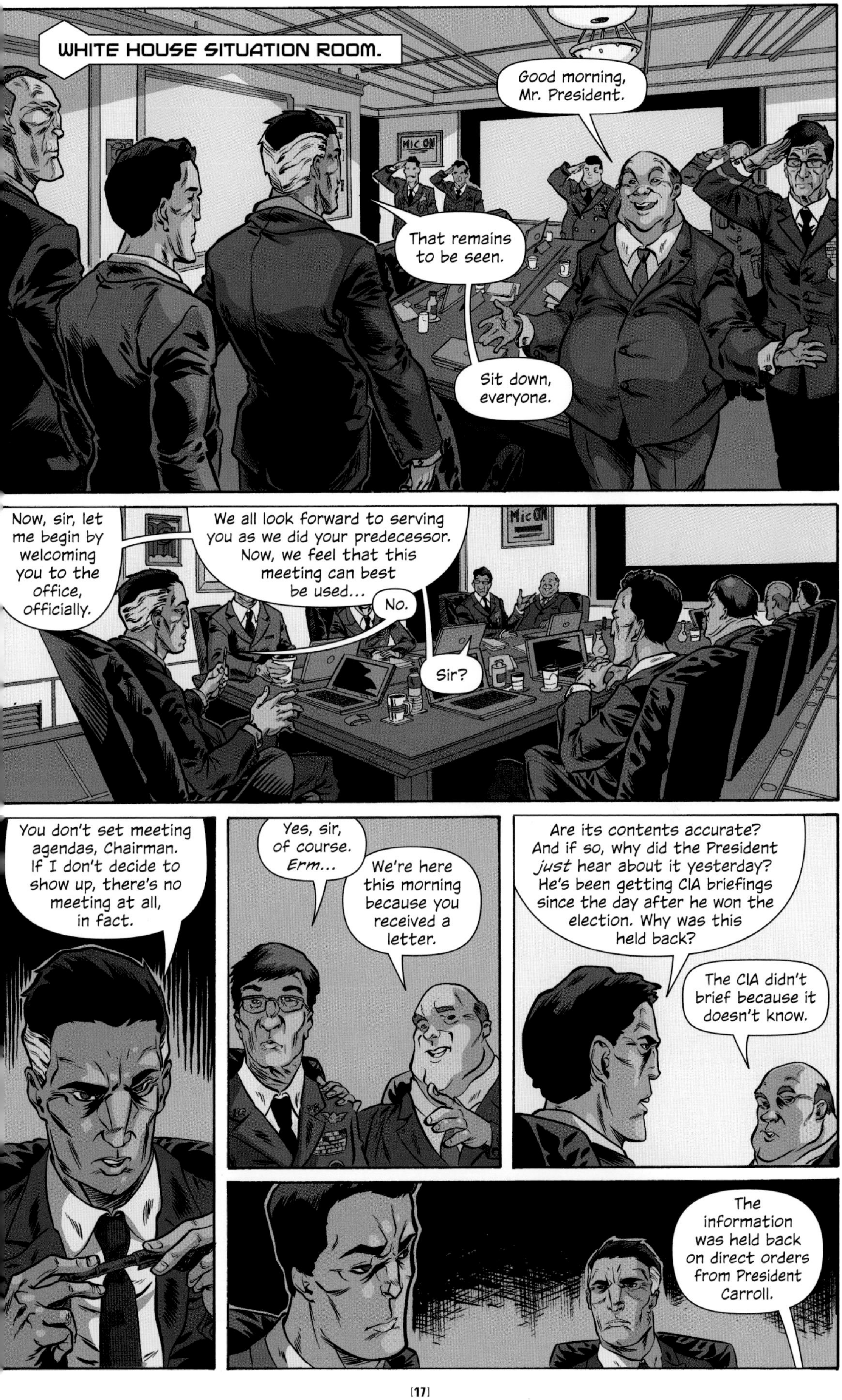
WHITE HOUSE SITUATION ROOM.
MIC ON
Good morning, Mr. President.
That remains to be seen.
Sit down, everyone.
Now, sir, let me begin by welcoming you to the office, officially.
We all look forward to serving you as we did your predecessor. Now, we feel that this meeting can best be used...
No.
Sir?
You don't set meeting agendas, Chairman. If I don't decide to show up, there's no meeting at all, in fact.
Yes, sir, of course. *Erm...*
We're here this morning because you received a letter.
Are its contents accurate? And if so, why did the President *just* hear about it yesterday? He's been getting CIA briefings since the day after he won the election. Why was this held back?
The CIA didn't brief because it doesn't know.
The information was held back on direct orders from President Carroll.

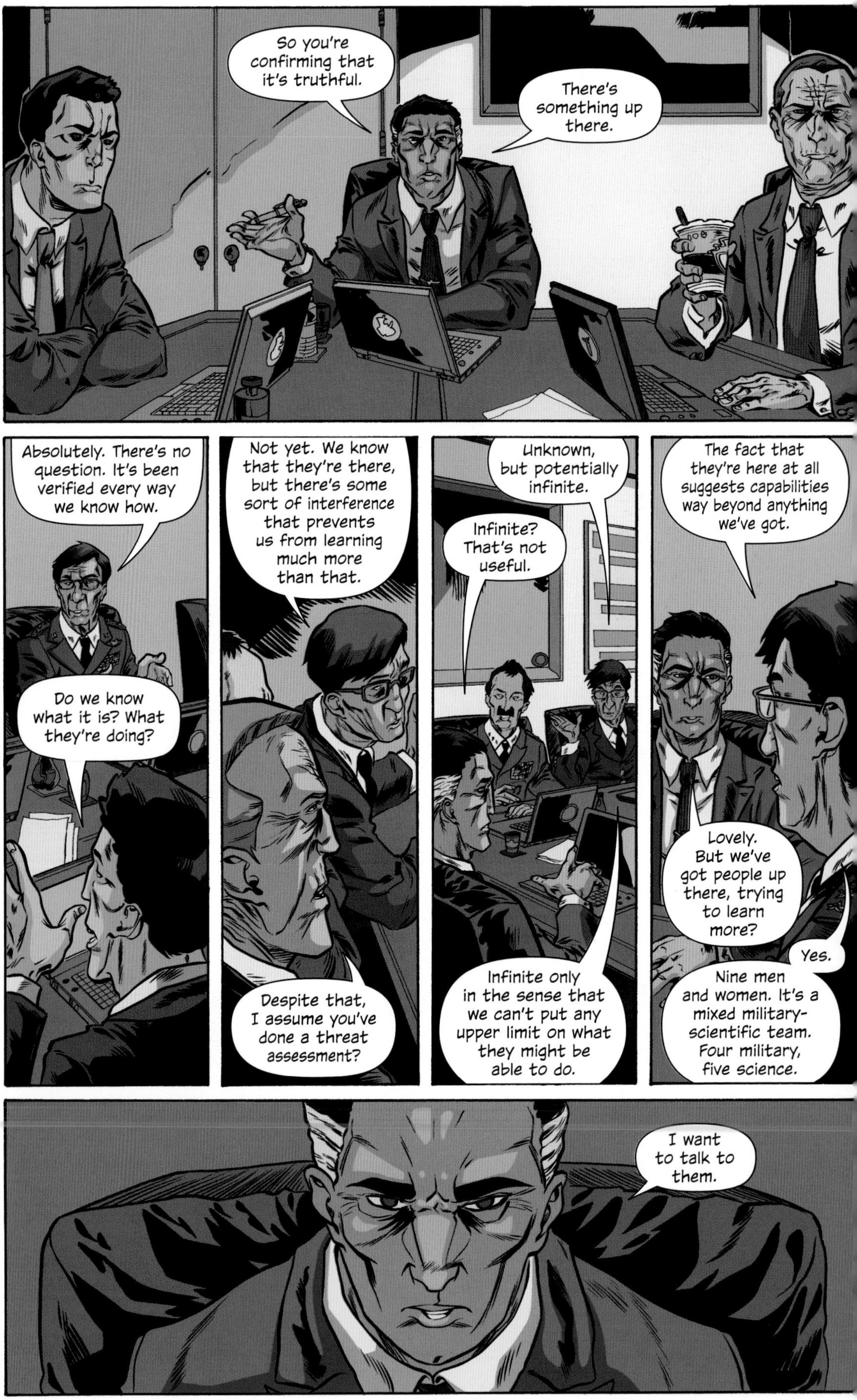

So you're confirming that it's truthful.
There's something up there.
Absolutely. There's no question. It's been verified every way we know how.
Do we know what it is? What they're doing?
Not yet. We know that they're there, but there's some sort of interference that prevents us from learning much more than that.
Despite that, I assume you've done a threat assessment?
Unknown, but potentially infinite.
Infinite? That's not useful.
Infinite only in the sense that we can't put any upper limit on what they might be able to do.
The fact that they're here at all suggests capabilities way beyond anything we've got.
Lovely. But we've got people up there, trying to learn more?
Yes.
Nine men and women. It's a mixed military-scientific team. Four military, five science.
I want to talk to them.

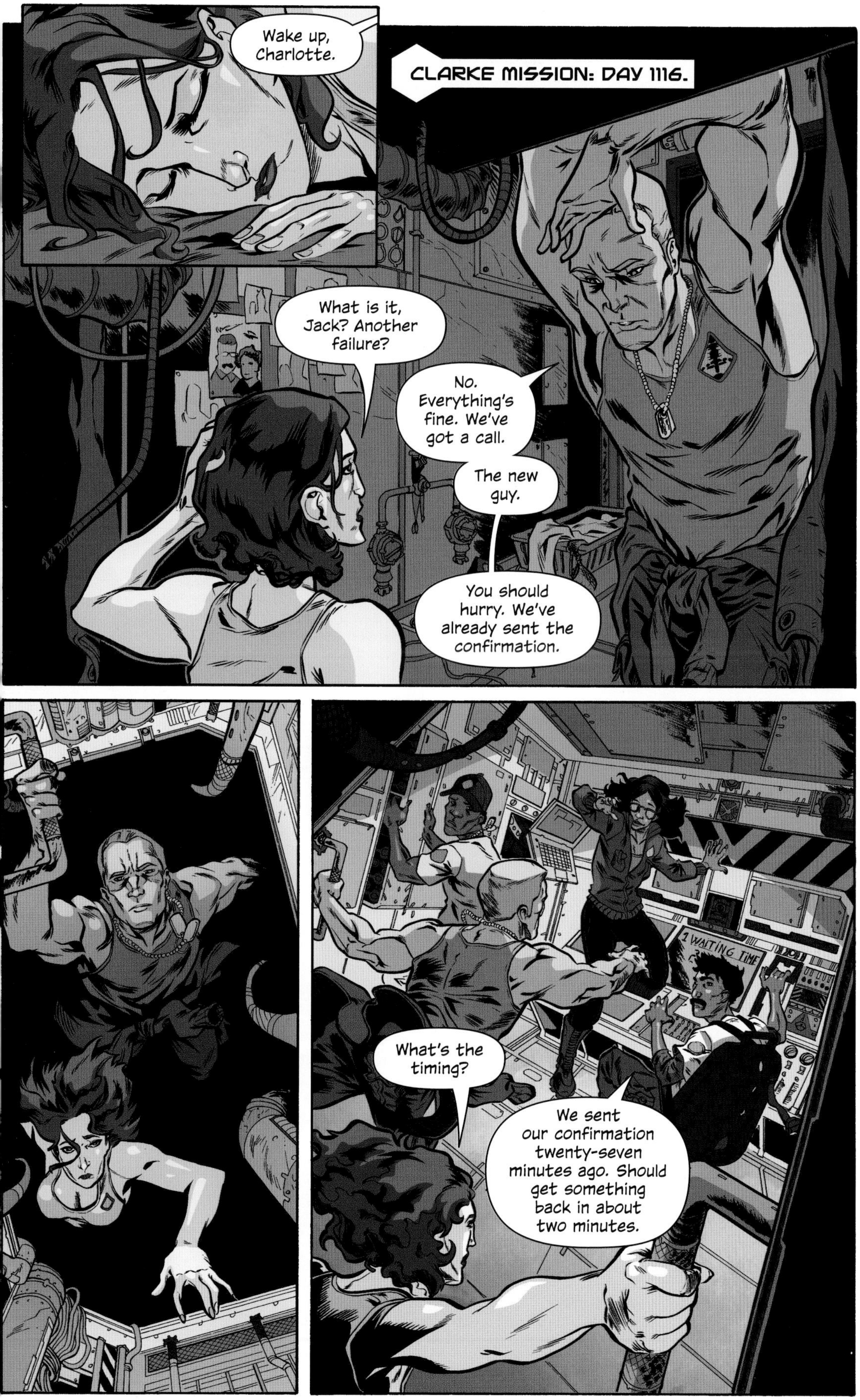
Wake up, Charlotte.
CLARKE MISSION: DAY 1116.
What is it, Jack? Another failure?
No. Everything's fine. We've got a call.
The new guy.
You should hurry. We've already sent the confirmation.
1 WAITING TIME
What's the timing?
We sent our confirmation twenty-seven minutes ago. Should get something back in about two minutes.

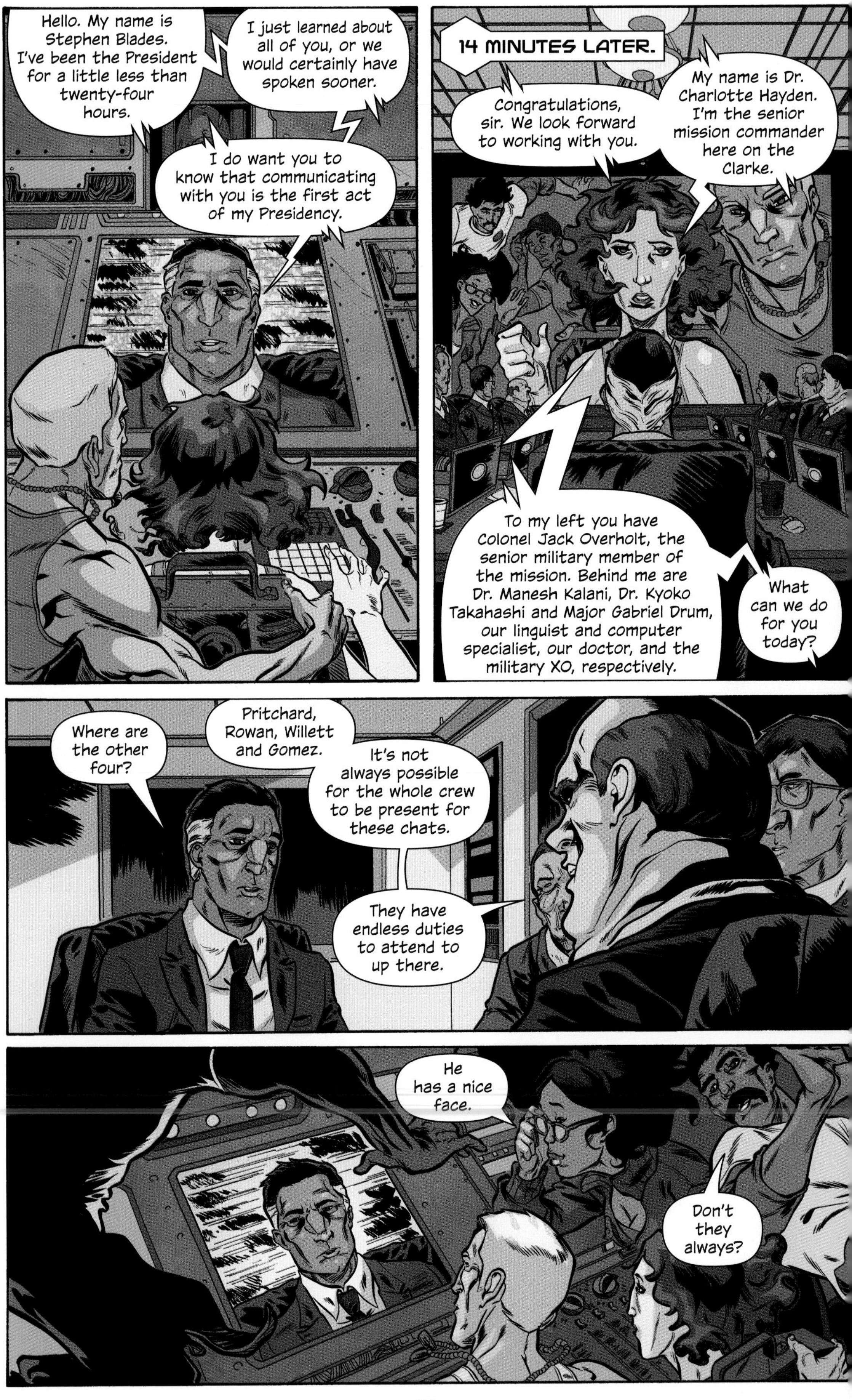

Hello. My name is Stephen Blades. I've been the President for a little less than twenty-four hours.
I just learned about all of you, or we would certainly have spoken sooner.
I do want you to know that communicating with you is the first act of my Presidency.
14 MINUTES LATER.
Congratulations, sir. We look forward to working with you.
My name is Dr. Charlotte Hayden. I'm the senior mission commander here on the Clarke.
To my left you have Colonel Jack Overholt, the senior military member of the mission. Behind me are Dr. Manesh Kalani, Dr. Kyoko Takahashi and Major Gabriel Drum, our linguist and computer specialist, our doctor, and the military XO, respectively.
What can we do for you today?
Where are the other four?
Pritchard, Rowan, Willett and Gomez.
It's not always possible for the whole crew to be present for these chats.
They have endless duties to attend to up there.
He has a nice face.
Don't they always?

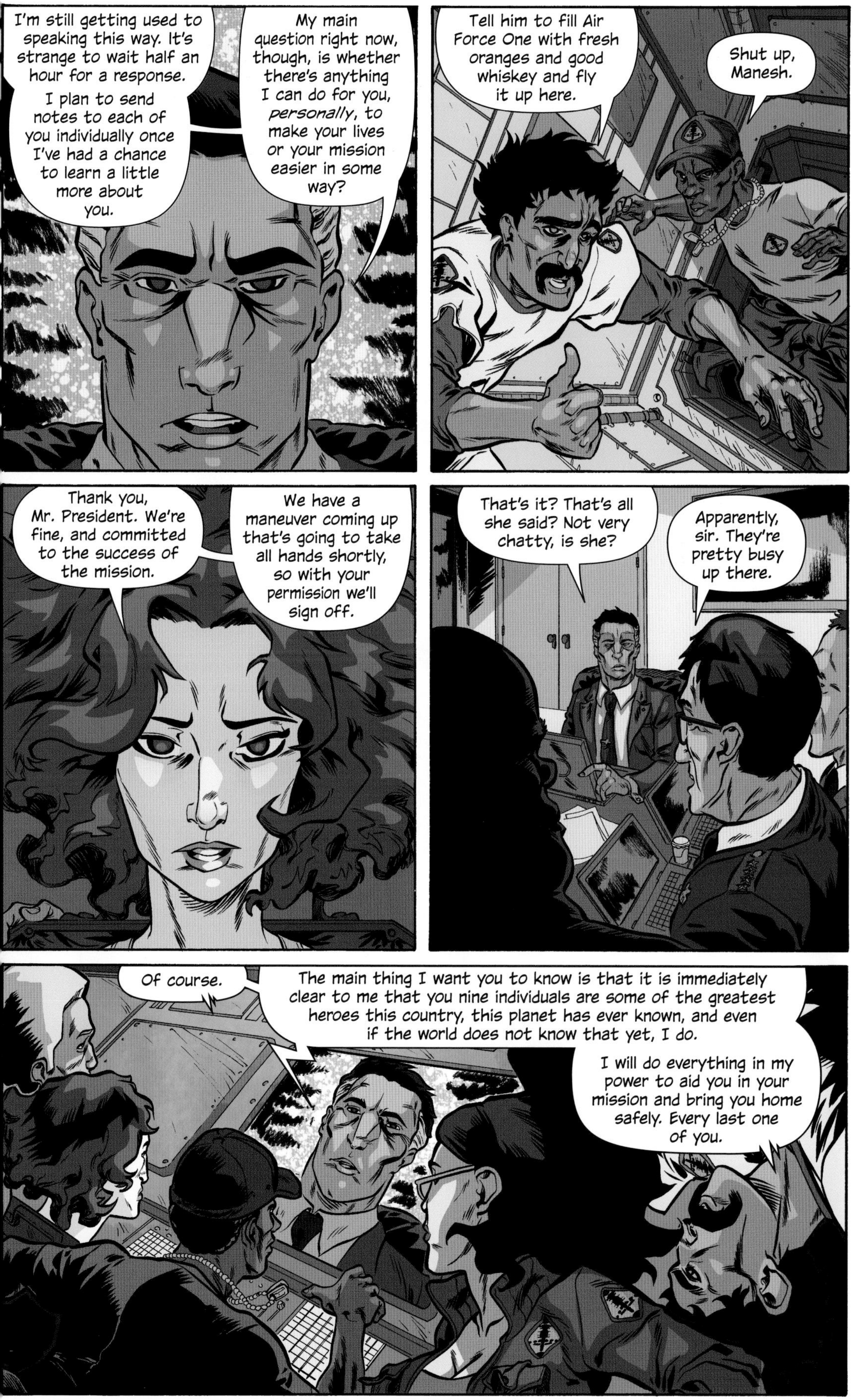
I'm still getting used to speaking this way. It's strange to wait half an hour for a response.
I plan to send notes to each of you individually once I've had a chance to learn a little more about you.
My main question right now, though, is whether there's anything I can do for you, *personally*, to make your lives or your mission easier in some way?
Tell him to fill Air Force One with fresh oranges and good whiskey and fly it up here.
Shut up, Manesh.
Thank you, Mr. President. We're fine, and committed to the success of the mission.
We have a maneuver coming up that's going to take all hands shortly, so with your permission we'll sign off.
That's it? That's all she said? Not very chatty, is she?
Apparently, sir. They're pretty busy up there.
Of course.
The main thing I want you to know is that it is immediately clear to me that you nine individuals are some of the greatest heroes this country, this planet has ever known, and even if the world does not know that yet, I do.
I will do everything in my power to aid you in your mission and bring you home safely. Every last one of you.

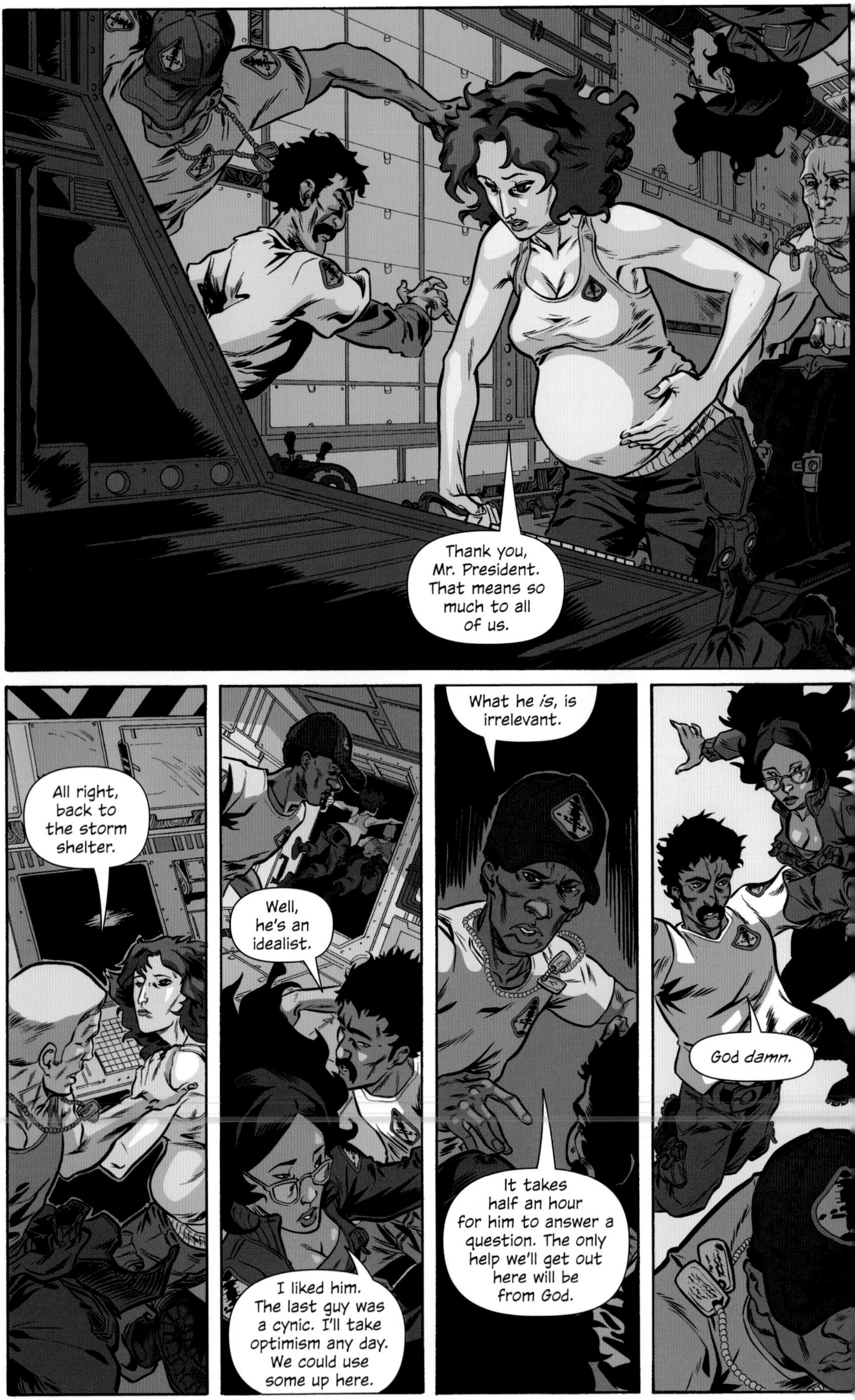
Thank you, Mr. President. That means so much to all of us.
All right, back to the storm shelter.
Well, he's an idealist.
I liked him. The last guy was a cynic. I'll take optimism any day. We could use some up here.
What he *is*, is irrelevant.
It takes half an hour for him to answer a question. The only help we'll get out here will be from God.
God damn.

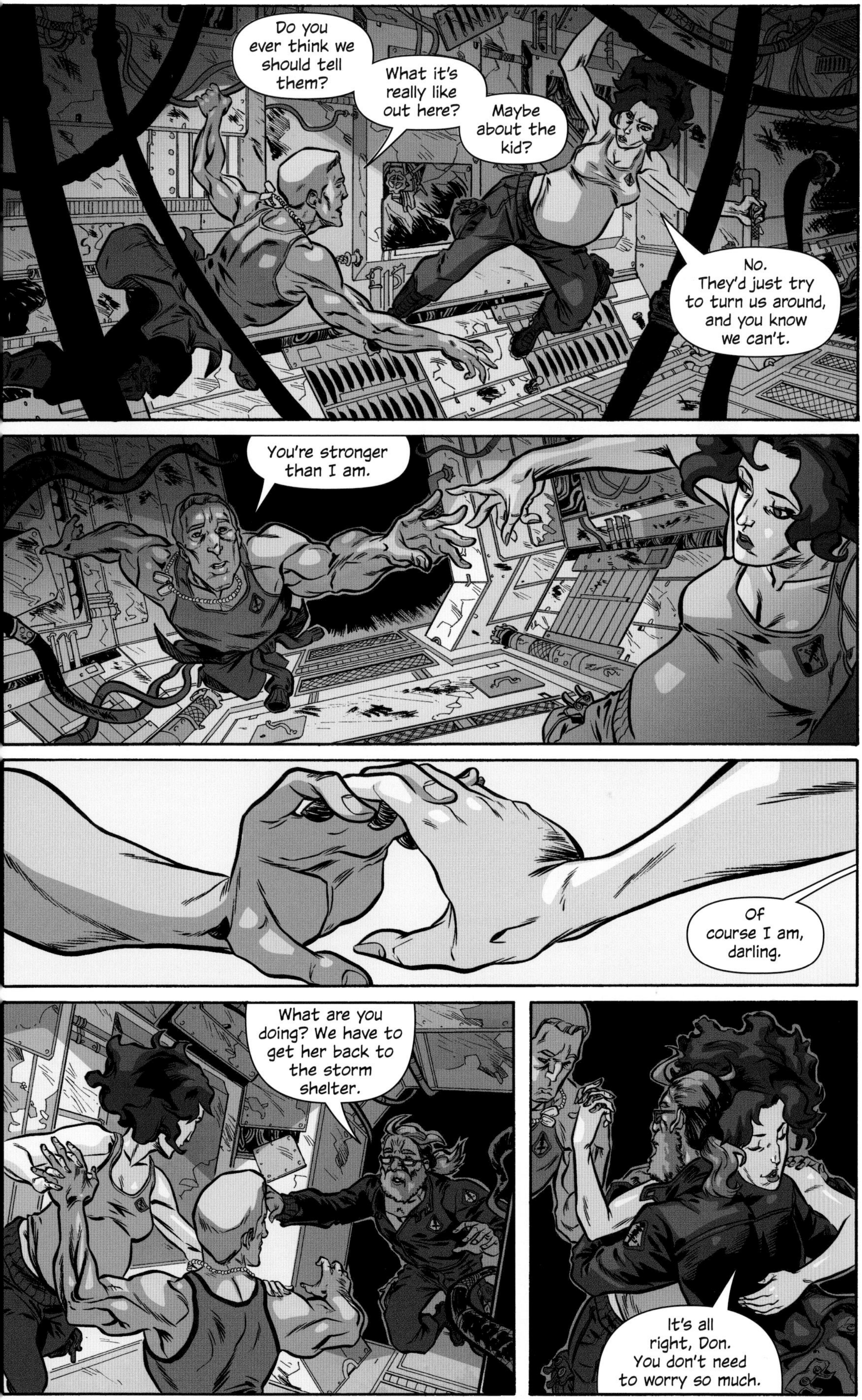
Do you ever think we should tell them?
What it's really like out here?
Maybe about the kid?
No. They'd just try to turn us around, and you know we can't.
You're stronger than I am.
Of course I am, darling.
What are you doing? We have to get her back to the storm shelter.
It's all right, Don. You don't need to worry so much.

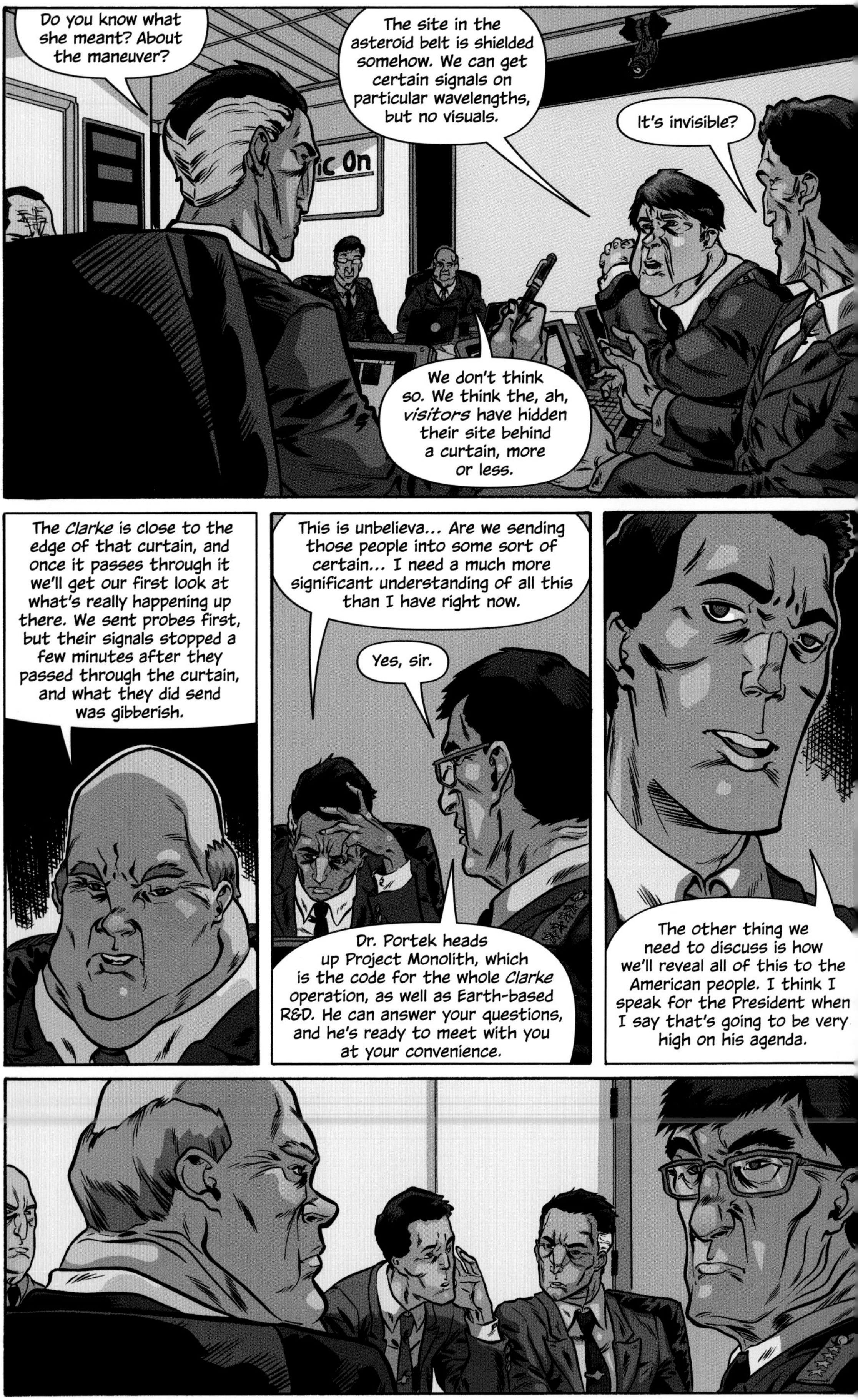
Do you know what she meant? About the maneuver?
The site in the asteroid belt is shielded somehow. We can get certain signals on particular wavelengths, but no visuals.
It's invisible?
We don't think so. We think the, ah, *visitors* have hidden their site behind a curtain, more or less.
The *Clarke* is close to the edge of that curtain, and once it passes through it we'll get our first look at what's really happening up there. We sent probes first, but their signals stopped a few minutes after they passed through the curtain, and what they did send was gibberish.
This is unbelieva... Are we sending those people into some sort of certain... I need a much more significant understanding of all this than I have right now.
Yes, sir.
Dr. Portek heads up Project Monolith, which is the code for the whole *Clarke* operation, as well as Earth-based R&D. He can answer your questions, and he's ready to meet with you at your convenience.
The other thing we need to discuss is how we'll reveal all of this to the American people. I think I speak for the President when I say that's going to be very high on his agenda.

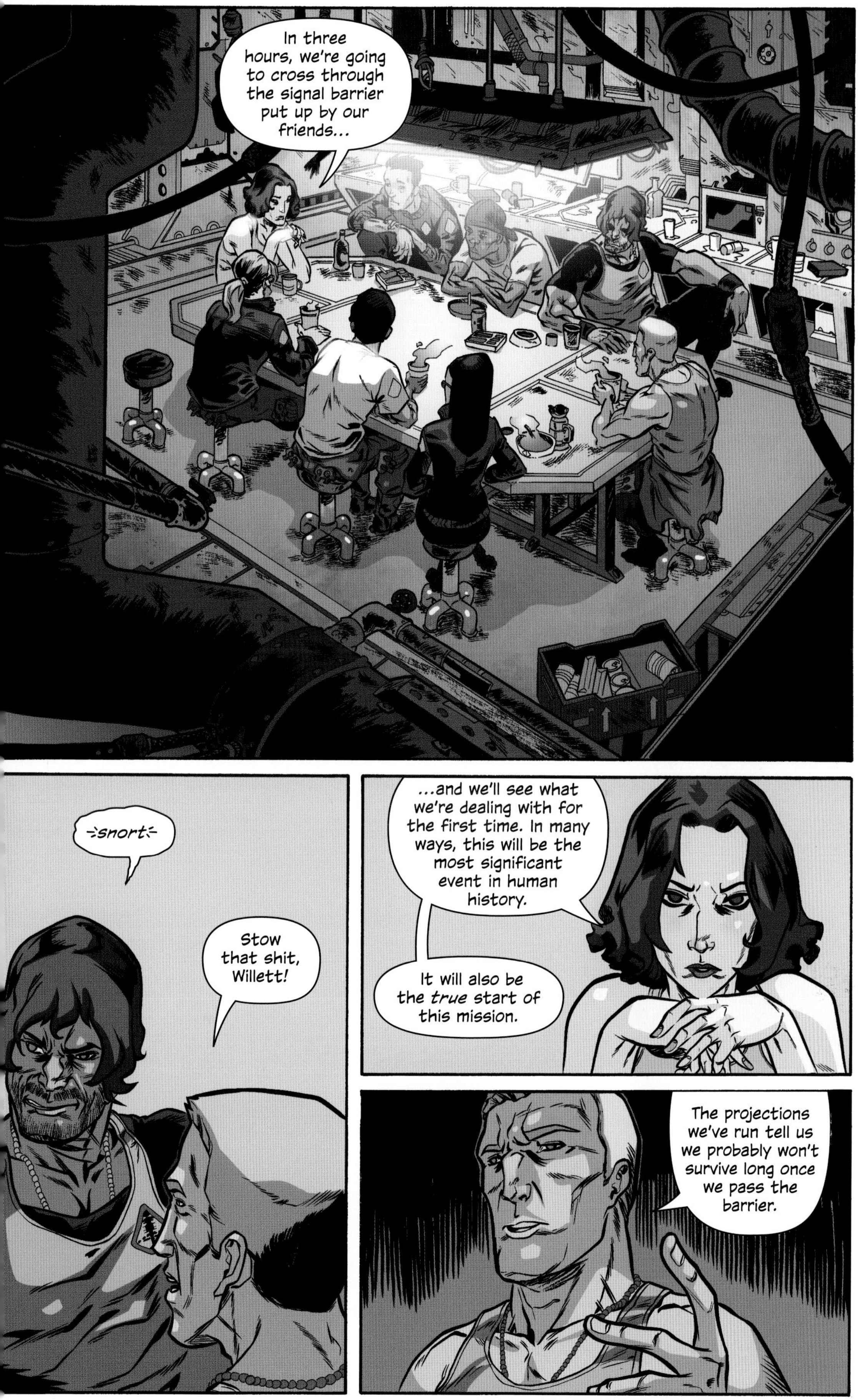

In three hours, we're going to cross through the signal barrier put up by our friends...
-snort-
Stow that shit, Willett!
...and we'll see what we're dealing with for the first time. In many ways, this will be the most significant event in human history.
It will also be the *true* start of this mission.
The projections we've run tell us we probably won't survive long once we pass the barrier.

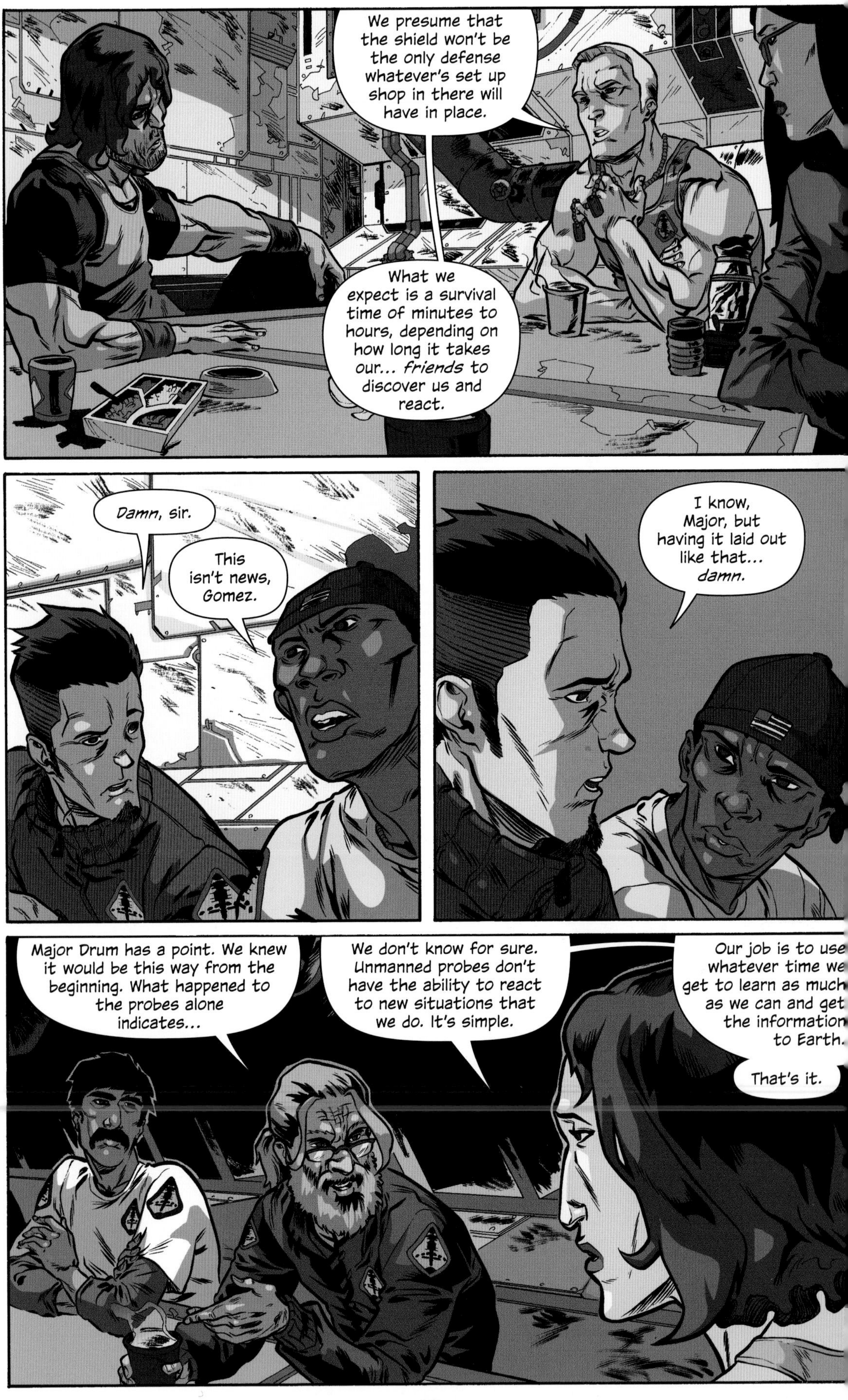
We presume that the shield won't be the only defense whatever's set up shop in there will have in place.
What we expect is a survival time of minutes to hours, depending on how long it takes our... *friends* to discover us and react.
Damn, sir.
This isn't news, Gomez.
I know, Major, but having it laid out like that... *damn.*
Major Drum has a point. We knew it would be this way from the beginning. What happened to the probes alone indicates...
We don't know for sure. Unmanned probes don't have the ability to react to new situations that we do. It's simple.
Our job is to use whatever time we get to learn as much as we can and get the information to Earth.
That's it.

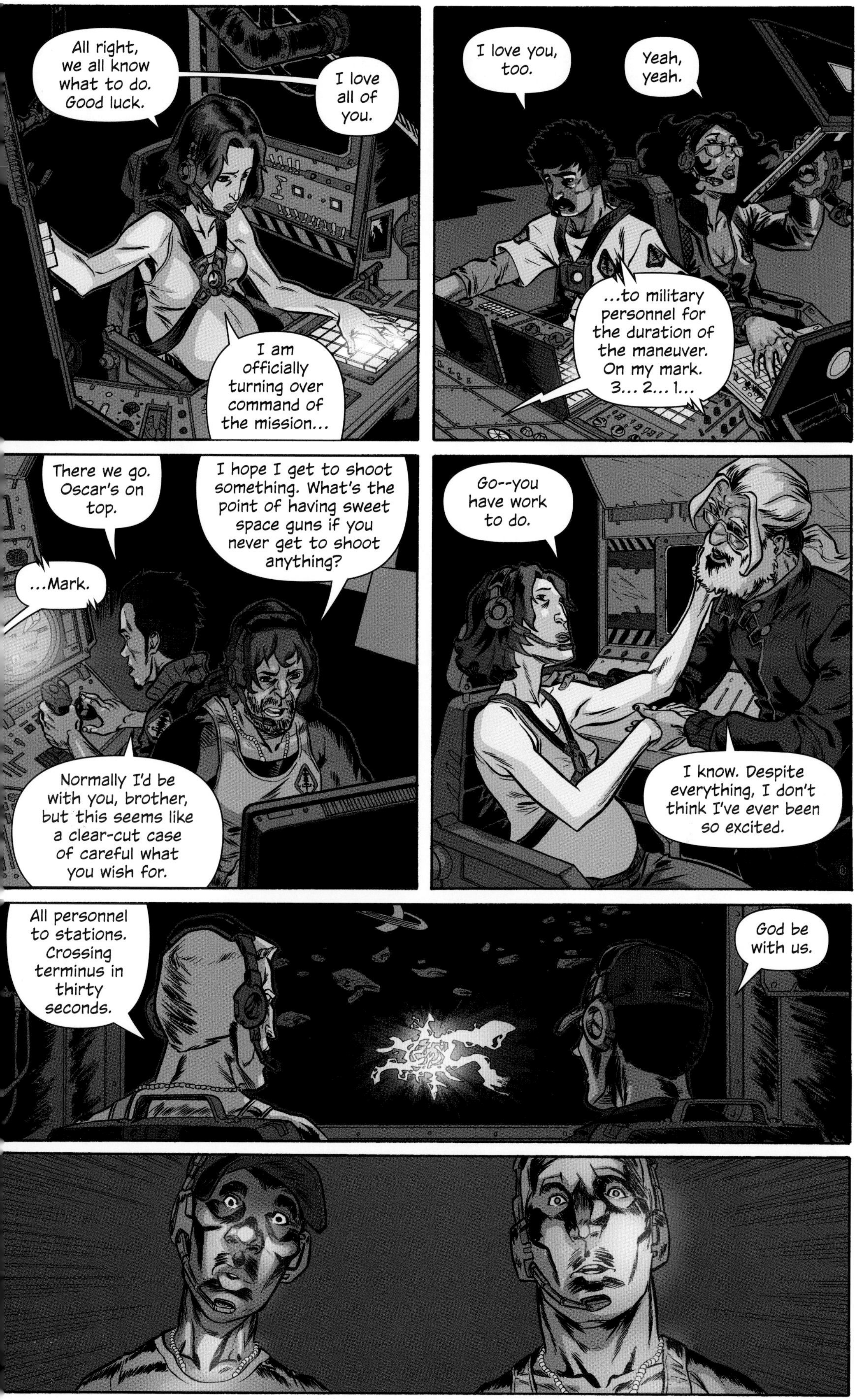
All right, we all know what to do. Good luck.
I love all of you.
I am officially turning over command of the mission...
I love you, too.
Yeah, yeah.
...to military personnel for the duration of the maneuver. On my mark. 3... 2... 1...
There we go. Oscar's on top.
...Mark.
I hope I get to shoot something. What's the point of having sweet space guns if you never get to shoot anything?
Normally I'd be with you, brother, but this seems like a clear-cut case of careful what you wish for.
Go--you have work to do.
I know. Despite everything, I don't think I've ever been so excited.
All personnel to stations. Crossing terminus in thirty seconds.
God be with us.

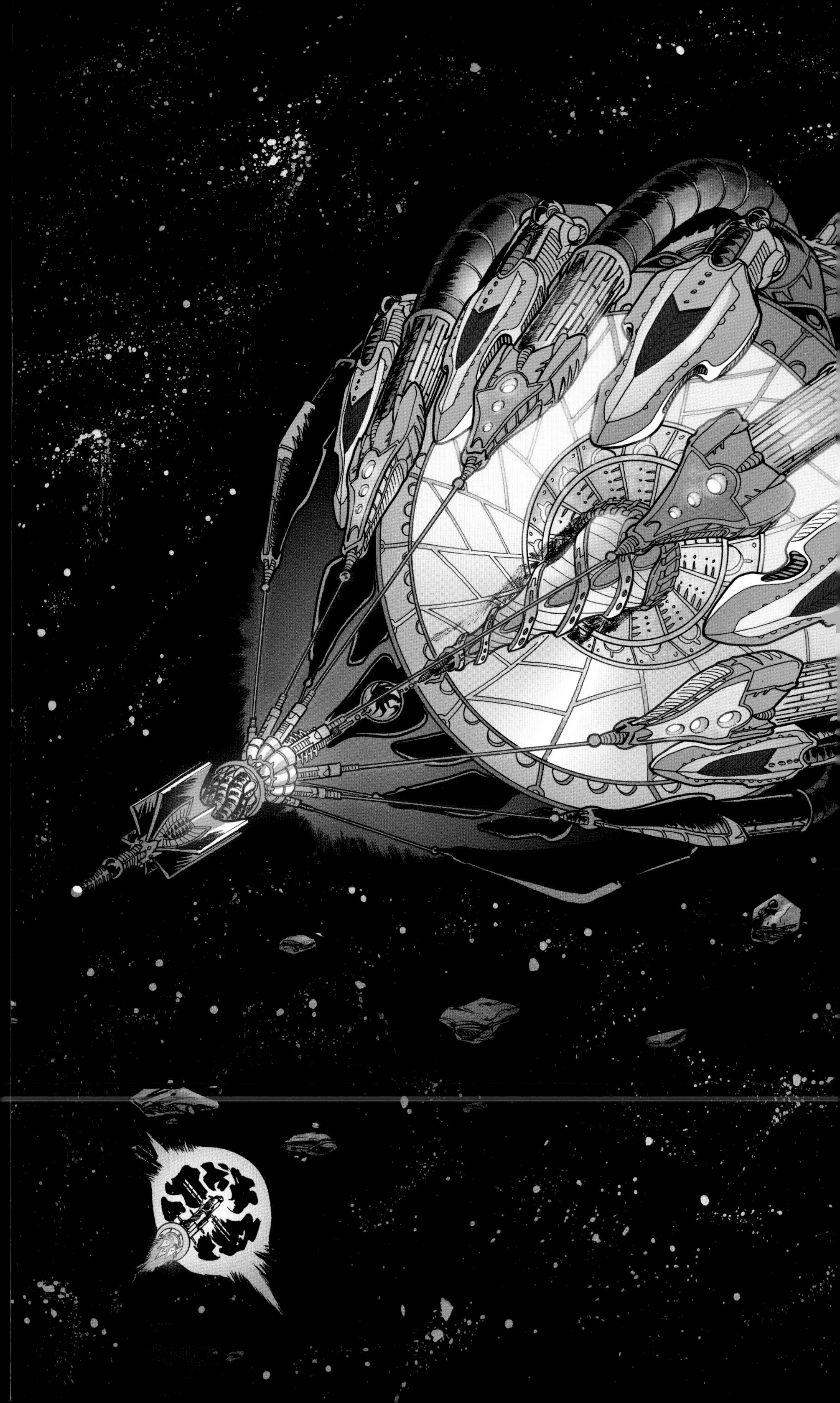

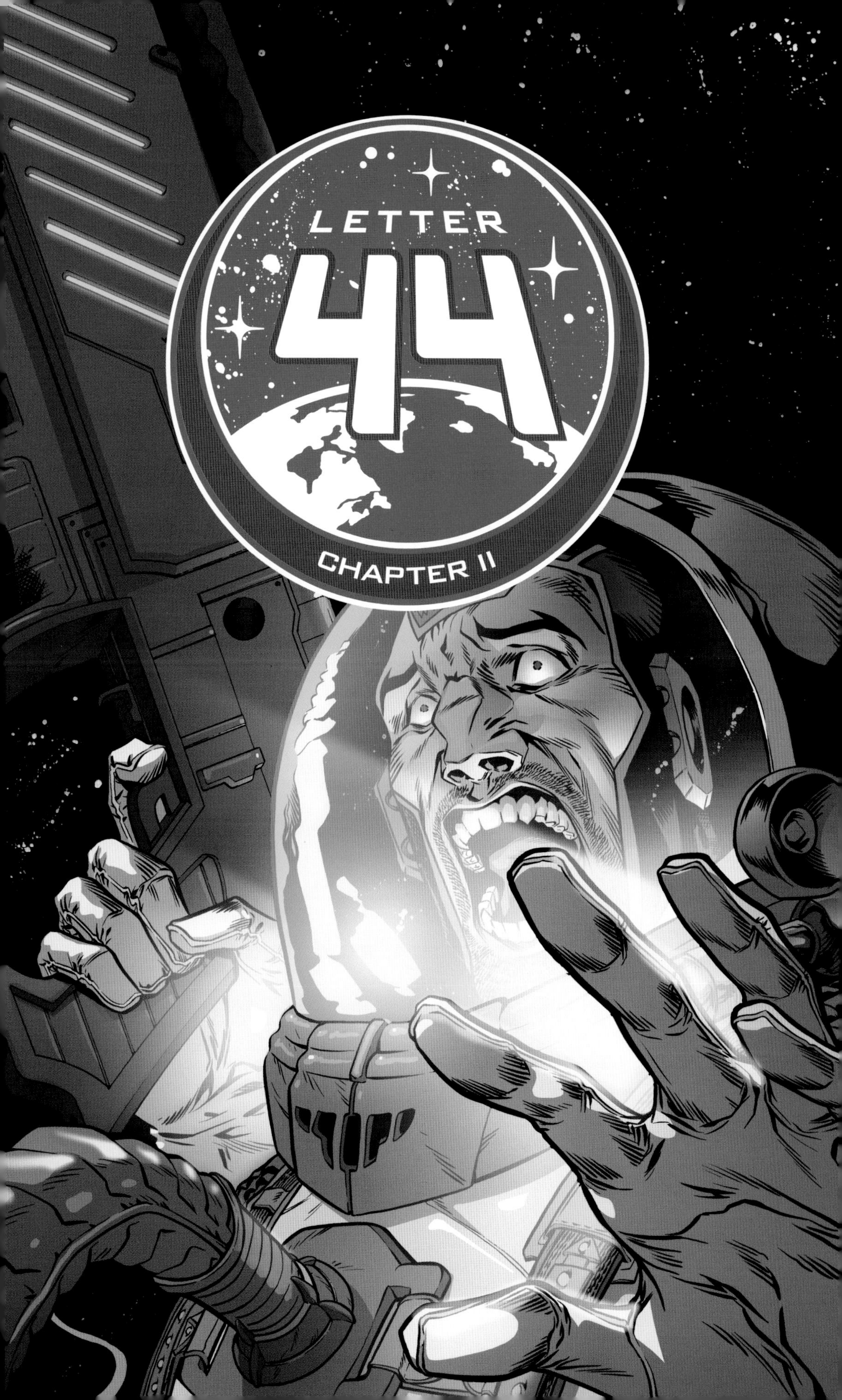
LETTER
44
CHAPTER II

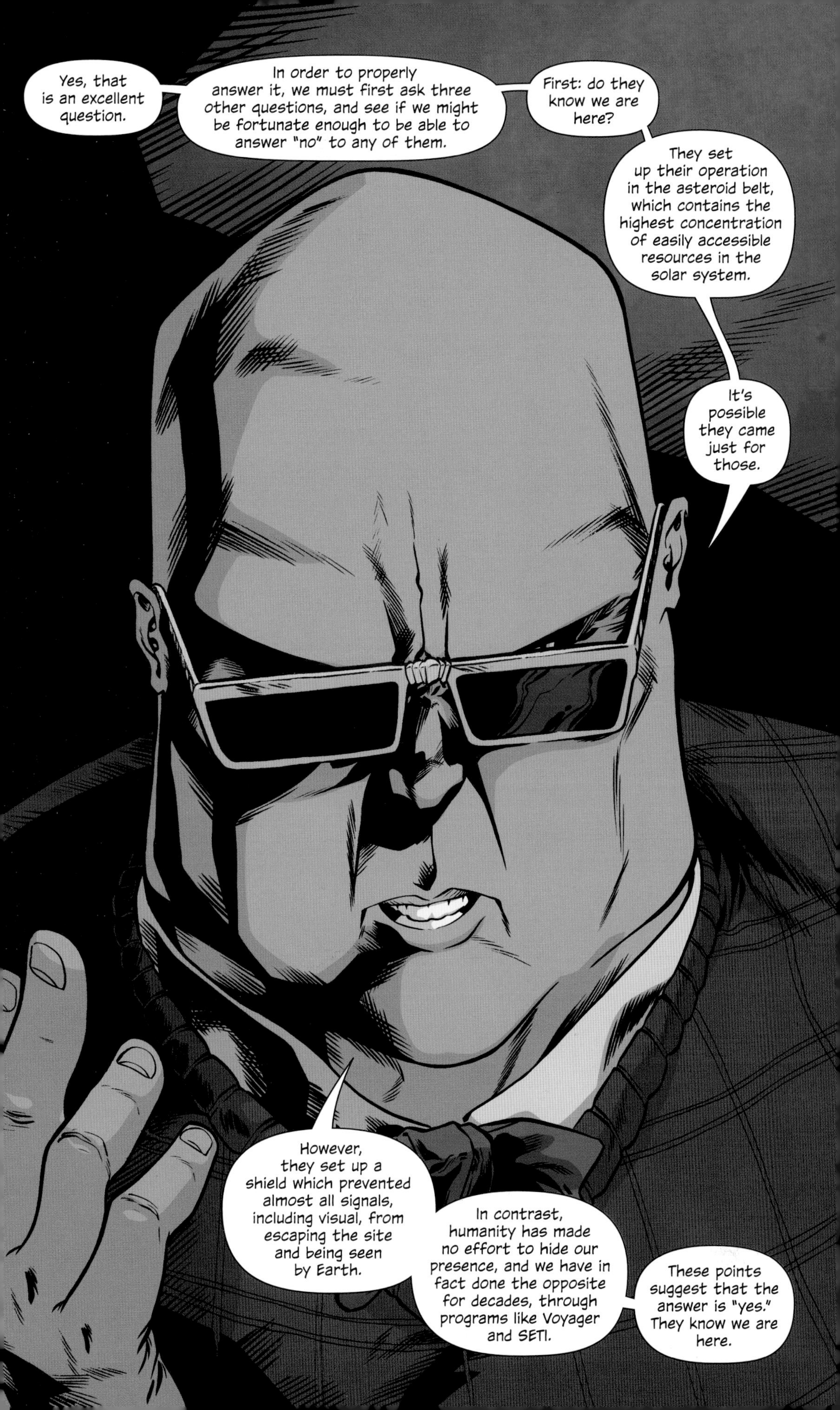
Yes, that is an excellent question.
In order to properly answer it, we must first ask three other questions, and see if we might be fortunate enough to be able to answer "no" to any of them.
First: do they know we are here?
They set up their operation in the asteroid belt, which contains the highest concentration of easily accessible resources in the solar system.
It's possible they came just for those.
However, they set up a shield which prevented almost all signals, including visual, from escaping the site and being seen by Earth.
In contrast, humanity has made no effort to hide our presence, and we have in fact done the opposite for decades, through programs like Voyager and SETI.
These points suggest that the answer is "yes." They know we are here.

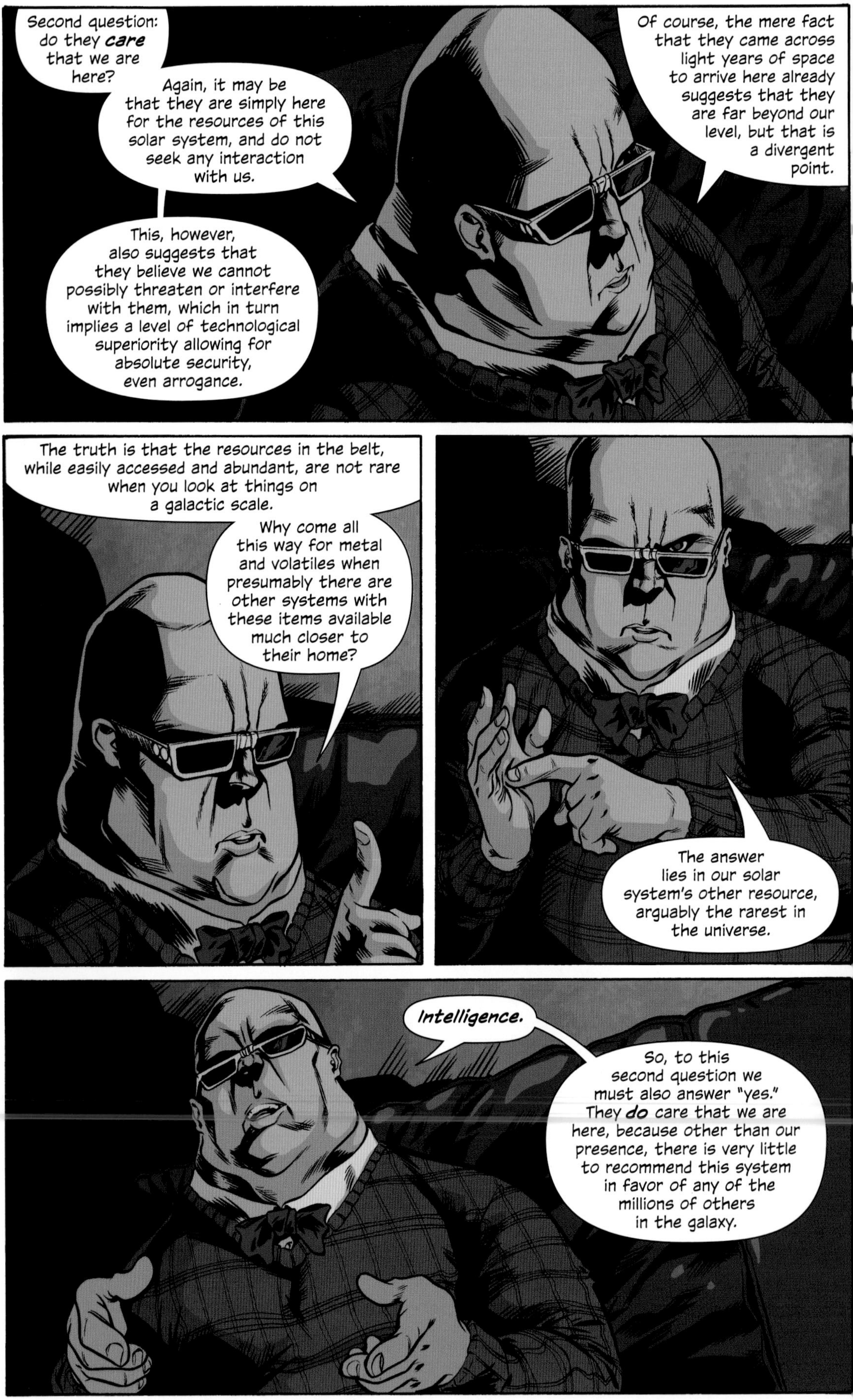
Second question: do they *care* that we are here?
Again, it may be that they are simply here for the resources of this solar system, and do not seek any interaction with us.
This, however, also suggests that they believe we cannot possibly threaten or interfere with them, which in turn implies a level of technological superiority allowing for absolute security, even arrogance.
Of course, the mere fact that they came across light years of space to arrive here already suggests that they are far beyond our level, but that is a divergent point.
The truth is that the resources in the belt, while easily accessed and abundant, are not rare when you look at things on a galactic scale.
Why come all this way for metal and volatiles when presumably there are other systems with these items available much closer to their home?
The answer lies in our solar system's other resource, arguably the rarest in the universe.
Intelligence.
So, to this second question we must also answer "yes." They *do* care that we are here, because other than our presence, there is very little to recommend this system in favor of any of the millions of others in the galaxy.

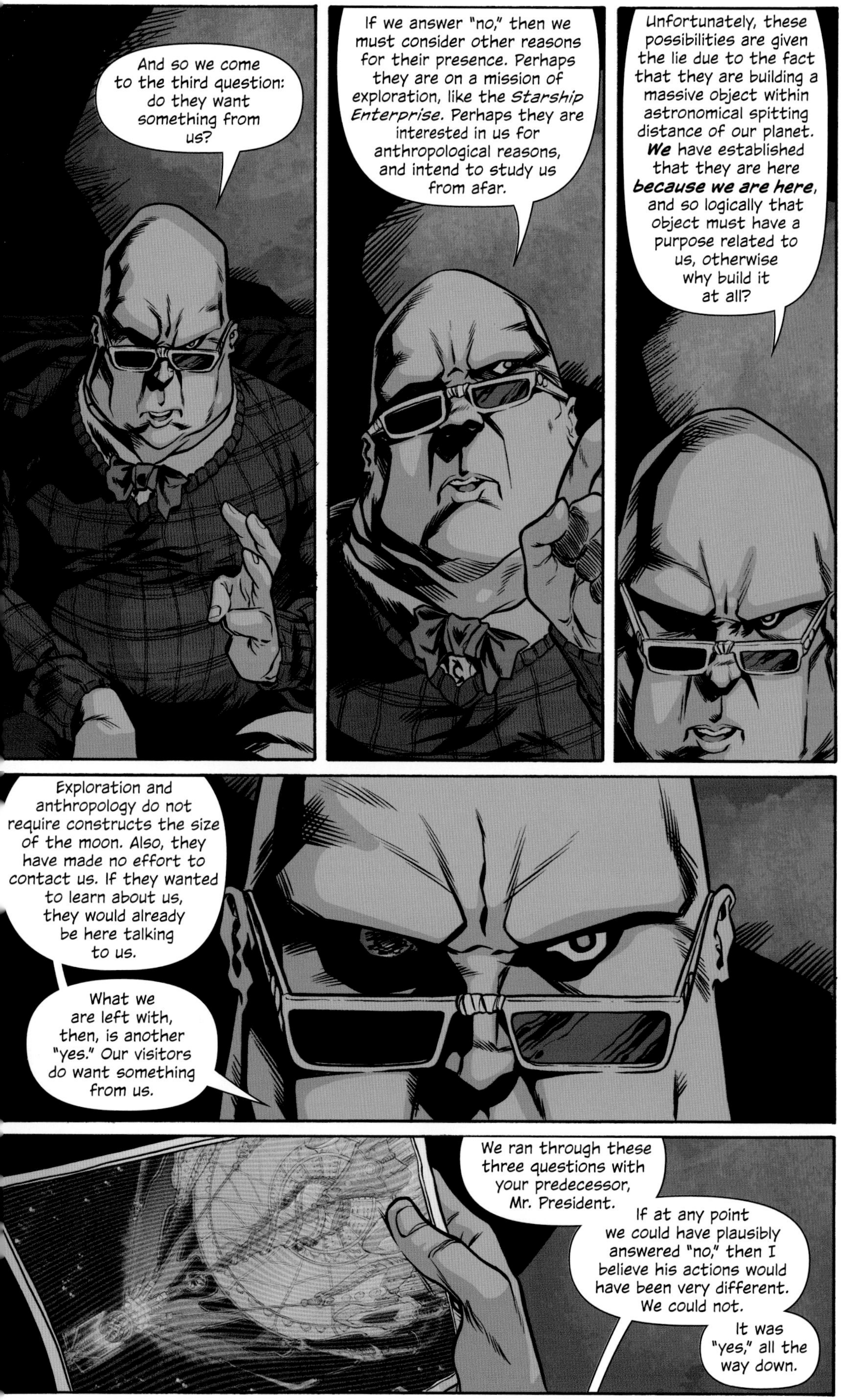
And so we come to the third question: do they want something from us?
If we answer "no," then we must consider other reasons for their presence. Perhaps they are on a mission of exploration, like the *Starship Enterprise*. Perhaps they are interested in us for anthropological reasons, and intend to study us from afar.
Unfortunately, these possibilities are given the lie due to the fact that they are building a massive object within astronomical spitting distance of our planet. ***We*** have established that they are here ***because we are here***, and so logically that object must have a purpose related to us, otherwise why build it at all?
Exploration and anthropology do not require constructs the size of the moon. Also, they have made no effort to contact us. If they wanted to learn about us, they would already be here talking to us.
What we are left with, then, is another "yes." Our visitors do want something from us.
We ran through these three questions with your predecessor, Mr. President.
If at any point we could have plausibly answered "no," then I believe his actions would have been very different. We could not.
It was "yes," all the way down.

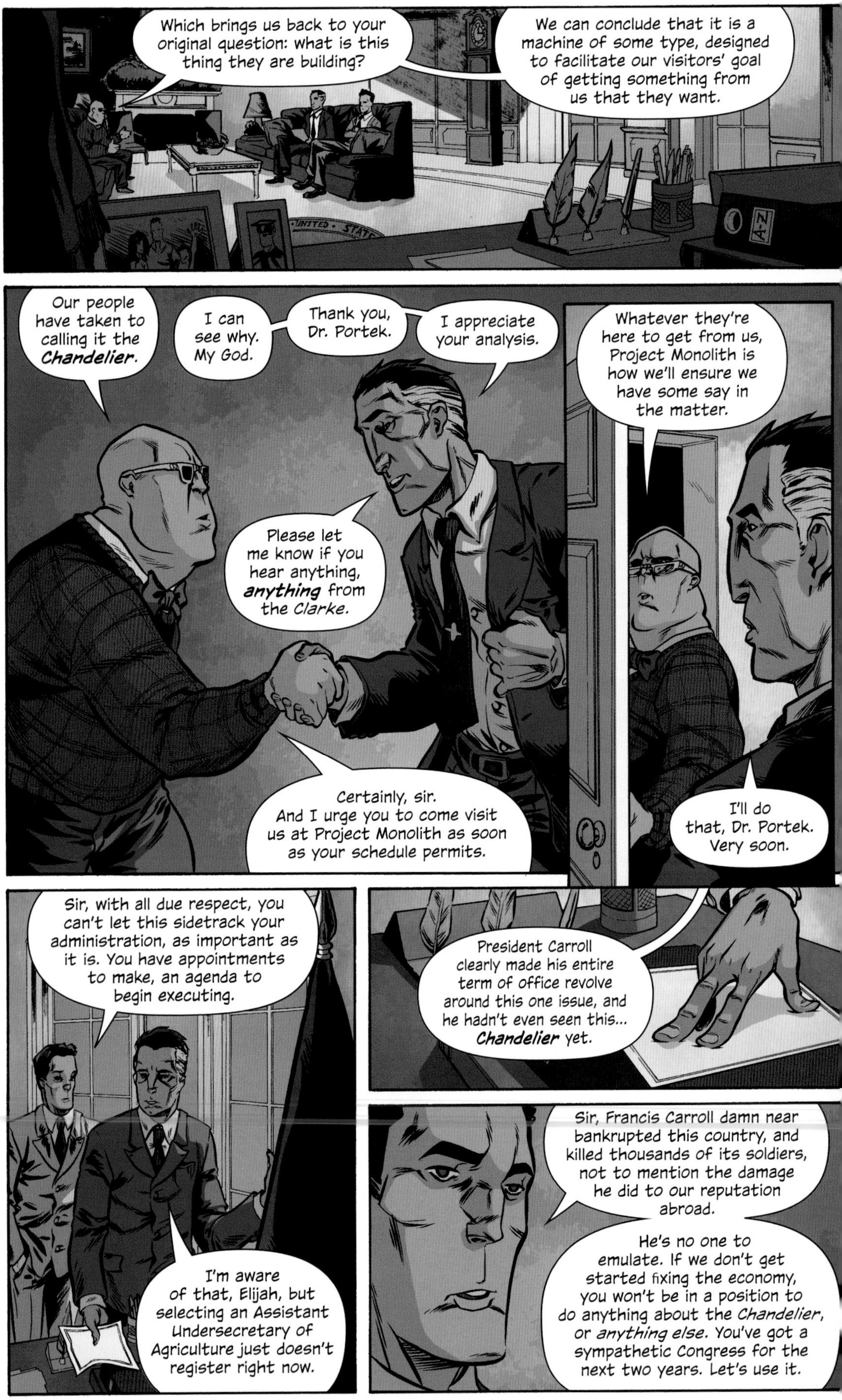
Which brings us back to your original question: what is this thing they are building?
We can conclude that it is a machine of some type, designed to facilitate our visitors' goal of getting something from us that they want.
UNITED STATES
A-Z
Our people have taken to calling it the ***Chandelier***.
I can see why. My God.
Thank you, Dr. Portek.
I appreciate your analysis.
Please let me know if you hear anything, ***anything*** from the *Clarke*.
Certainly, sir. And I urge you to come visit us at Project Monolith as soon as your schedule permits.
Whatever they're here to get from us, Project Monolith is how we'll ensure we have some say in the matter.
I'll do that, Dr. Portek. Very soon.
Sir, with all due respect, you can't let this sidetrack your administration, as important as it is. You have appointments to make, an agenda to begin executing.
I'm aware of that, Elijah, but selecting an Assistant Undersecretary of Agriculture just doesn't register right now.
President Carroll clearly made his entire term of office revolve around this one issue, and he hadn't even seen this... ***Chandelier*** yet.
Sir, Francis Carroll damn near bankrupted this country, and killed thousands of its soldiers, not to mention the damage he did to our reputation abroad.
He's no one to emulate. If we don't get started fixing the economy, you won't be in a position to do anything about the *Chandelier*, or *anything else*. You've got a sympathetic Congress for the next two years. Let's use it.

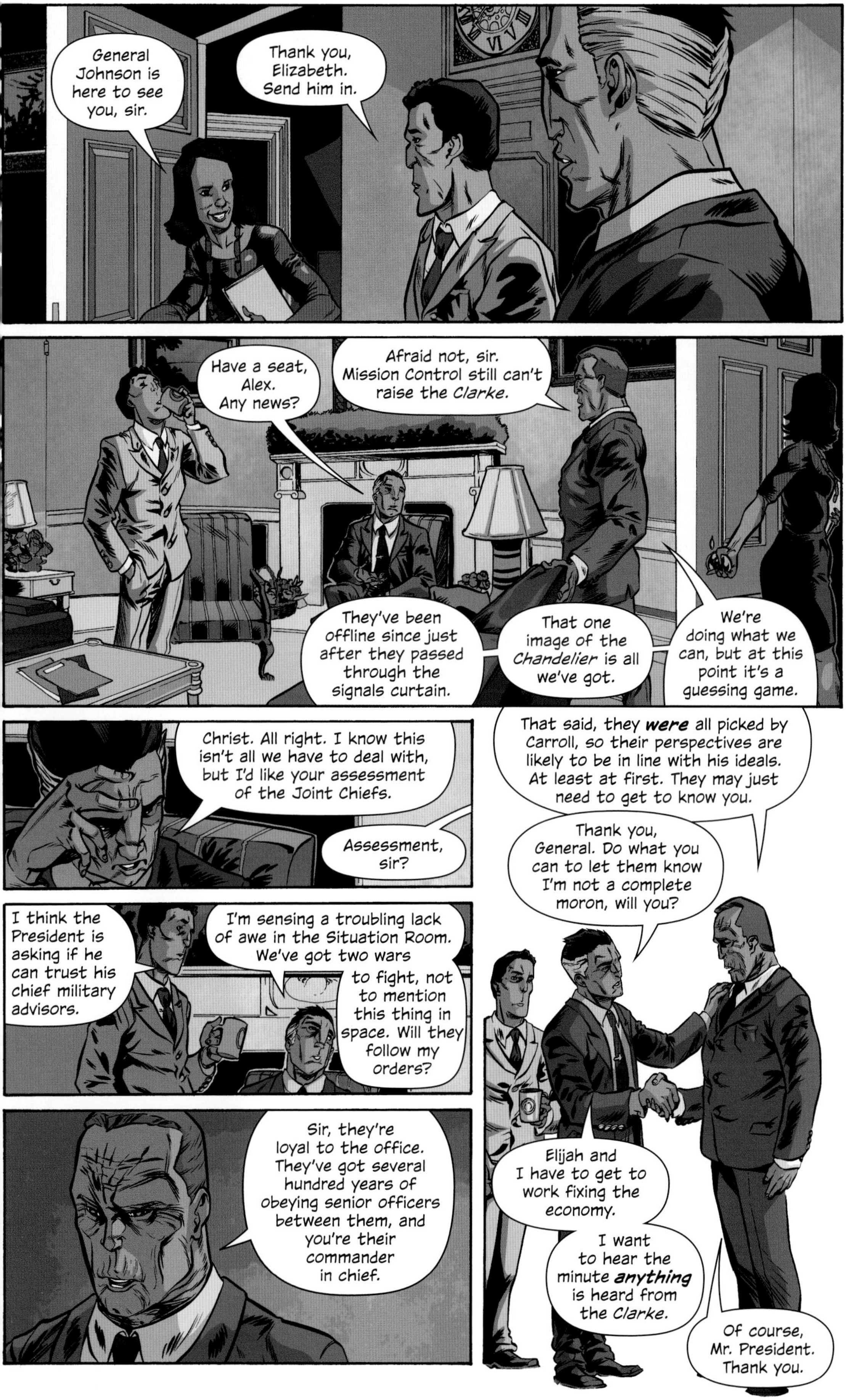
General Johnson is here to see you, sir.
Thank you, Elizabeth. Send him in.
Have a seat, Alex. Any news?
Afraid not, sir. Mission Control still can't raise the *Clarke*.
They've been offline since just after they passed through the signals curtain.
That one image of the *Chandelier* is all we've got.
We're doing what we can, but at this point it's a guessing game.
Christ. All right. I know this isn't all we have to deal with, but I'd like your assessment of the Joint Chiefs.
Assessment, sir?
I think the President is asking if he can trust his chief military advisors.
I'm sensing a troubling lack of awe in the Situation Room. We've got two wars
to fight, not to mention this thing in space. Will they follow my orders?
Sir, they're loyal to the office. They've got several hundred years of obeying senior officers between them, and you're their commander in chief.
That said, they **were** all picked by Carroll, so their perspectives are likely to be in line with his ideals. At least at first. They may just need to get to know you.
Thank you, General. Do what you can to let them know I'm not a complete moron, will you?
Elijah and I have to get to work fixing the economy.
I want to hear the minute **anything** is heard from the *Clarke*.
Of course, Mr. President. Thank you.

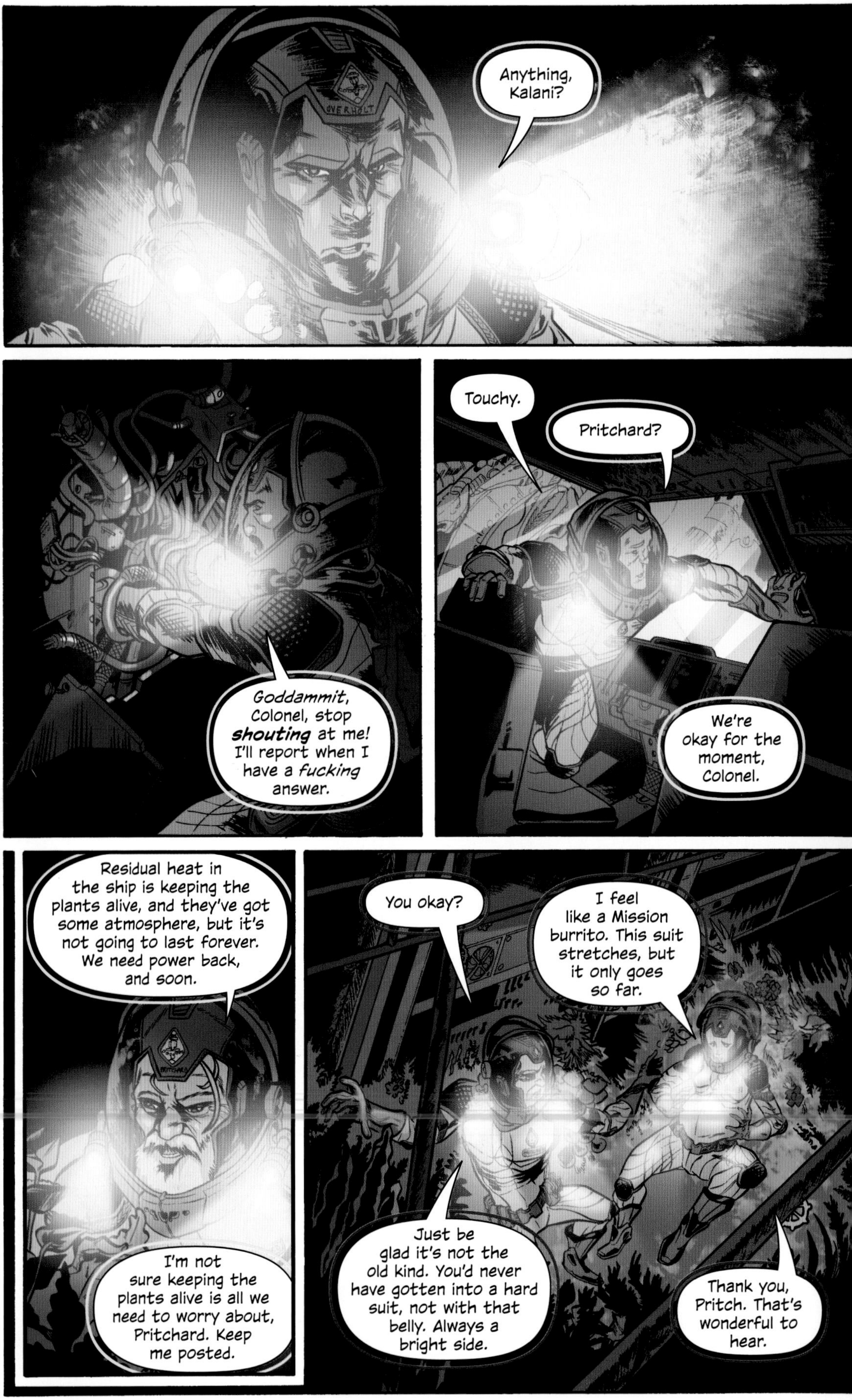
Anything, Kalani?
Goddammit, Colonel, stop shouting at me! I'll report when I have a fucking answer.
Touchy.
Pritchard?
We're okay for the moment, Colonel.
Residual heat in the ship is keeping the plants alive, and they've got some atmosphere, but it's not going to last forever. We need power back, and soon.
I'm not sure keeping the plants alive is all we need to worry about, Pritchard. Keep me posted.
You okay?
I feel like a Mission burrito. This suit stretches, but it only goes so far.
Just be glad it's not the old kind. You'd never have gotten into a hard suit, not with that belly. Always a bright side.
Thank you, Pritch. That's wonderful to hear.

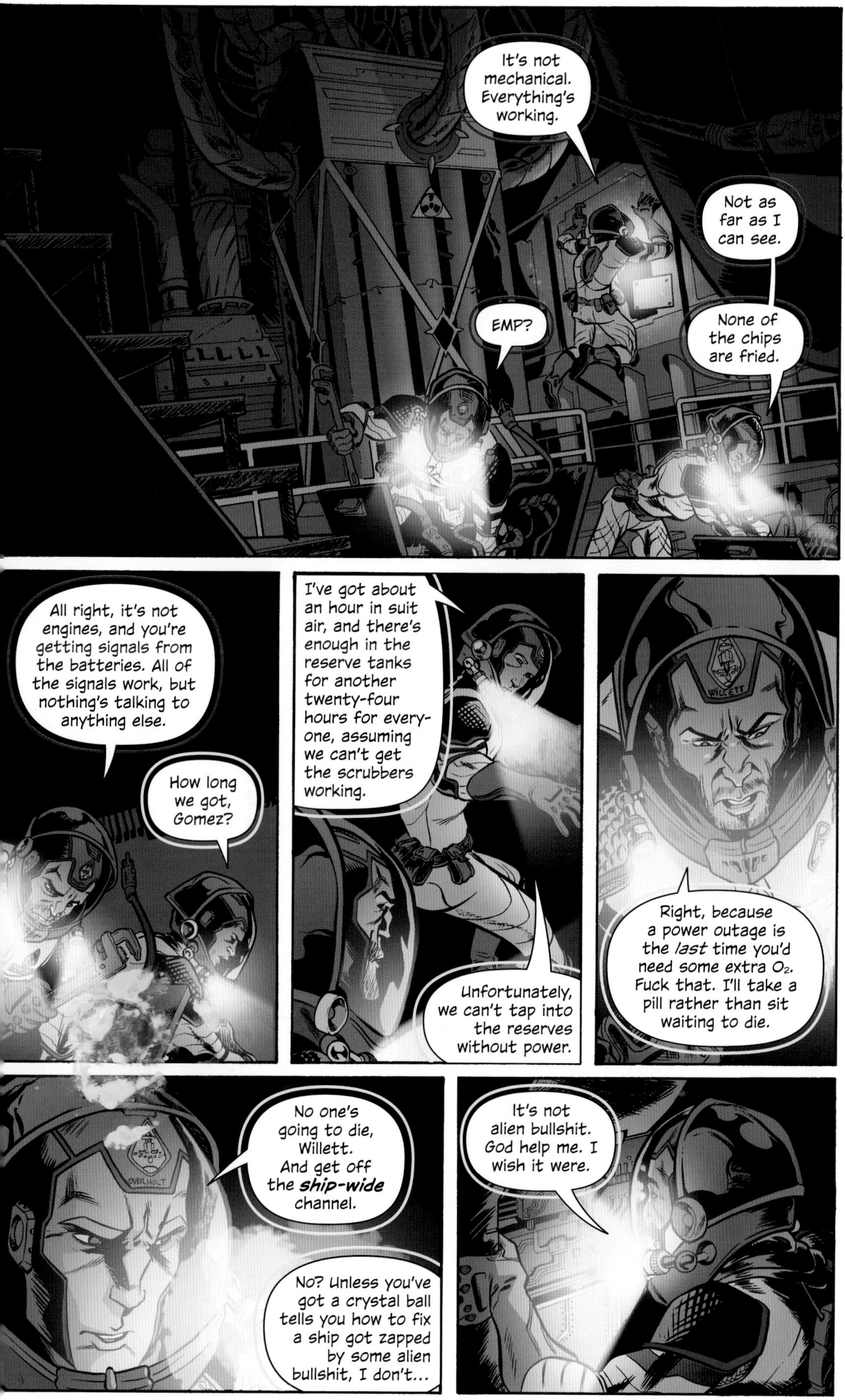
It's not mechanical. Everything's working.
EMP?
Not as far as I can see.
None of the chips are fried.
All right, it's not engines, and you're getting signals from the batteries. All of the signals work, but nothing's talking to anything else.
How long we got, Gomez?
I've got about an hour in suit air, and there's enough in the reserve tanks for another twenty-four hours for every-one, assuming we can't get the scrubbers working.
Unfortunately, we can't tap into the reserves without power.
WILLETT
Right, because a power outage is the *last* time you'd need some extra O₂. Fuck that. I'll take a pill rather than sit waiting to die.
OVERHOLT
No one's going to die, Willett. And get off the ***ship-wide*** channel.
No? Unless you've got a crystal ball tells you how to fix a ship got zapped by some alien bullshit, I don't...
It's not alien bullshit. God help me. I wish it were.

I hate it out here.

I love it! First chance I've had to bring this little girl out to play.

It's ridiculous. What are you supposed to shoot?

We're millions of kilometers from anything. What'll happen, something will *sneak up* on us?

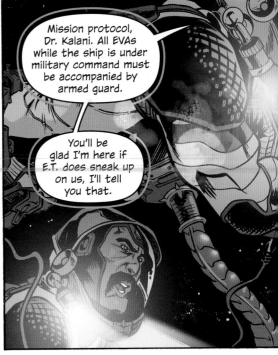

Mission protocol, Dr. Kalani. All EVAs while the ship is under military command must be accompanied by armed guard.

You'll be glad I'm here if E.T. does sneak up on us, I'll tell you that.

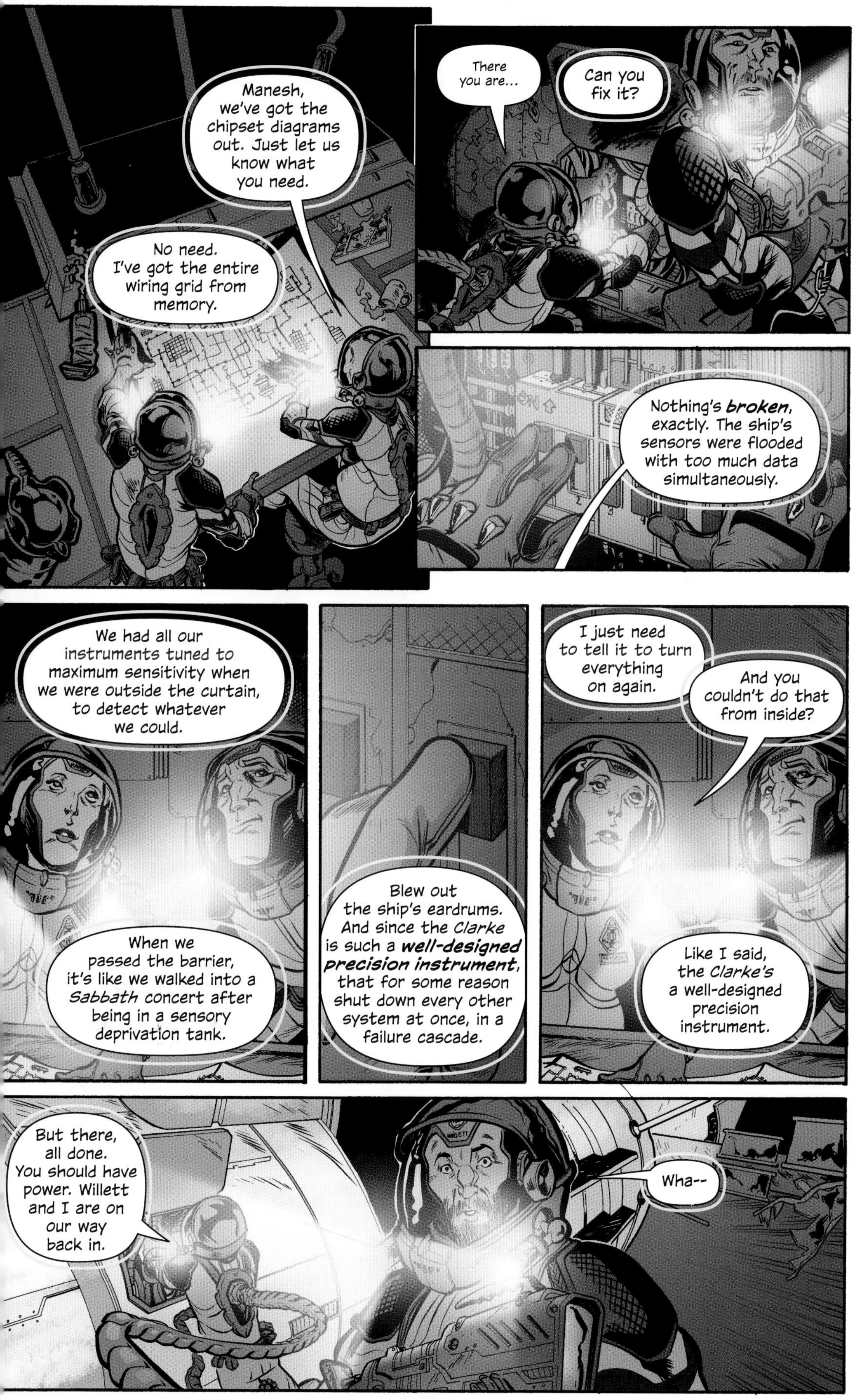

Manesh, we've got the chipset diagrams out. Just let us know what you need.
No need. I've got the entire wiring grid from memory.
There you are...
Can you fix it?
Nothing's **broken**, exactly. The ship's sensors were flooded with too much data simultaneously.
We had all our instruments tuned to maximum sensitivity when we were outside the curtain, to detect whatever we could.
When we passed the barrier, it's like we walked into a *Sabbath* concert after being in a sensory deprivation tank.
Blew out the ship's eardrums. And since the *Clarke* is such a ***well-designed precision instrument***, that for some reason shut down every other system at once, in a failure cascade.
I just need to tell it to turn everything on again.
And you couldn't do that from inside?
Like I said, the *Clarke's* a well-designed precision instrument.
But there, all done. You should have power. Willett and I are on our way back in.
Wha--

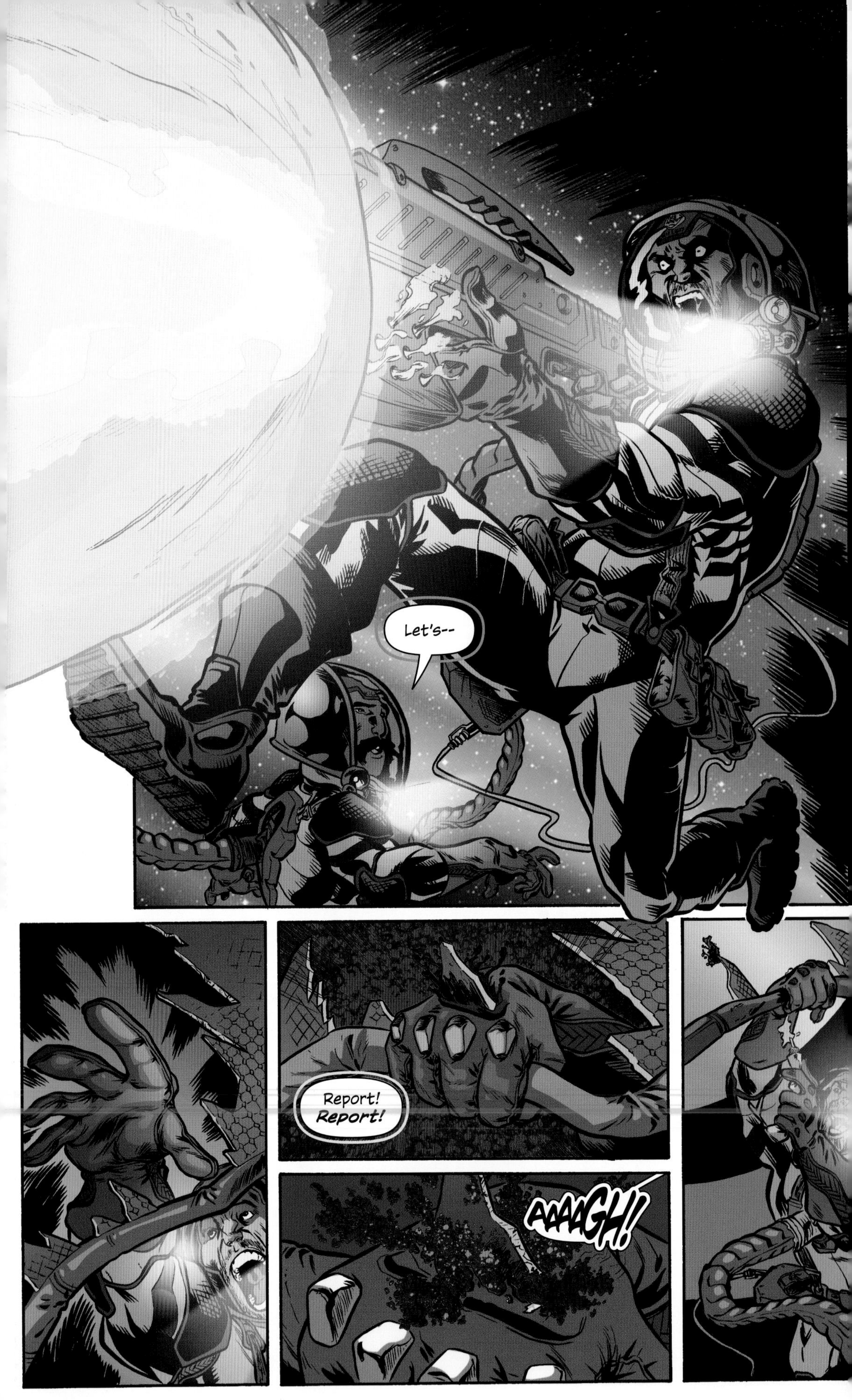
Let's--
Report! Report!
AAAAGH!

Oof
Oh God, the tether *snapped!* Oh God, **oh God...**
Manesh!* *Willett! What the *hell* is happening out there?
We're okay, Charlotte. Just a little trouble, but we're okay.
Little trouble my ass!
Manesh, you're a smart guy. Think this through. My rifle had a misfire-- you know how poorly tested this gear was.
We're safe now. No big deal. I think we'll both be a lot happier if we leave this situation outside the ship, don't you?
KALANI
Fucking asshole.
We're on our way back in. Please have medical standing by.
Roger that. Thanks, guys, good work.

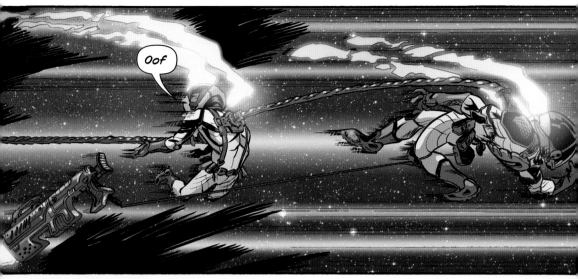

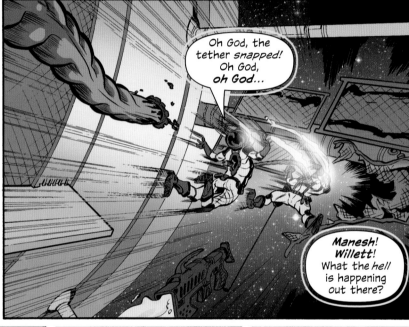

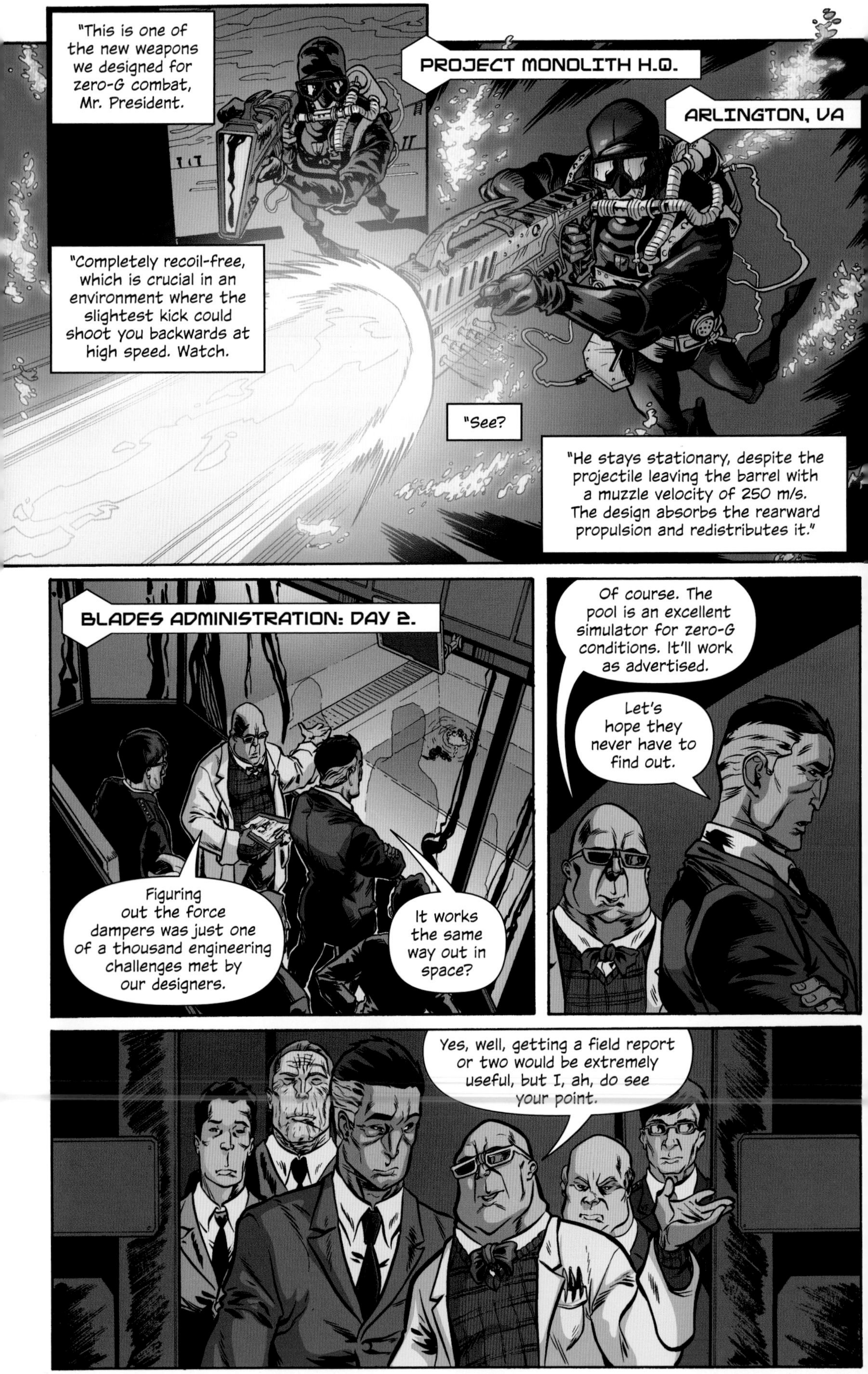
"This is one of the new weapons we designed for zero-G combat, Mr. President.
PROJECT MONOLITH H.Q.
ARLINGTON, VA
"Completely recoil-free, which is crucial in an environment where the slightest kick could shoot you backwards at high speed. Watch.
"See?
"He stays stationary, despite the projectile leaving the barrel with a muzzle velocity of 250 m/s. The design absorbs the rearward propulsion and redistributes it."
BLADES ADMINISTRATION: DAY 2.
Figuring out the force dampers was just one of a thousand engineering challenges met by our designers.
It works the same way out in space?
Of course. The pool is an excellent simulator for zero-G conditions. It'll work as advertised.
Let's hope they never have to find out.
Yes, well, getting a field report or two would be extremely useful, but I, ah, do see your point.

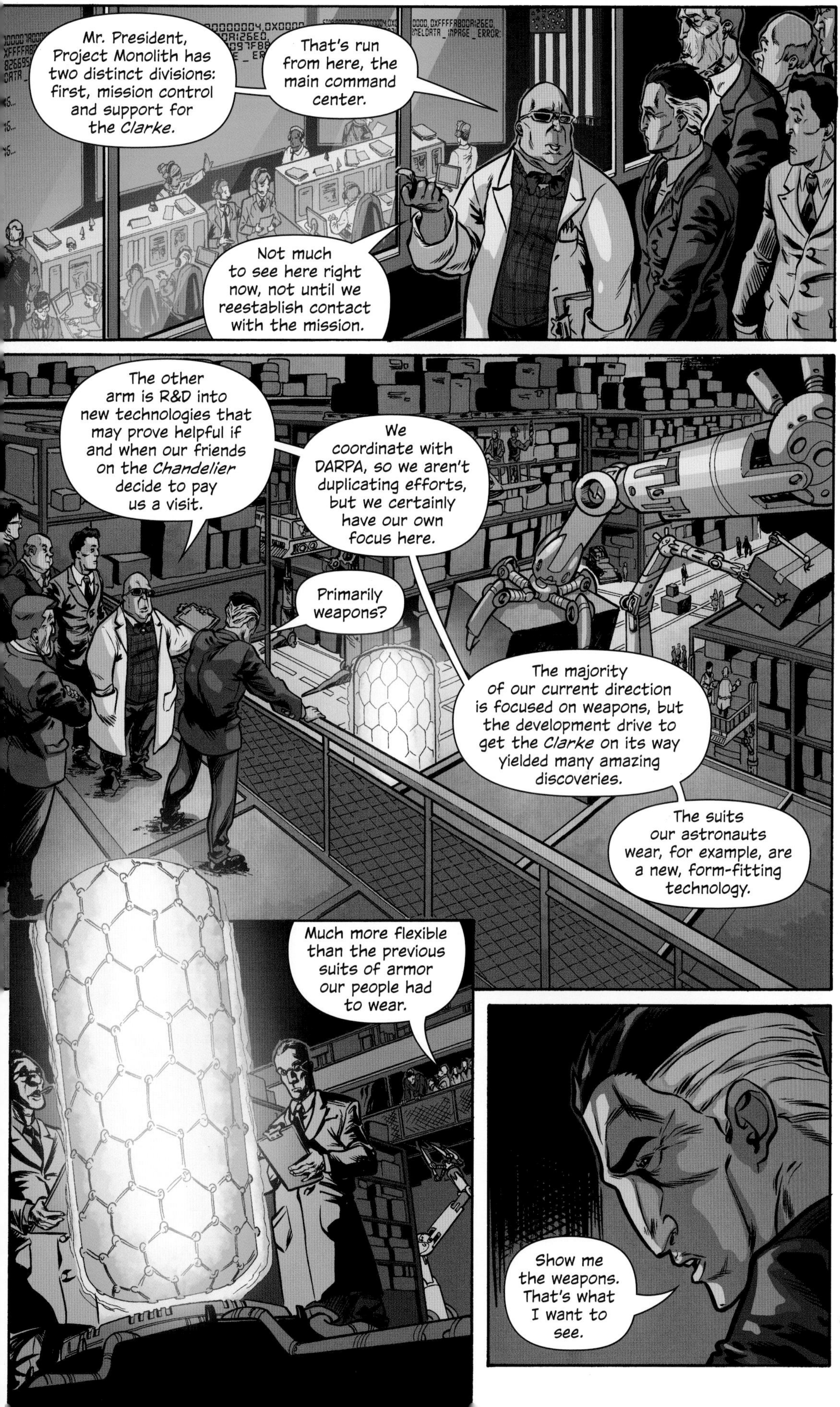
Mr. President, Project Monolith has two distinct divisions: first, mission control and support for the *Clarke.*
That's run from here, the main command center.
Not much to see here right now, not until we reestablish contact with the mission.
The other arm is R&D into new technologies that may prove helpful if and when our friends on the *Chandelier* decide to pay us a visit.
We coordinate with DARPA, so we aren't duplicating efforts, but we certainly have our own focus here.
Primarily weapons?
The majority of our current direction is focused on weapons, but the development drive to get the *Clarke* on its way yielded many amazing discoveries.
The suits our astronauts wear, for example, are a new, form-fitting technology.
Much more flexible than the previous suits of armor our people had to wear.
Show me the weapons. That's what I want to see.

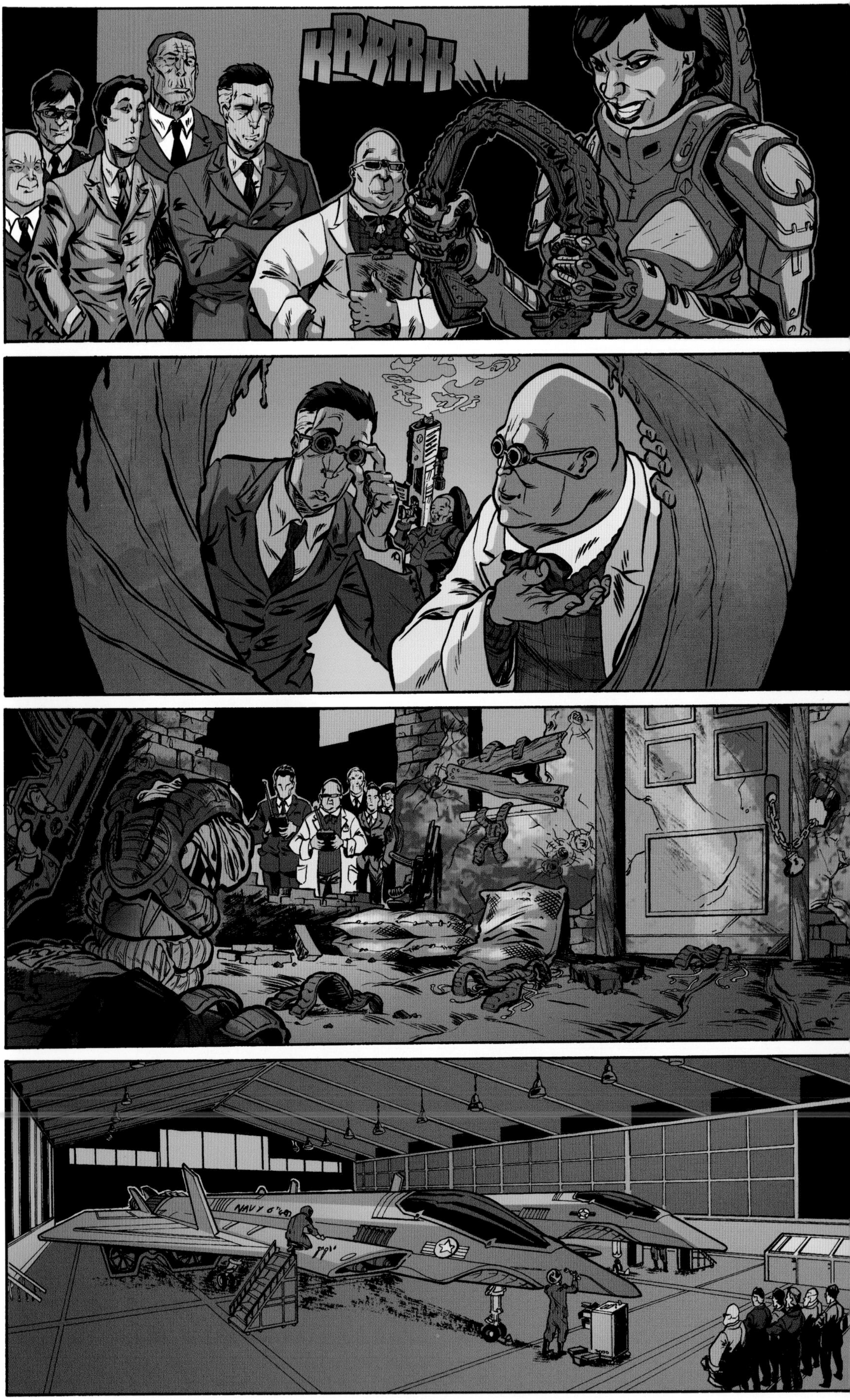
KRRRK

And all of this **works**? It's not experimental?

Oh, yes. Stress-tested and designed through multiple generations. Ready to be mass-produced as required.

The United States has been fighting two massively expensive wars in the Middle East and central Asia for **years**...

...Yet to my knowledge we aren't *using* any of this stuff.

No, sir, we are not.

Why? Seems like if we put even half of this in the field we could win those wars in a week.

Well, sir, there are, of course, military considerations--it's never as simple as...

Answer his question, General. Why *aren't* we deploying this technology, if it's ready to go?

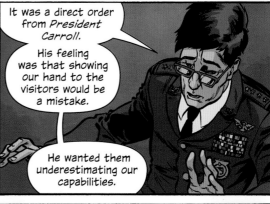

It was a direct order from *President Carroll*.

His feeling was that showing our hand to the visitors would be a mistake.

He wanted them underestimating our capabilities.

While we spend *billions* each month with thousands of our kids dead over there?

Yeah, that's **not** going to work for me.

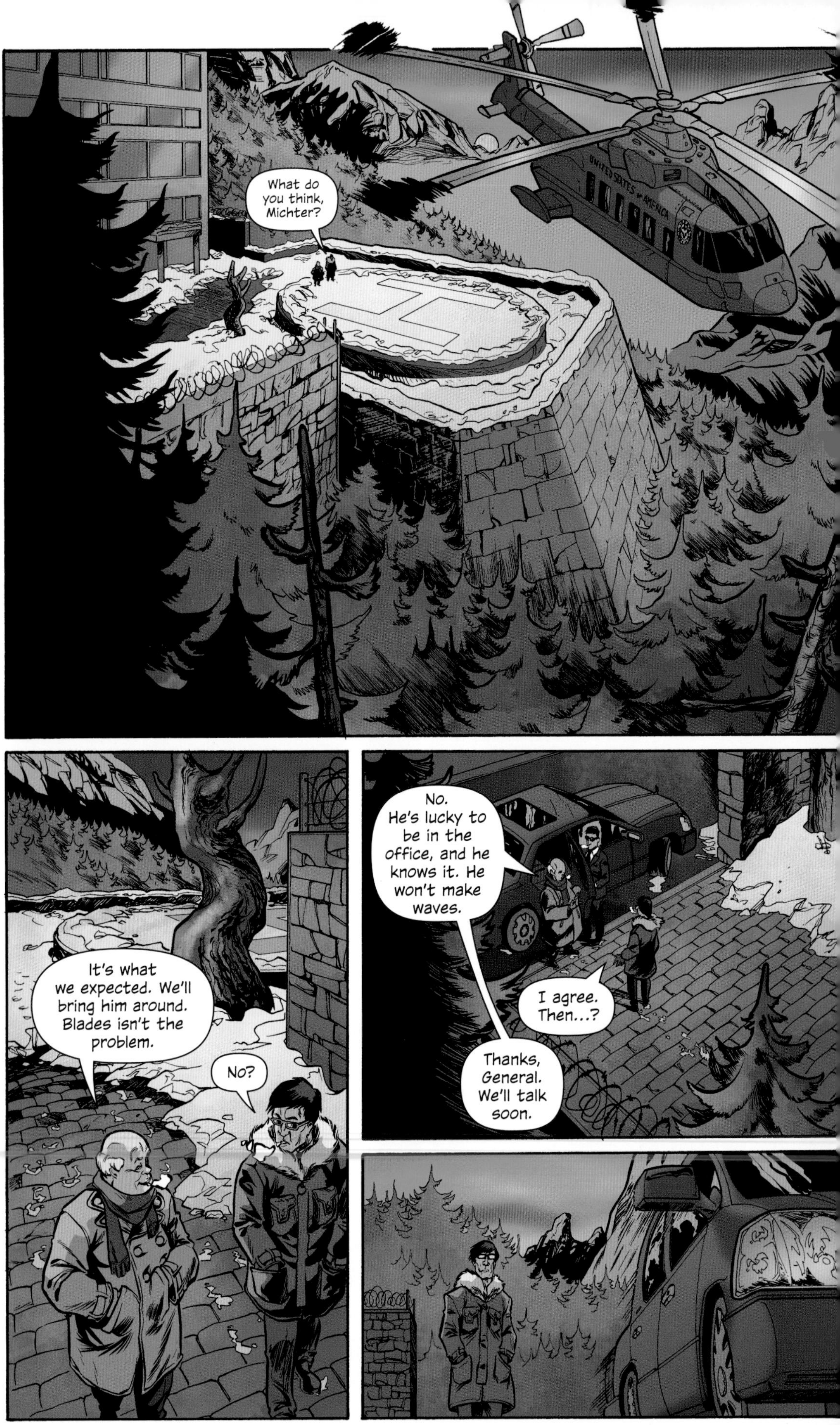
What do you think, Michter?
It's what we expected. We'll bring him around. Blades isn't the problem.
No?
No. He's lucky to be in the office, and he knows it. He won't make waves.
I agree. Then...?
Thanks, General. We'll talk soon.

What is this, **superglue**?

Yeah. Basically. It's suit sealant. I cut myself on the solar panel, and I needed to close it up before my blood boiled away.

Everything looks fine. What I wouldn't give for an ultrasound, but...

Thanks for checking. I was just worried, after being in that suit for that long.

It's going to feel like the mother of all sunburns on the exposed skin, but all things considered, for an exposure to full vacuum, it's not bad.

Thanks, doc.

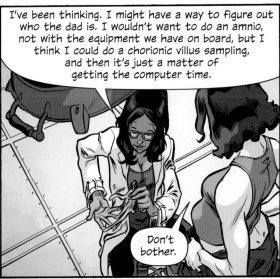

I've been thinking. I might have a way to figure out who the dad is. I wouldn't want to do an amnio, not with the equipment we have on board, but I think I could do a chorionic villus sampling, and then it's just a matter of getting the computer time.

Don't bother.

You fired your weapon out there, didn't you? Finally got your field test.

That's not why I fired. I *saw* something out there, on the hull. It looked like a rainbow--a *living* rainbow.

I don't know, man--I just squeezed the trigger. I thought I was past all this stuff. Those meds you gave me were really working.

Jesus, I hope all that isn't starting up again.

Don't **bother**?

It's **everyone's** baby. It was everyone's the second we voted to keep it.

We made it through the barrier, and the *Chandelier*... it's like standing on the rim of the Grand Canyon.

Nothing we do matters.

It's gotten *very* exciting.

There's nothing we can do that will affect that thing.

Don't get me wrong. I'm not defeatist.

Sometimes you just have to accept how small you are.

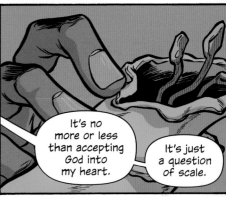

It's no more or less than accepting God into my heart.

It's just a question of scale.

Gabriel? Everyone's in the common room--

Of course. I'll be right there.

I'd give Willett's hand for something stronger than water.

Still, to the crew of the *Clarke*, for keeping this under-designed *tub* flying another day!

HEAR HEAR!

I am, at this time, formally transferring command back to civilian control, as the current threat assessment is nil.

Thank you, Colonel.

I accept command.

All right. This is the first chance we've had to breathe since we crossed the barrier.

We've all seen the *Chandelier*, and I know there's a ton of analysis yet to come, but I'd like to have preliminary assessments.

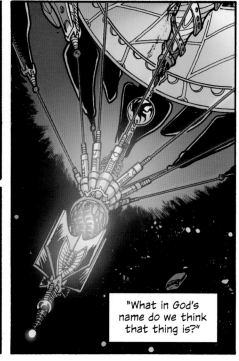

"What in God's name do we think that thing is?"

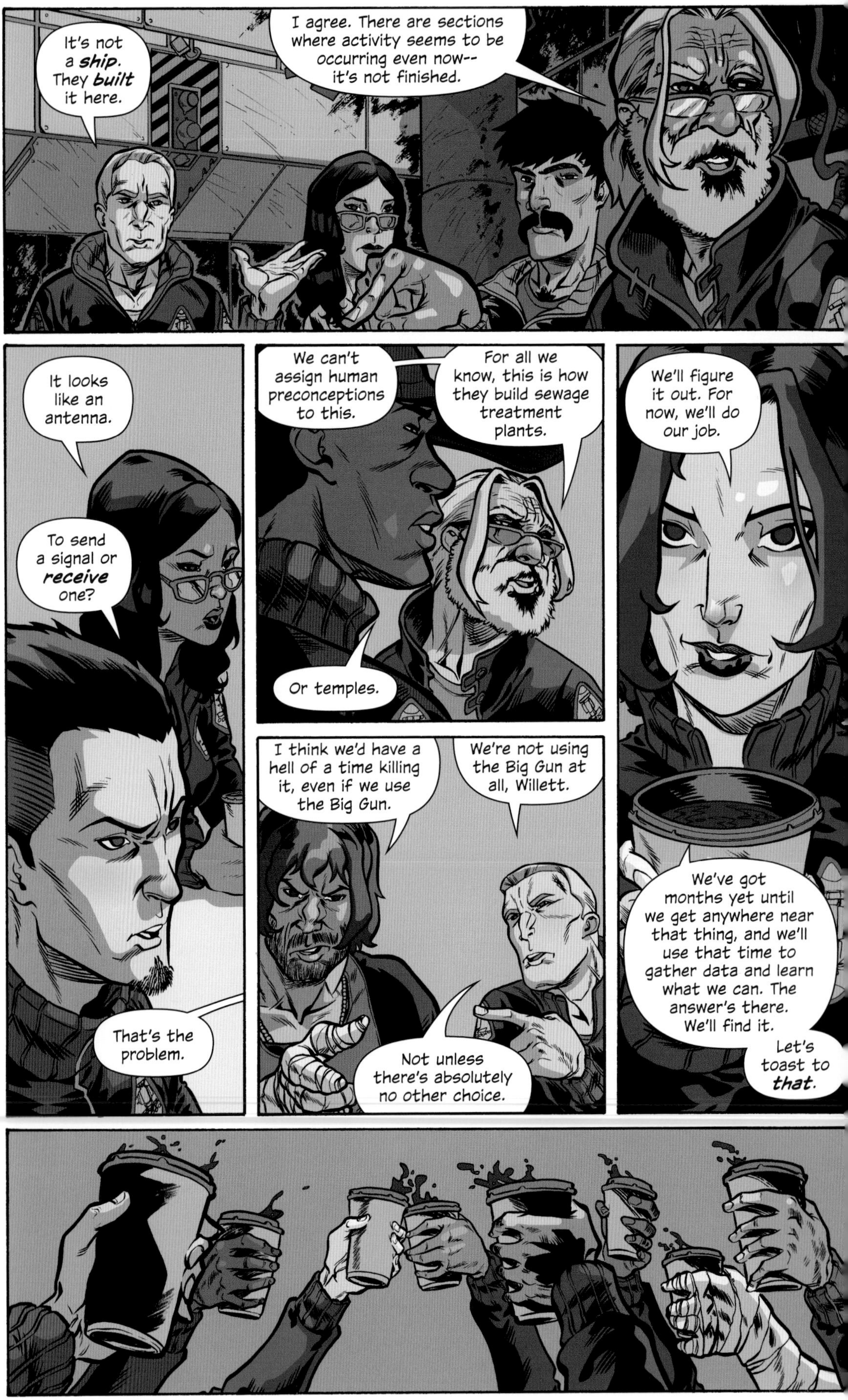

It's not a *ship*. They *built* it here.
I agree. There are sections where activity seems to be occurring even now-- it's not finished.
It looks like an antenna.
To send a signal or *receive* one?
That's the problem.
We can't assign human preconceptions to this.
For all we know, this is how they build sewage treatment plants.
Or temples.
I think we'd have a hell of a time killing it, even if we use the Big Gun.
We're not using the Big Gun at all, Willett.
Not unless there's absolutely no other choice.
We'll figure it out. For now, we'll do our job.
We've got months yet until we get anywhere near that thing, and we'll use that time to gather data and learn what we can. The answer's there. We'll find it.
Let's toast to *that*.

Excuse me, sir, Dr. Portek calling in for you.

Put him through.

Mr. President, we have re-established contact with the *Clarke*. They're sending down reams of data. It's quite wonderful.

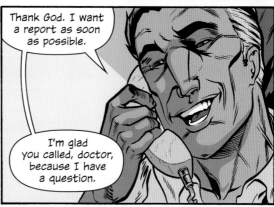

Thank God. I want a report as soon as possible.

I'm glad you called, doctor, because I have a question.

I was running through the dossier you gave me on the *Clarke*.

I'm not an engineer, but if I'm understanding what these papers tell me, they don't have enough fuel to get home.

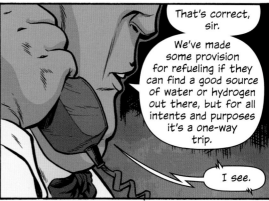

That's correct, sir.

We've made some provision for refueling if they can find a good source of water or hydrogen out there, but for all intents and purposes it's a one-way trip.

I see.

But you must realize, sir, that every person on the *Clarke* is there entirely by choice.

They're scientists.

This is an opportunity beyond their wildest dreams.

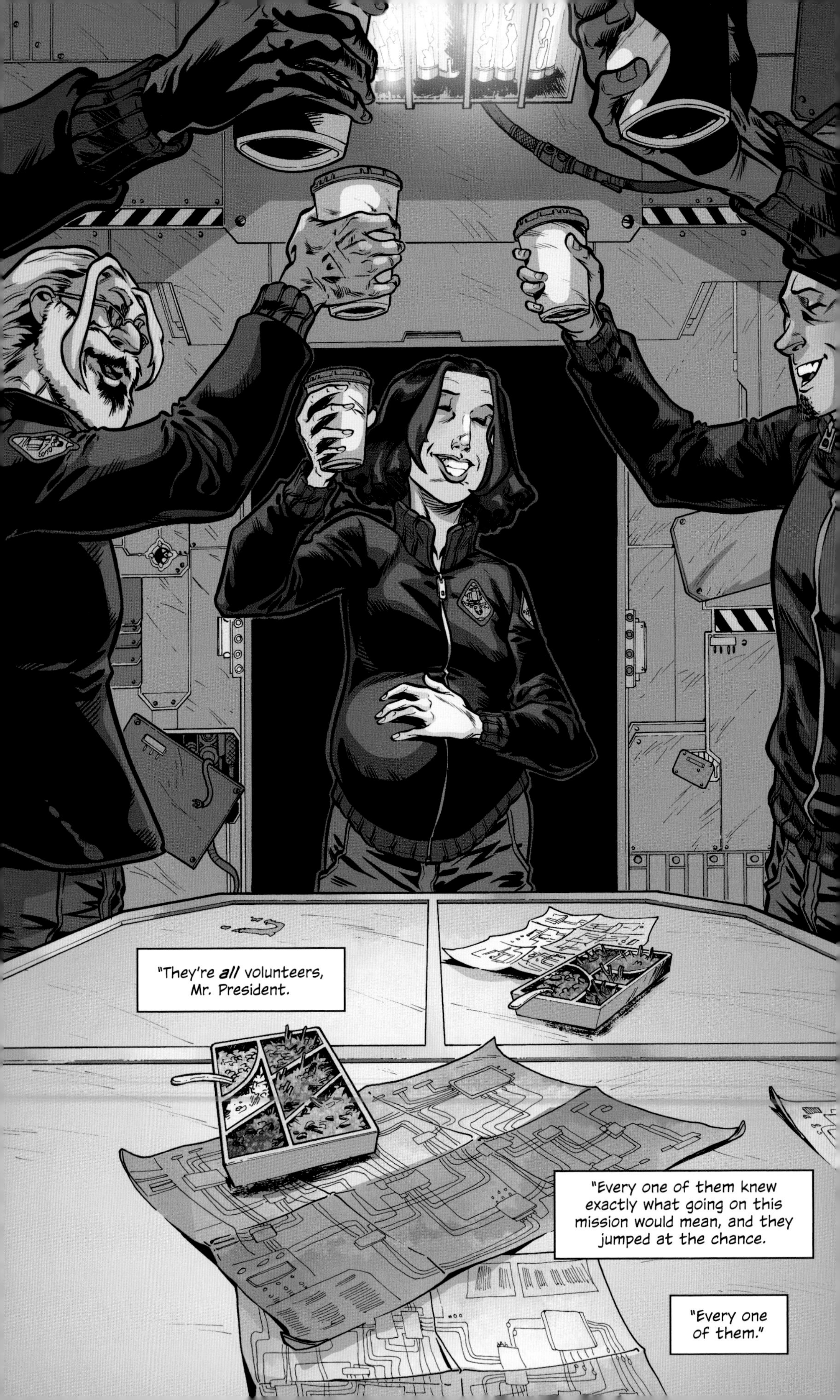
"They're *all* volunteers, Mr. President.
"Every one of them knew exactly what going on this mission would mean, and they jumped at the chance.
"Every one of them."

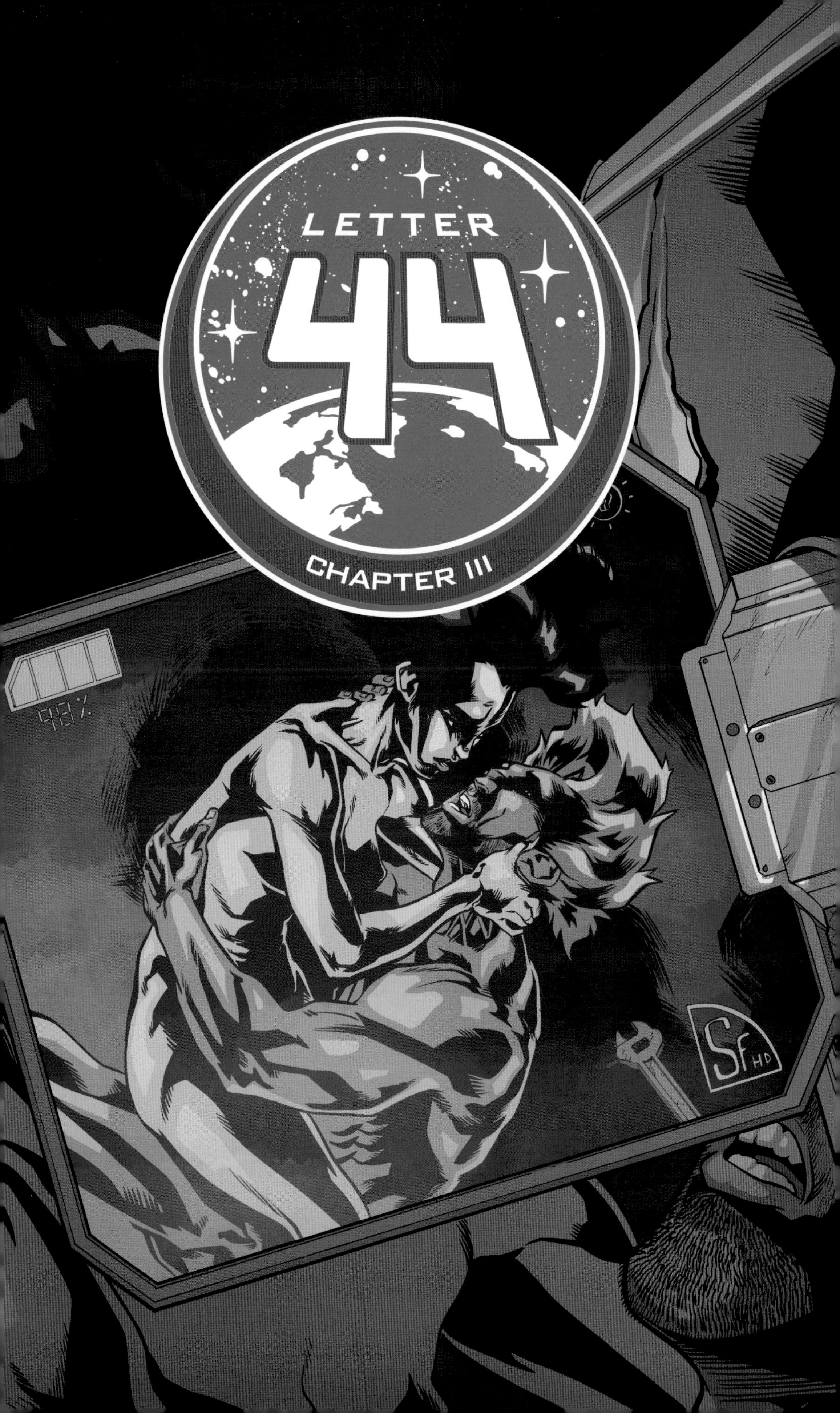
LETTER
44
CHAPTER III
98%

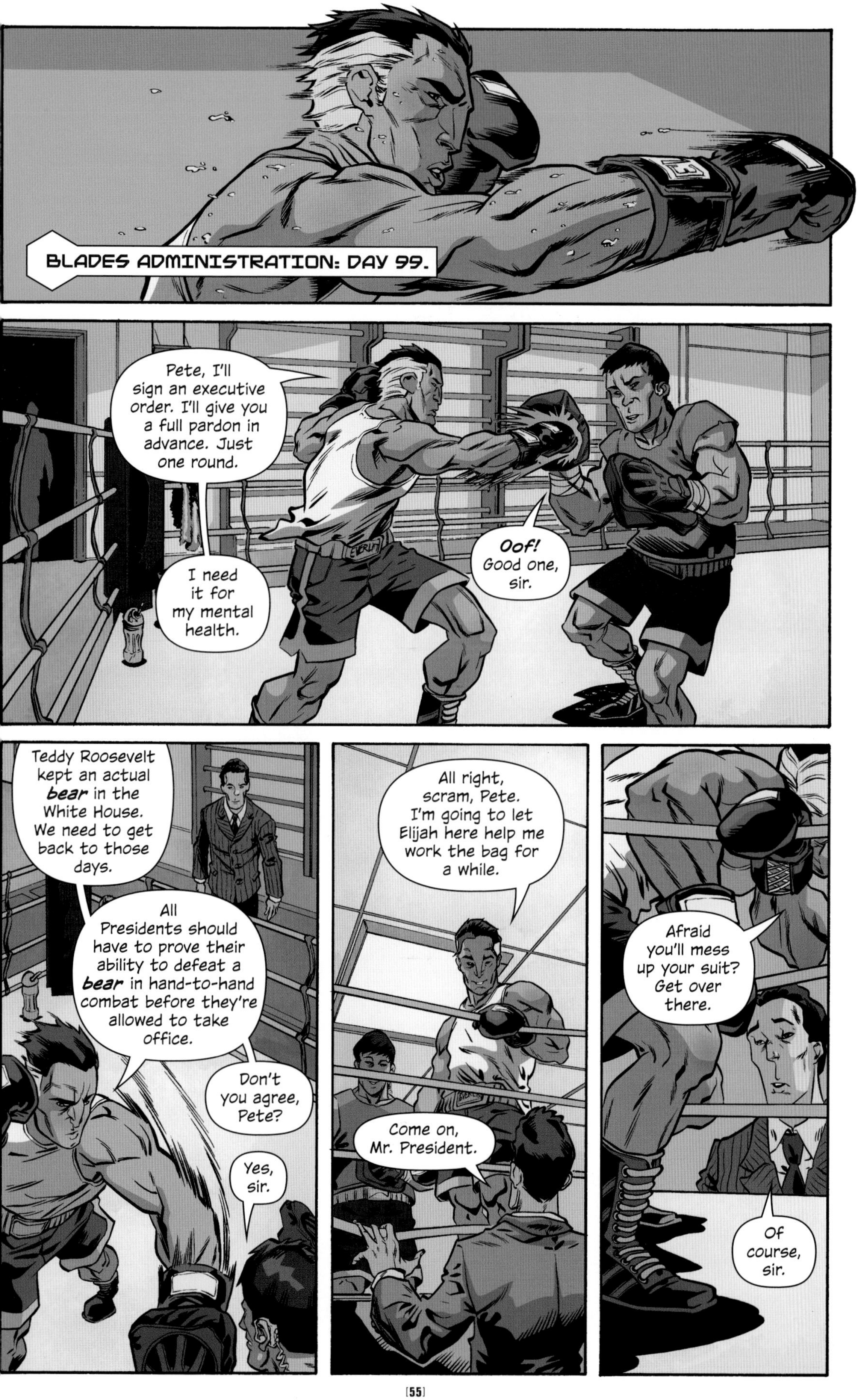
BLADES ADMINISTRATION: DAY 99.
Pete, I'll sign an executive order. I'll give you a full pardon in advance. Just one round.
I need it for my mental health.
Oof! Good one, sir.
Teddy Roosevelt kept an actual bear in the White House. We need to get back to those days.
All Presidents should have to prove their ability to defeat a bear in hand-to-hand combat before they're allowed to take office.
Don't you agree, Pete?
Yes, sir.
All right, scram, Pete. I'm going to let Elijah here help me work the bag for a while.
Come on, Mr. President.
Afraid you'll mess up your suit? Get over there.
Of course, sir.

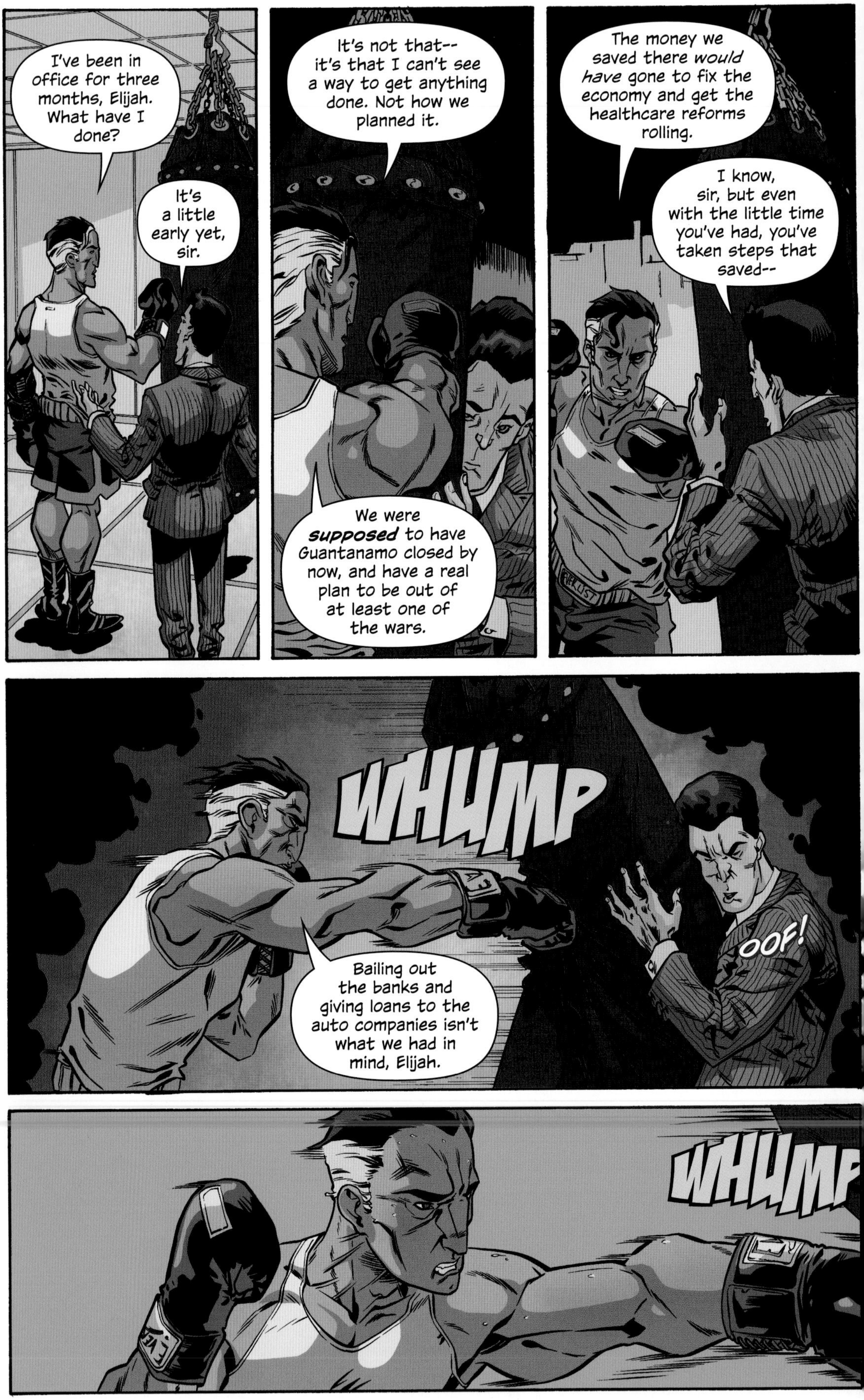

I've been in office for three months, Elijah. What have I done?
It's a little early yet, sir.
It's not that-- it's that I can't see a way to get anything done. Not how we planned it.
We were *supposed* to have Guantanamo closed by now, and have a real plan to be out of at least one of the wars.
The money we saved there *would have* gone to fix the economy and get the healthcare reforms rolling.
I know, sir, but even with the little time you've had, you've taken steps that saved--
WHUMP
OOF!
Bailing out the banks and giving loans to the auto companies isn't what we had in mind, Elijah.
WHUMP

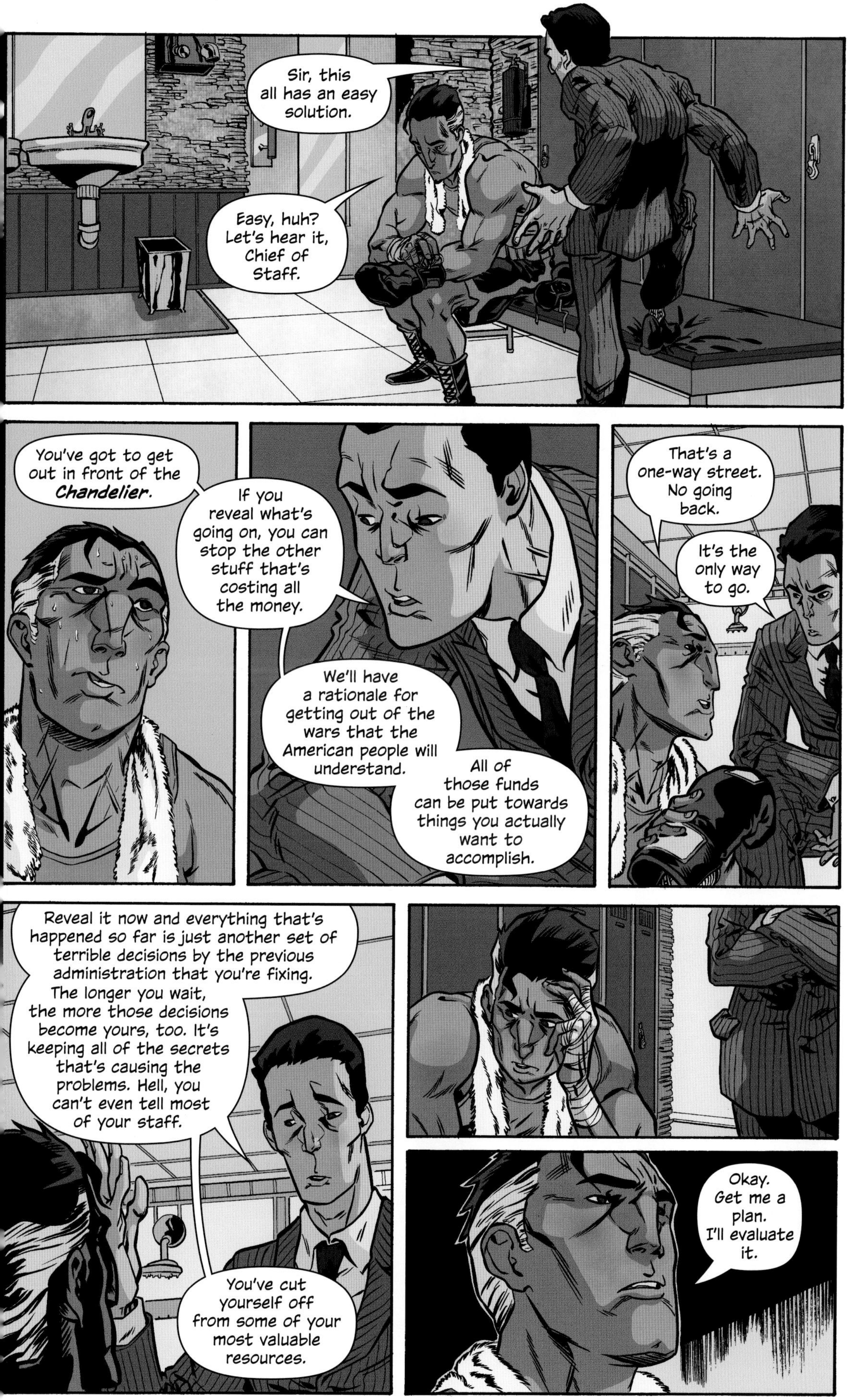
Sir, this all has an easy solution.
Easy, huh? Let's hear it, Chief of Staff.
You've got to get out in front of the *Chandelier*.
If you reveal what's going on, you can stop the other stuff that's costing all the money.
We'll have a rationale for getting out of the wars that the American people will understand.
All of those funds can be put towards things you actually want to accomplish.
That's a one-way street. No going back.
It's the only way to go.
Reveal it now and everything that's happened so far is just another set of terrible decisions by the previous administration that you're fixing.
The longer you wait, the more those decisions become yours, too. It's keeping all of the secrets that's causing the problems. Hell, you can't even tell most of your staff.
You've cut yourself off from some of your most valuable resources.
Okay. Get me a plan. I'll evaluate it.

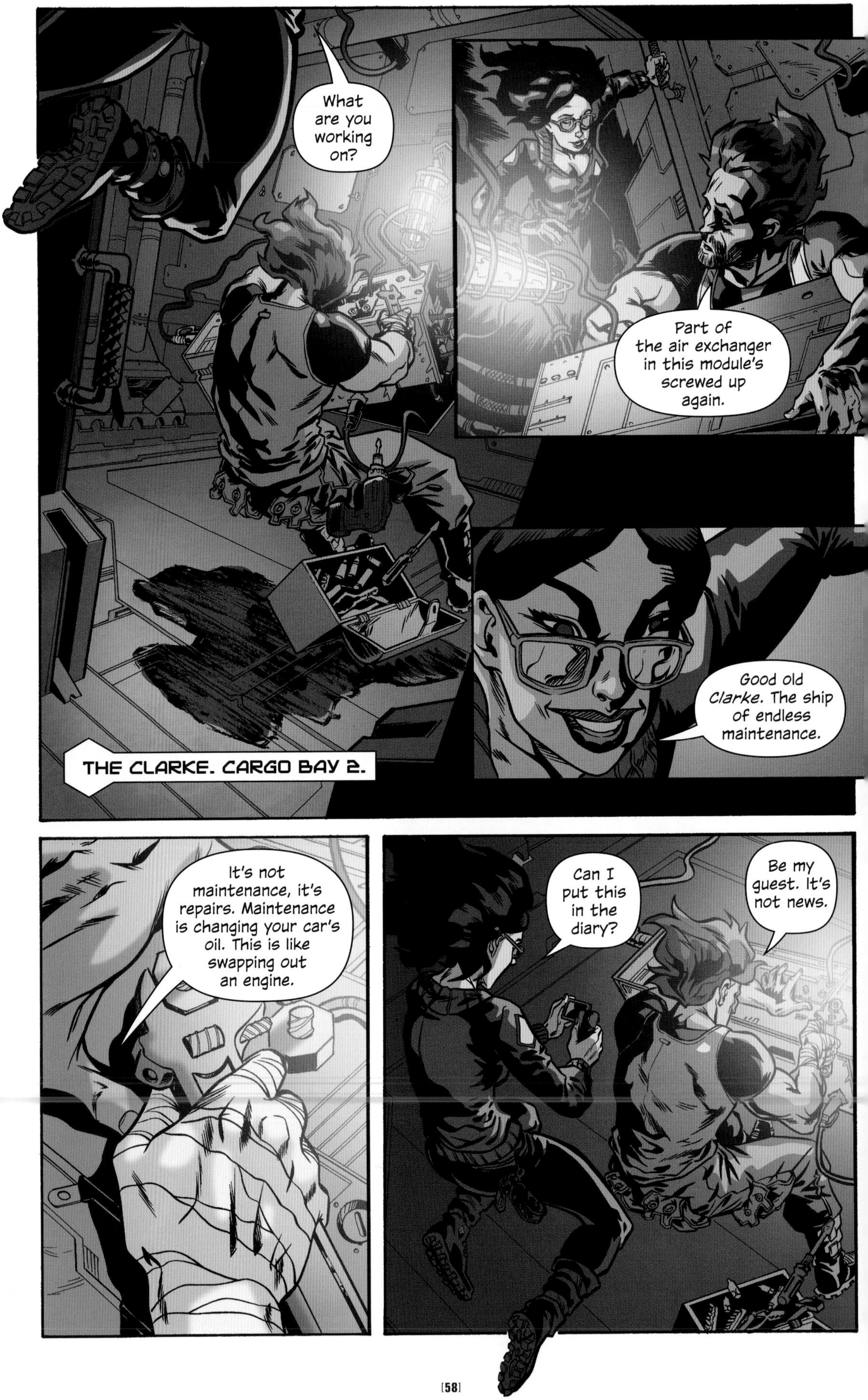
What are you working on?
Part of the air exchanger in this module's screwed up again.
Good old *Clarke*. The ship of endless maintenance.
THE CLARKE. CARGO BAY 2.
It's not maintenance, it's repairs. Maintenance is changing your car's oil. This is like swapping out an engine.
Can I put this in the diary?
Be my guest. It's not news.

So, this is chapter... what... three hundred and fifty in the ongoing chronicles of keeping the *Clarke* afloat?

What do you mean?

TOSHIBA

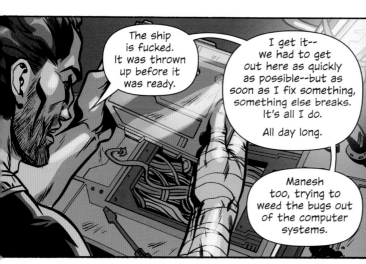

The ship is fucked. It was thrown up before it was ready.

I get it-- we had to get out here as quickly as possible--but as soon as I fix something, something else breaks. It's all I do.

All day long.

Manesh too, trying to weed the bugs out of the computer systems.

Sometime it's going to be something big enough that Manesh and I can't fix it, and that'll be that.

God, that's grim as hell. Turn that off, Kyoko. Or leave it on--I'll give you something to get on tape.

Big talker.

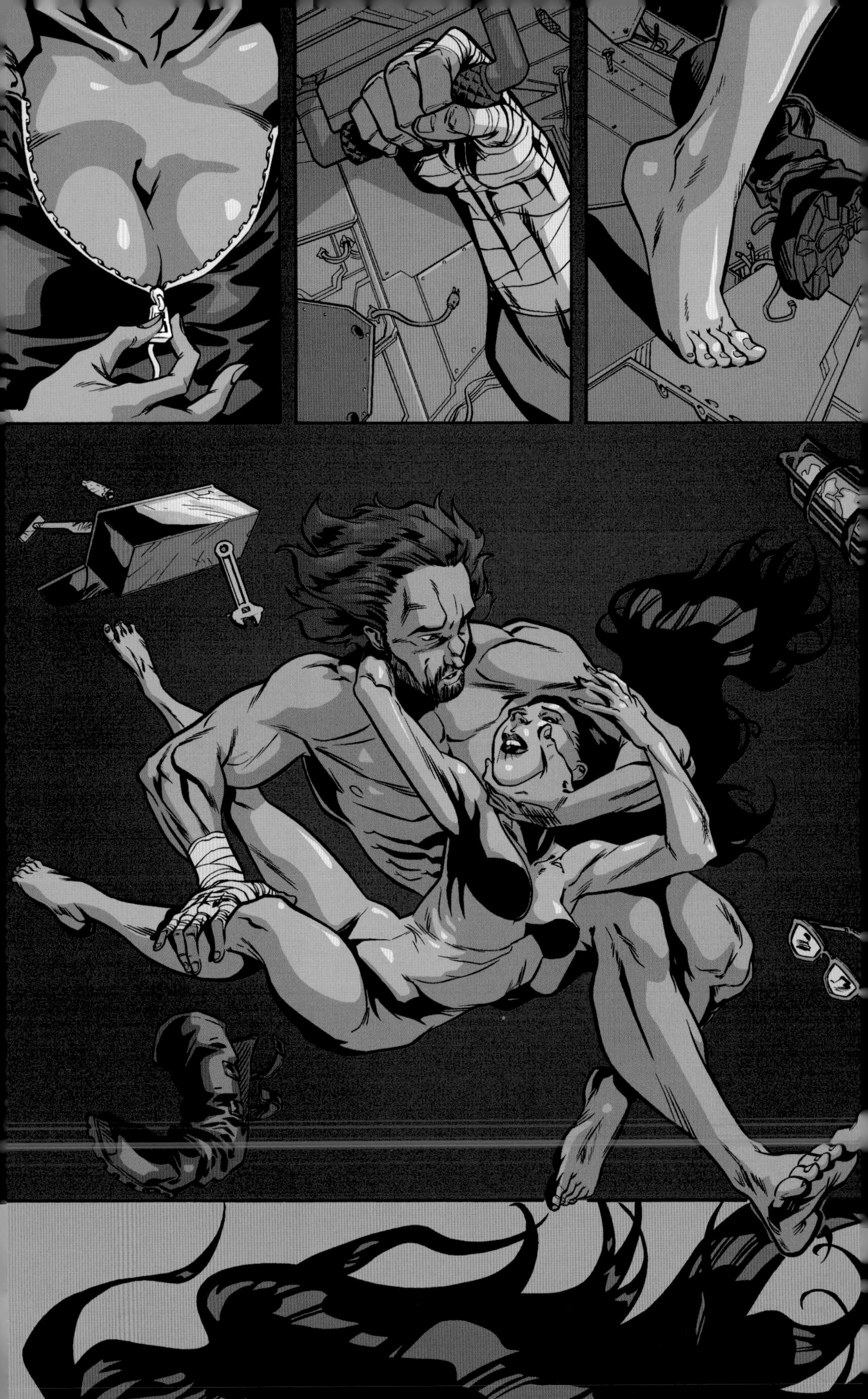

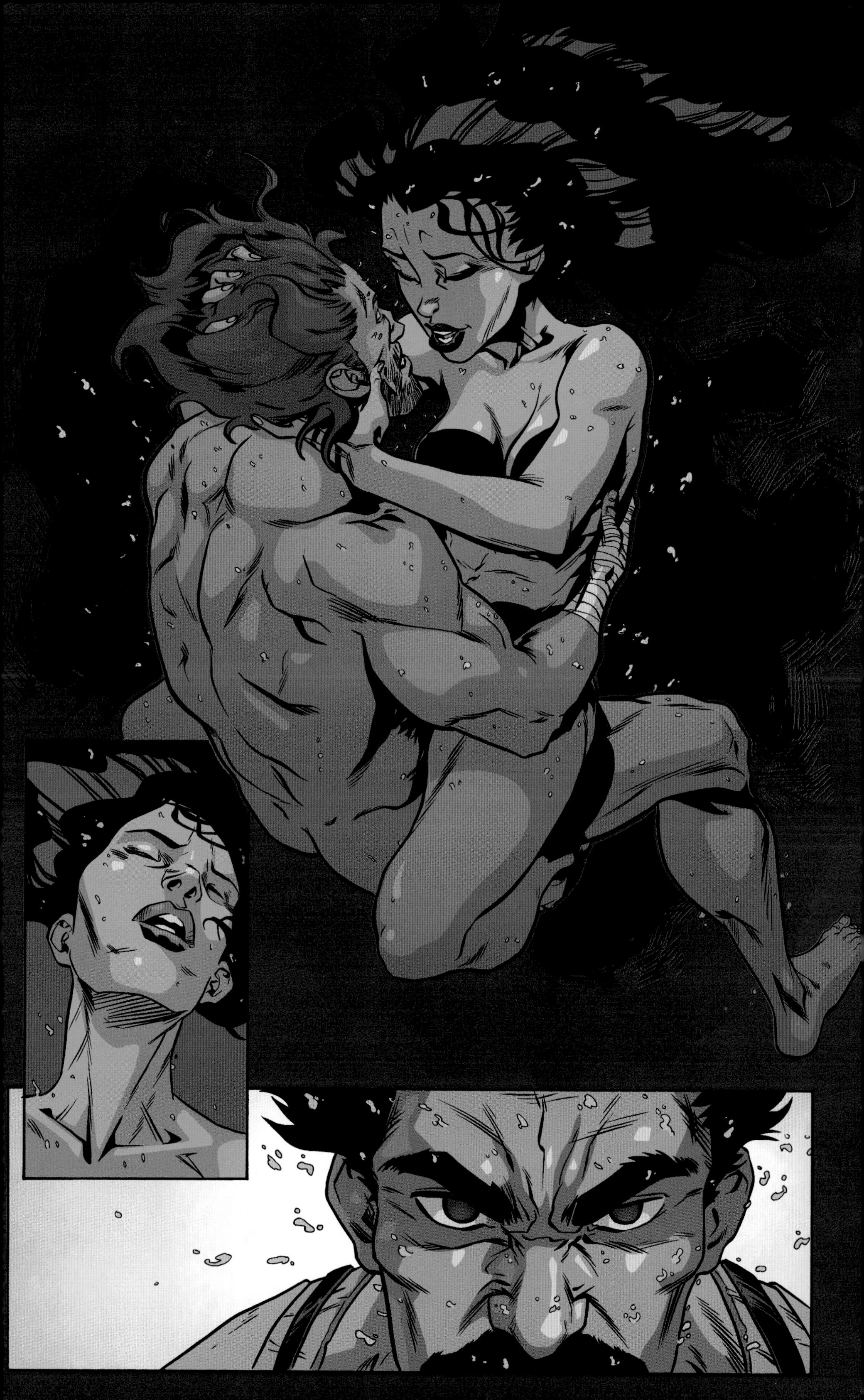

Jesus, Manesh, take it easy.

What choice do I have?

My friend, you need to put it out of your mind. Zen.

There are exactly two women on this ship. One is seven months pregnant, and she's spoken for by Pritchard and the Colonel.

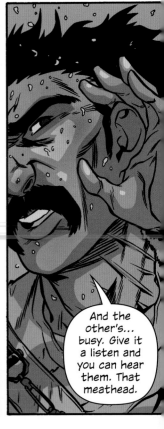

And the other's... busy. Give it a listen and you can hear them. That meathead.

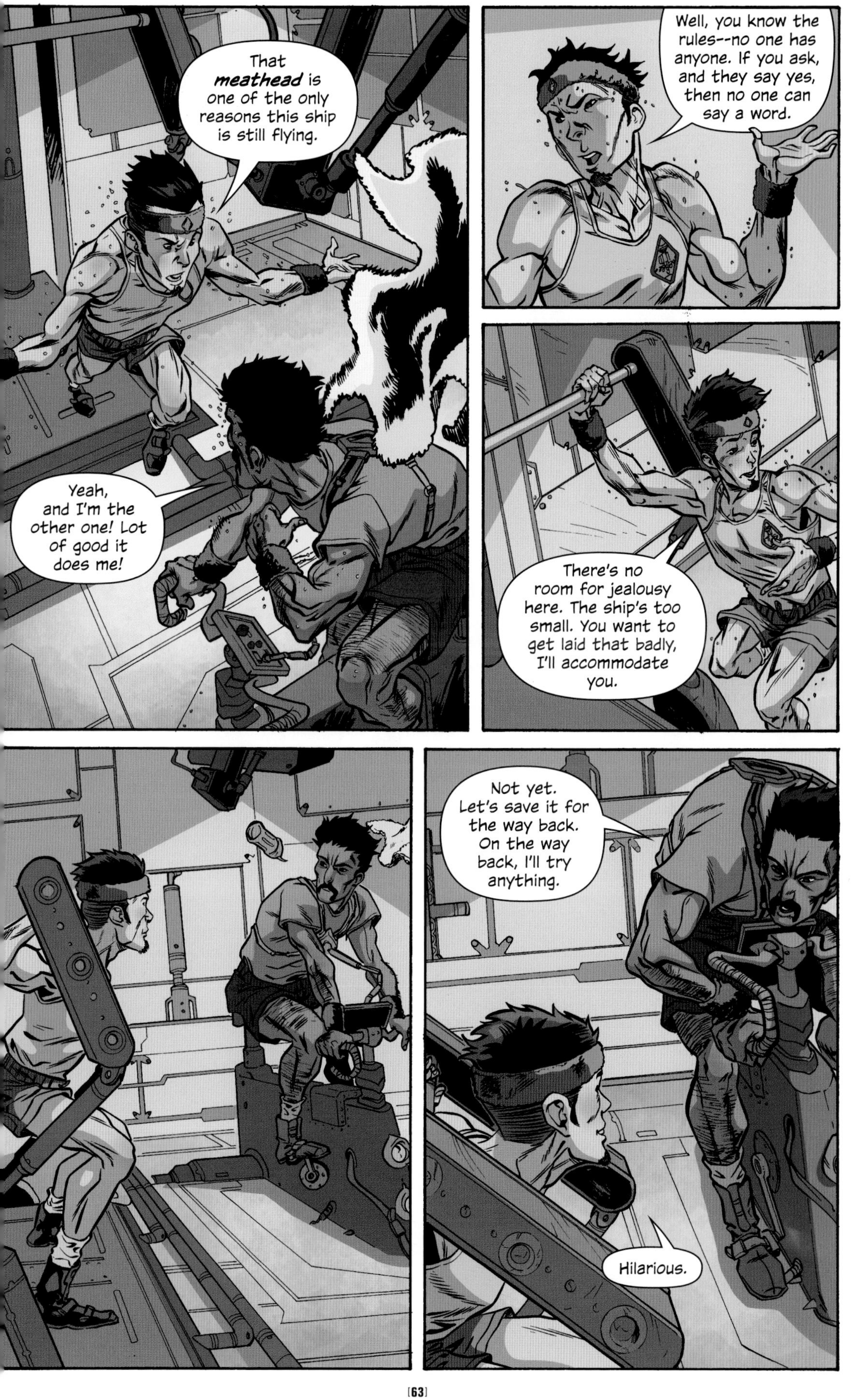
That *meathead* is one of the only reasons this ship is still flying.
Yeah, and I'm the other one! Lot of good it does me!
Well, you know the rules--no one has anyone. If you ask, and they say yes, then no one can say a word.
There's no room for jealousy here. The ship's too small. You want to get laid that badly, I'll accommodate you.
Not yet. Let's save it for the way back. On the way back, I'll try anything.
Hilarious.

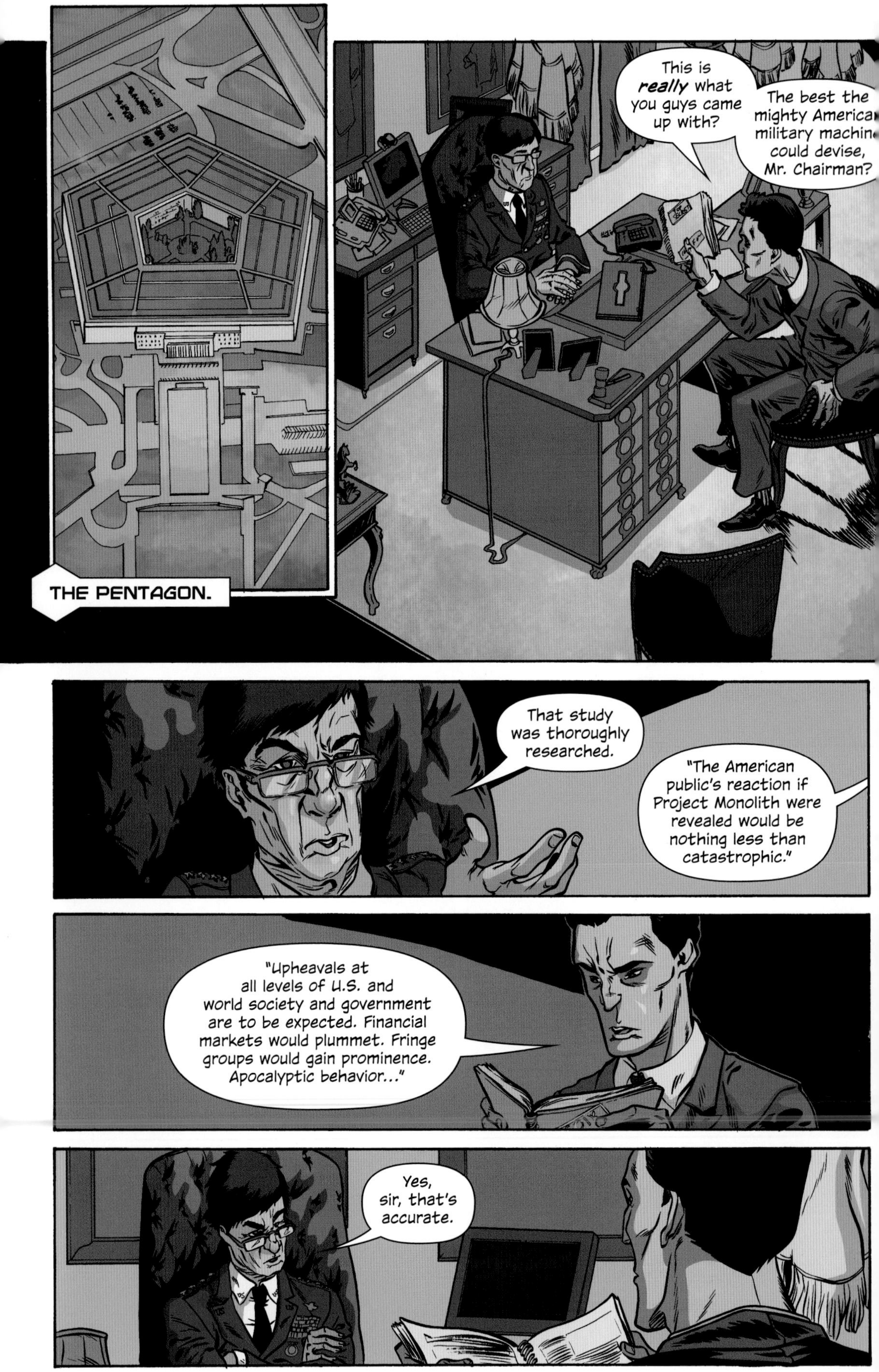
THE PENTAGON.
This is *really* what you guys came up with?
The best the mighty America military machin could devise, Mr. Chairman?
That study was thoroughly researched.
"The American public's reaction if Project Monolith were revealed would be nothing less than catastrophic."
"Upheavals at all levels of U.S. and world society and government are to be expected. Financial markets would plummet. Fringe groups would gain prominence. Apocalyptic behavior..."
Yes, sir, that's accurate.

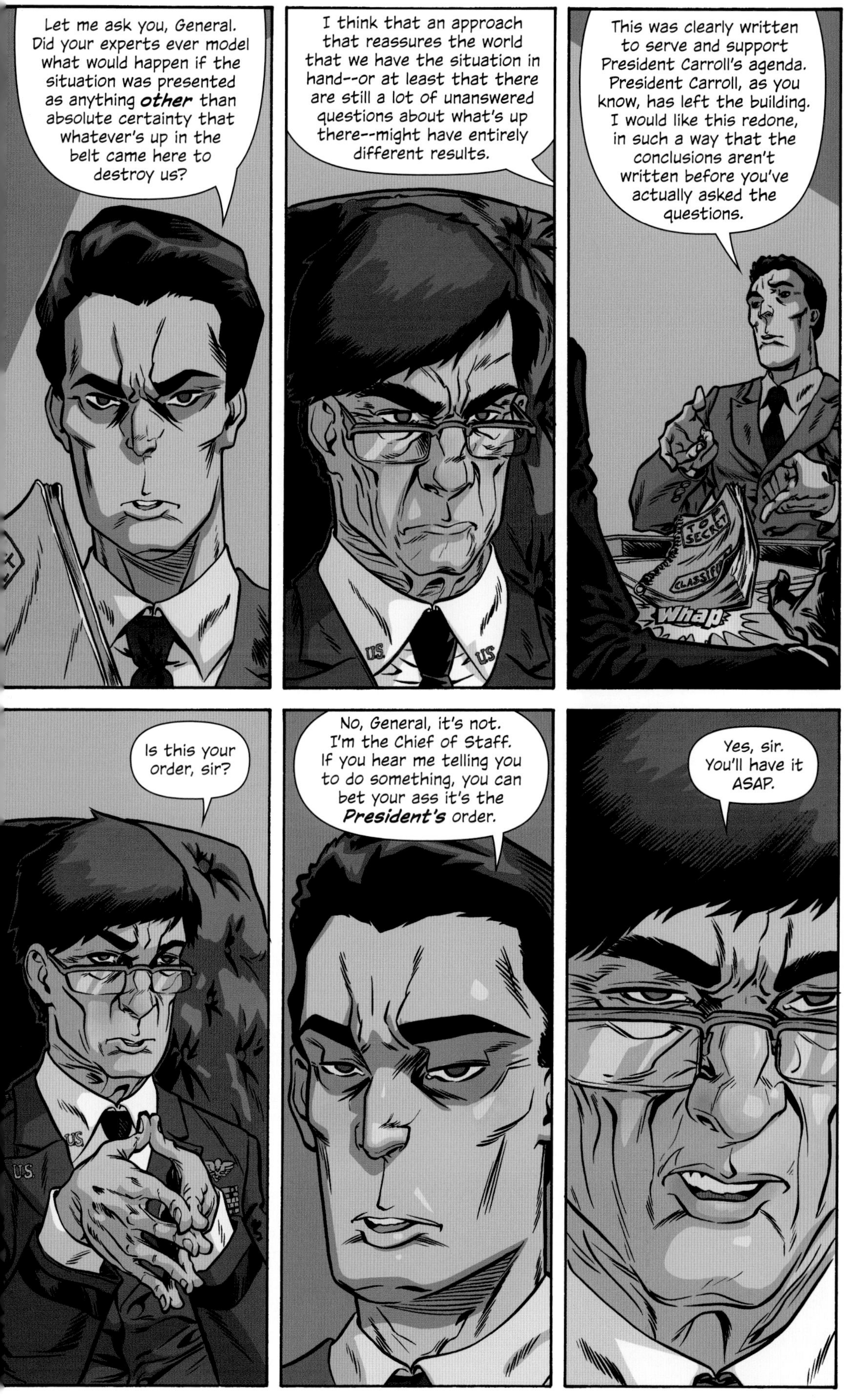
Let me ask you, General. Did your experts ever model what would happen if the situation was presented as anything *other* than absolute certainty that whatever's up in the belt came here to destroy us?
I think that an approach that reassures the world that we have the situation in hand--or at least that there are still a lot of unanswered questions about what's up there--might have entirely different results.
This was clearly written to serve and support President Carroll's agenda. President Carroll, as you know, has left the building. I would like this redone, in such a way that the conclusions aren't written before you've actually asked the questions.
TOP SECRET
CLASSIFI
Whap
Is this your order, sir?
No, General, it's not. I'm the Chief of Staff. If you hear me telling you to do something, you can bet your ass it's the *President's* order.
Yes, sir. You'll have it ASAP.

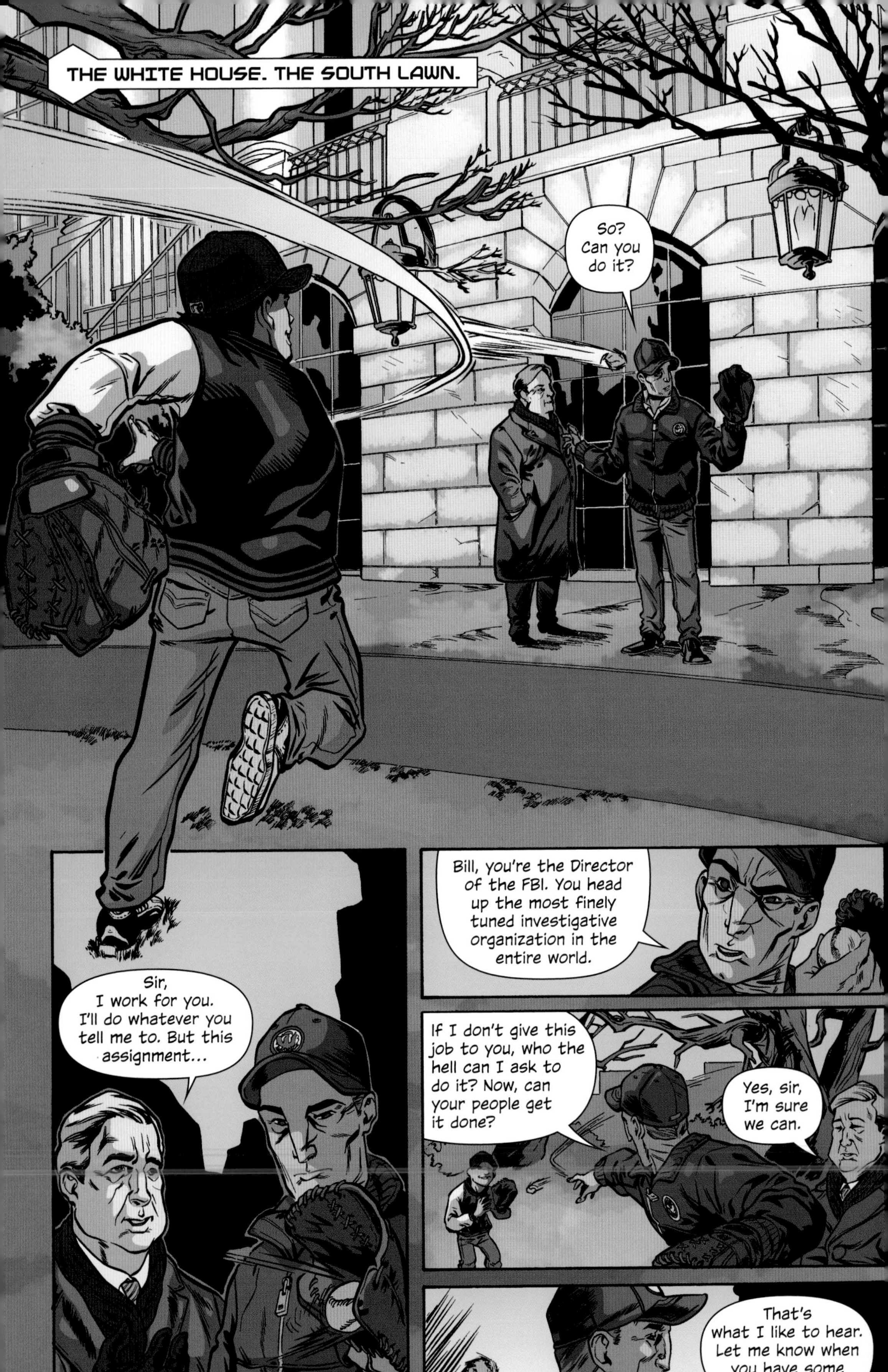
THE WHITE HOUSE. THE SOUTH LAWN.
So? Can you do it?
Sir, I work for you. I'll do whatever you tell me to. But this assignment...
Bill, you're the Director of the FBI. You head up the most finely tuned investigative organization in the entire world.
If I don't give this job to you, who the hell can I ask to do it? Now, can your people get it done?
Yes, sir, I'm sure we can.
That's what I like to hear. Let me know when you have some news.

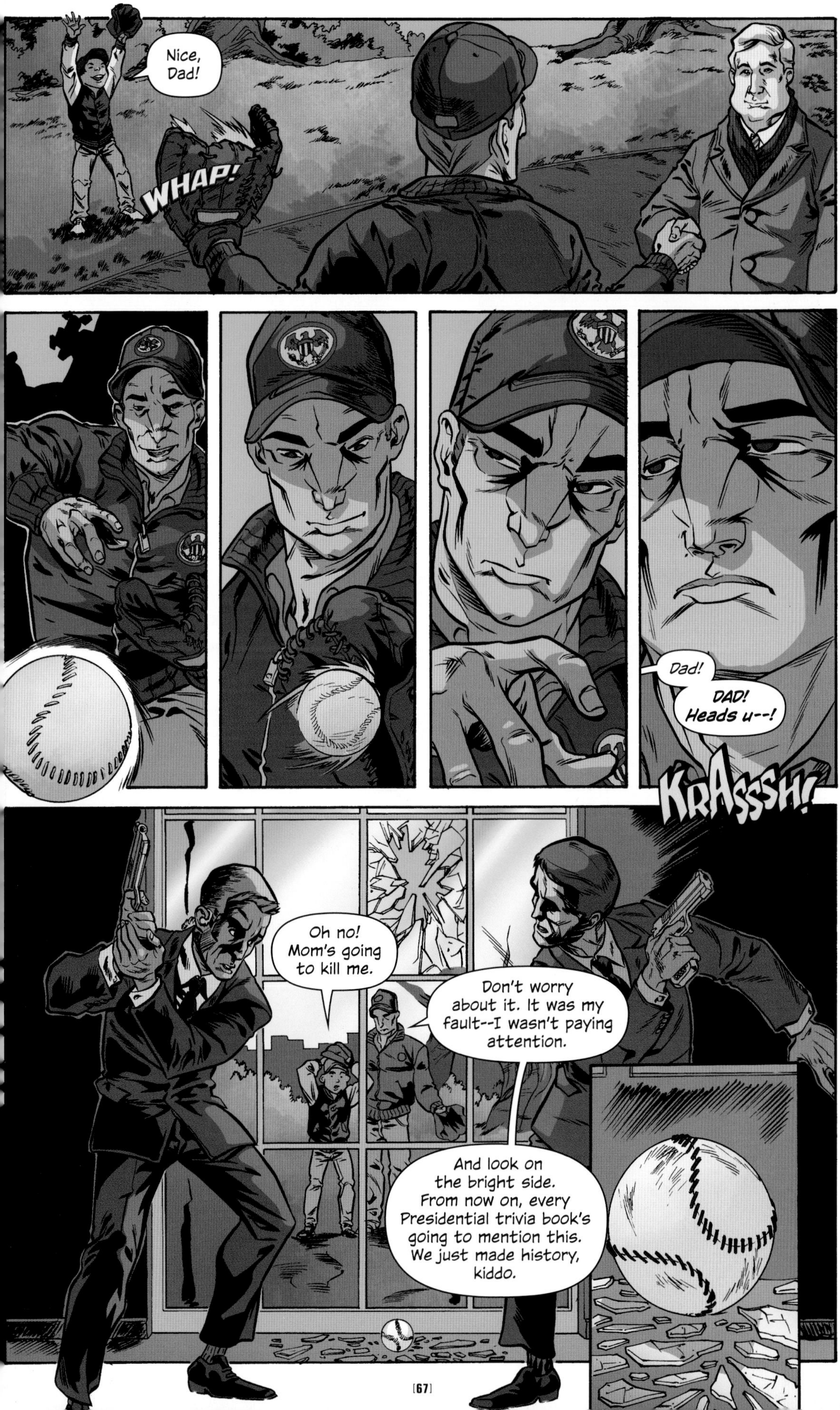

Nice, Dad!
WHAP!
Dad!
DAD! Heads u--!
KRASSSH!
Oh no! Mom's going to kill me.
Don't worry about it. It was my fault--I wasn't paying attention.
And look on the bright side. From now on, every Presidential trivia book's going to mention this. We just made history, kiddo.

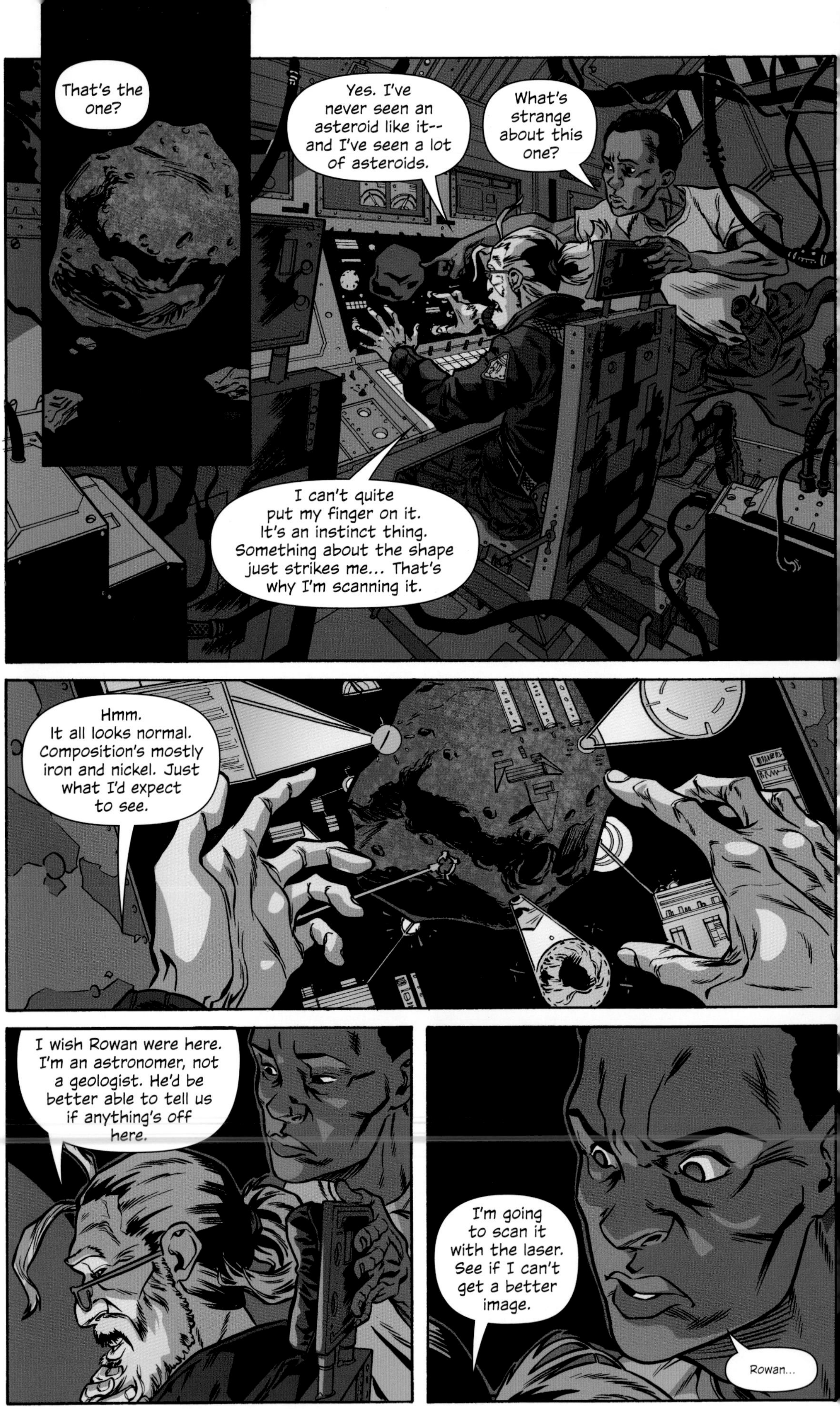
That's the one?
Yes. I've never seen an asteroid like it-- and I've seen a lot of asteroids.
What's strange about this one?
I can't quite put my finger on it. It's an instinct thing. Something about the shape just strikes me... That's why I'm scanning it.
Hmm. It all looks normal. Composition's mostly iron and nickel. Just what I'd expect to see.
I wish Rowan were here. I'm an astronomer, not a geologist. He'd be better able to tell us if anything's off here.
I'm going to scan it with the laser. See if I can't get a better image.
Rowan...

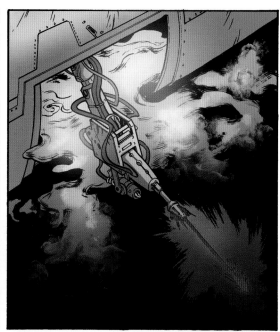
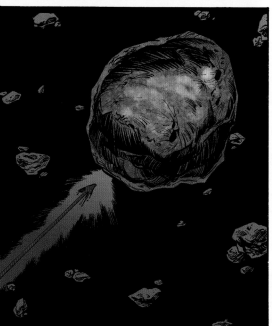
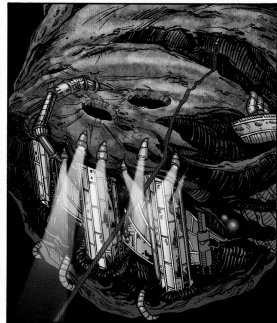

Wow.

You're sure it's not just a reflection of your original signal?

Of course it's not a reflection! I never...

Easy, Pritchard.

The signal was returned to us at exactly the same strength as the one we sent out. No degradation at all.

Even in space, even with a laser, there would be things in the way.

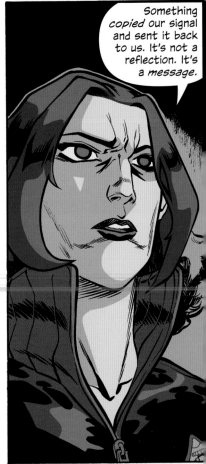

Something *copied* our signal and sent it back to us. It's not a reflection. It's a *message*.

Dust and so on--enough to diffuse the beam a little, so even if it was a reflection, it would come back a little weaker than what we sent out.

Not to mention that an asteroid reflective enough to bounce our laser back at us would be reflecting sunlight like a searchlight in space. It would be impossible to miss.

So what does this mean?

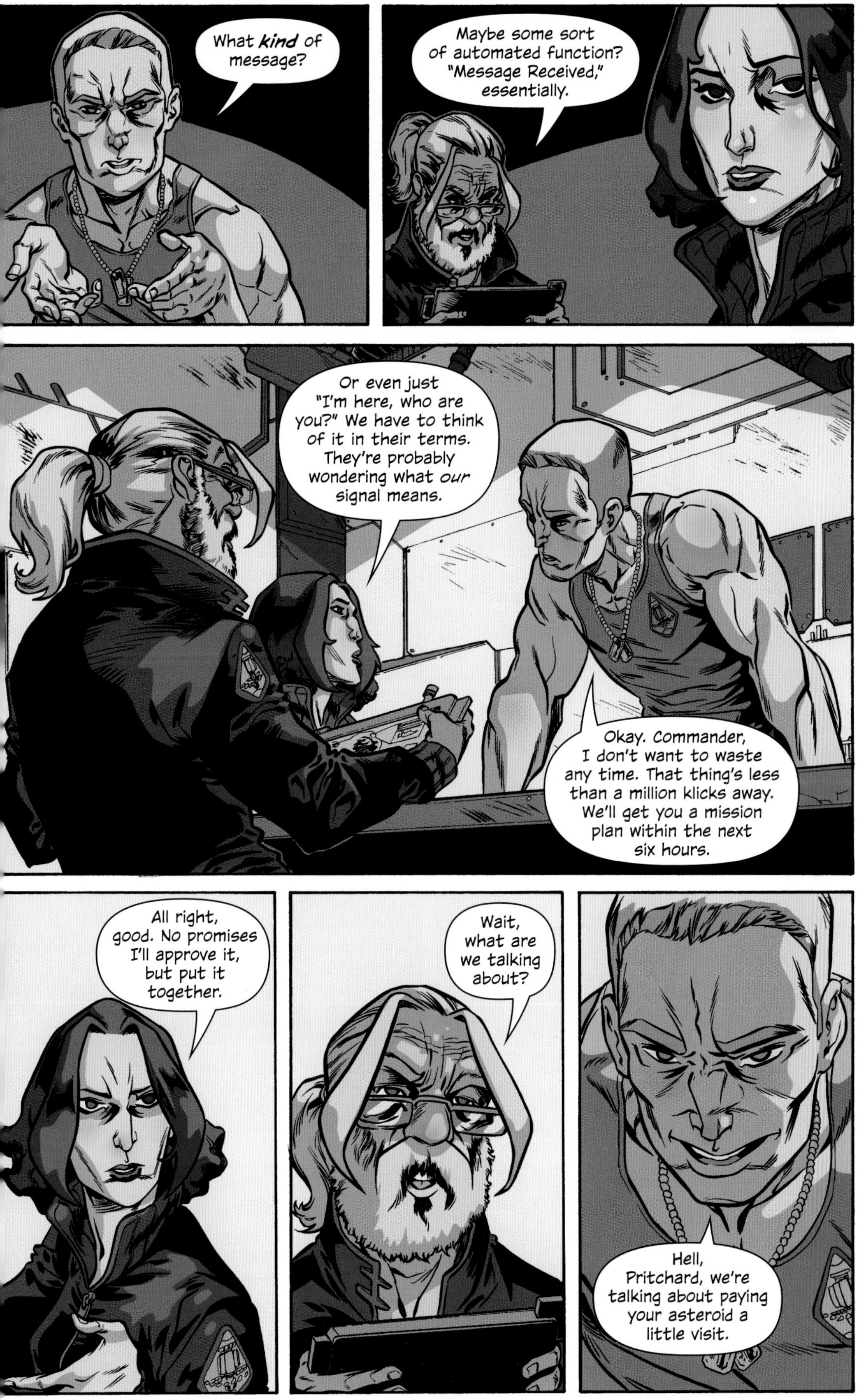
What *kind* of message?
Maybe some sort of automated function? "Message Received," essentially.
Or even just "I'm here, who are you?" We have to think of it in their terms. They're probably wondering what *our* signal means.
Okay. Commander, I don't want to waste any time. That thing's less than a million klicks away. We'll get you a mission plan within the next six hours.
All right, good. No promises I'll approve it, but put it together.
Wait, what are we talking about?
Hell, Pritchard, we're talking about paying your asteroid a little visit.

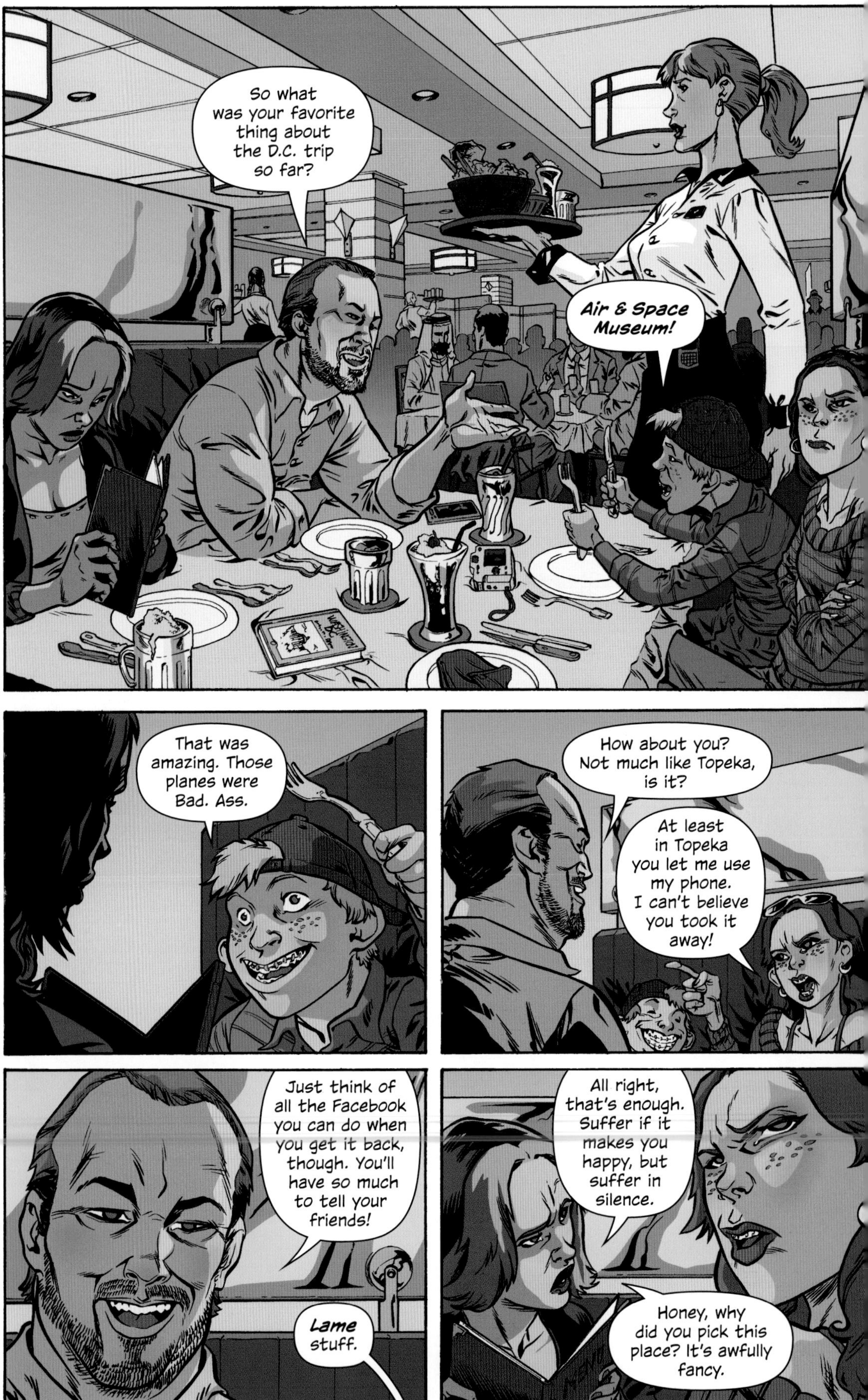
So what was your favorite thing about the D.C. trip so far?
Air & Space Museum!
That was amazing. Those planes were Bad. Ass.
How about you? Not much like Topeka, is it?
At least in Topeka you let me use my phone. I can't believe you took it away!
Just think of all the Facebook you can do when you get it back, though. You'll have so much to tell your friends!
Lame stuff.
All right, that's enough. Suffer if it makes you happy, but suffer in silence.
Honey, why did you pick this place? It's awfully fancy.

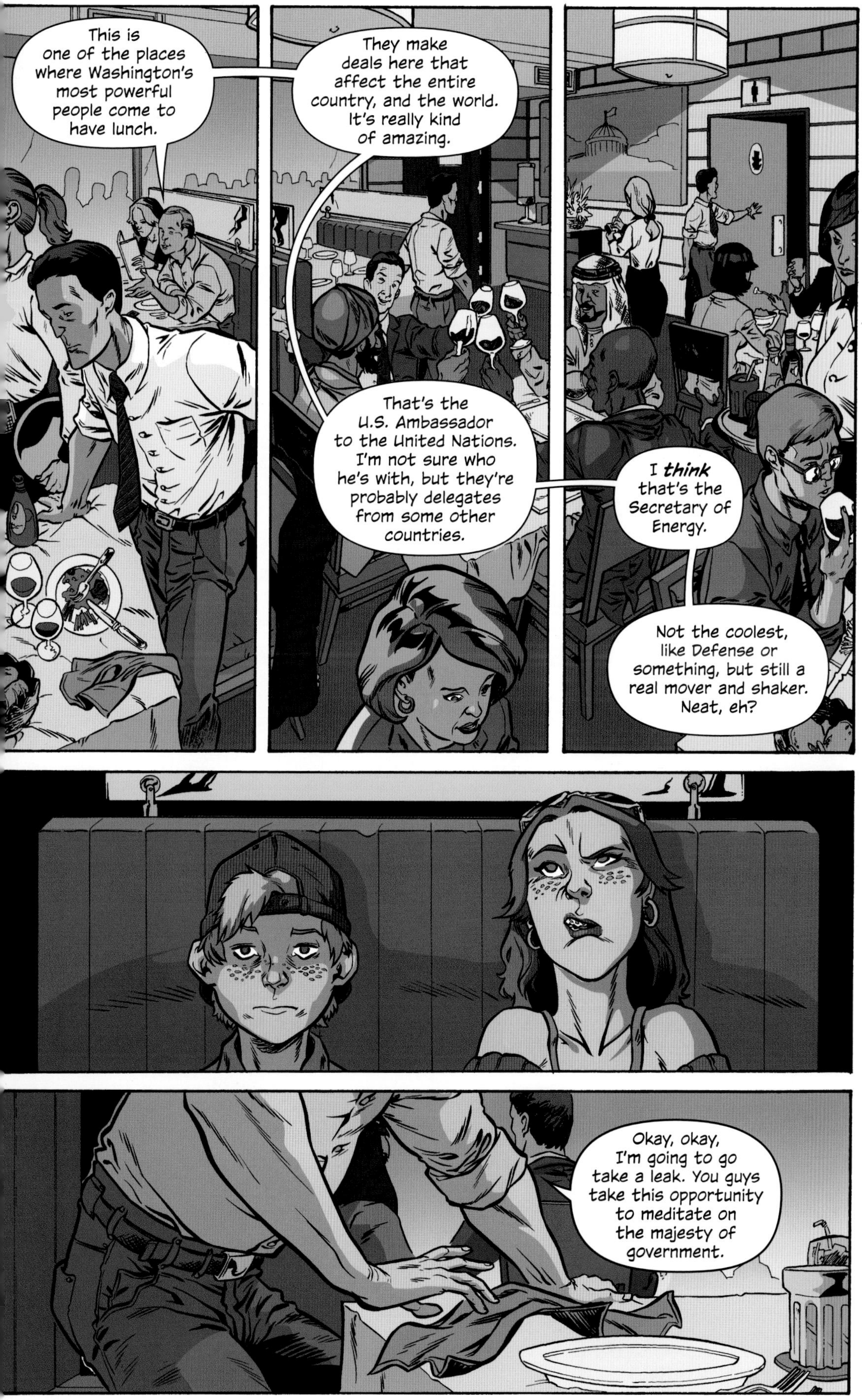
This is one of the places where Washington's most powerful people come to have lunch.
They make deals here that affect the entire country, and the world. It's really kind of amazing.
That's the U.S. Ambassador to the United Nations. I'm not sure who he's with, but they're probably delegates from some other countries.
I *think* that's the Secretary of Energy.
Not the coolest, like Defense or something, but still a real mover and shaker. Neat, eh?
Okay, okay, I'm going to go take a leak. You guys take this opportunity to meditate on the majesty of government.

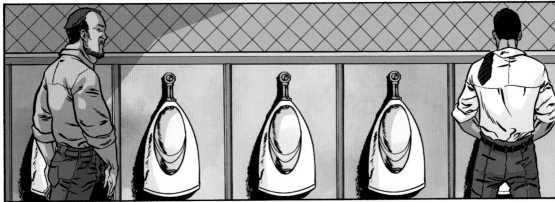

Say, you're Elijah Green, the President's Chief of Staff!

I love Washington. Some of the most powerful people in the world, right out with us regular folks. I feel like I'm peeing next to Bruce Springsteen.

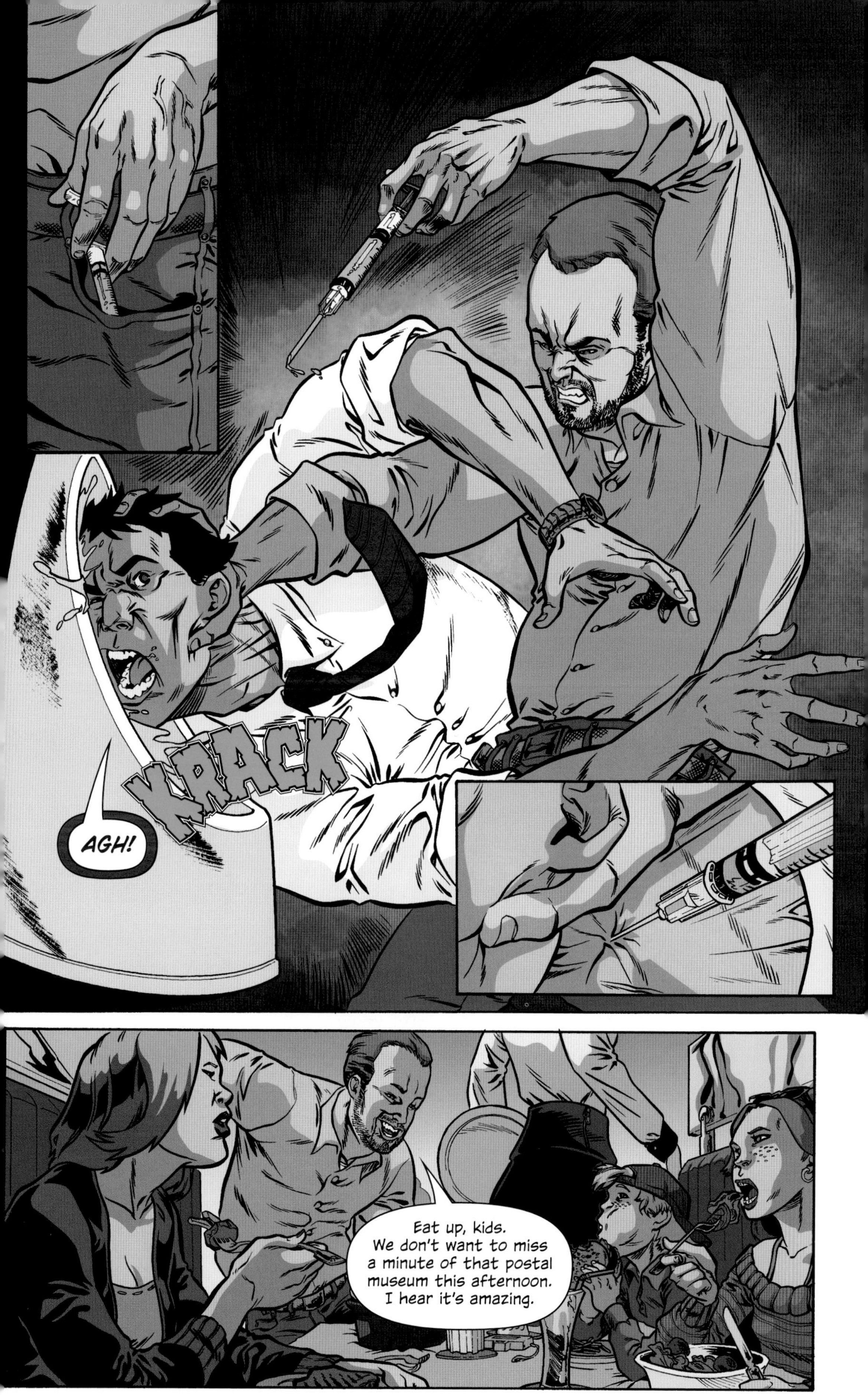
KRACK
AGH!
Eat up, kids.
We don't want to miss
a minute of that postal
museum this afternoon.
I hear it's amazing.

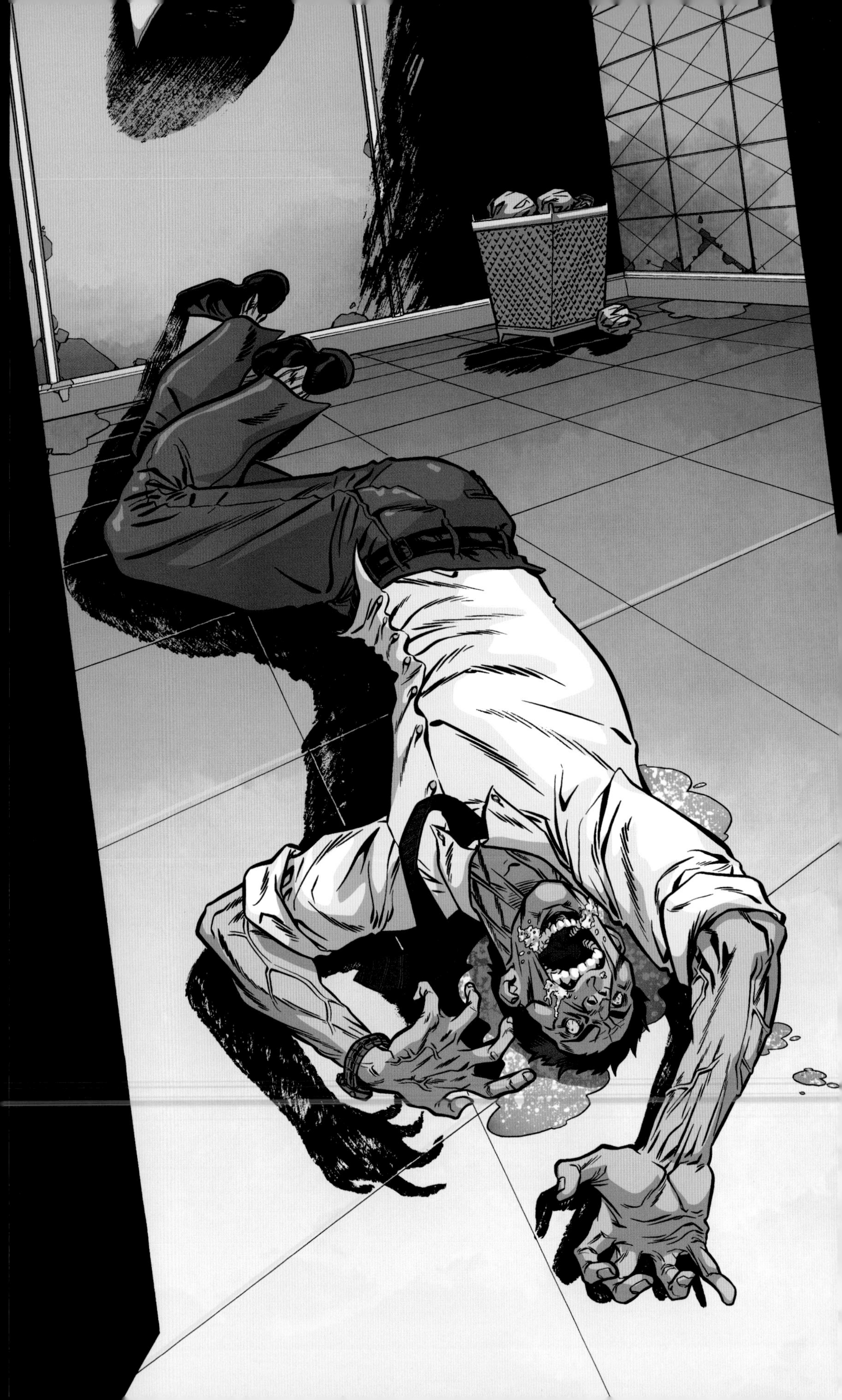

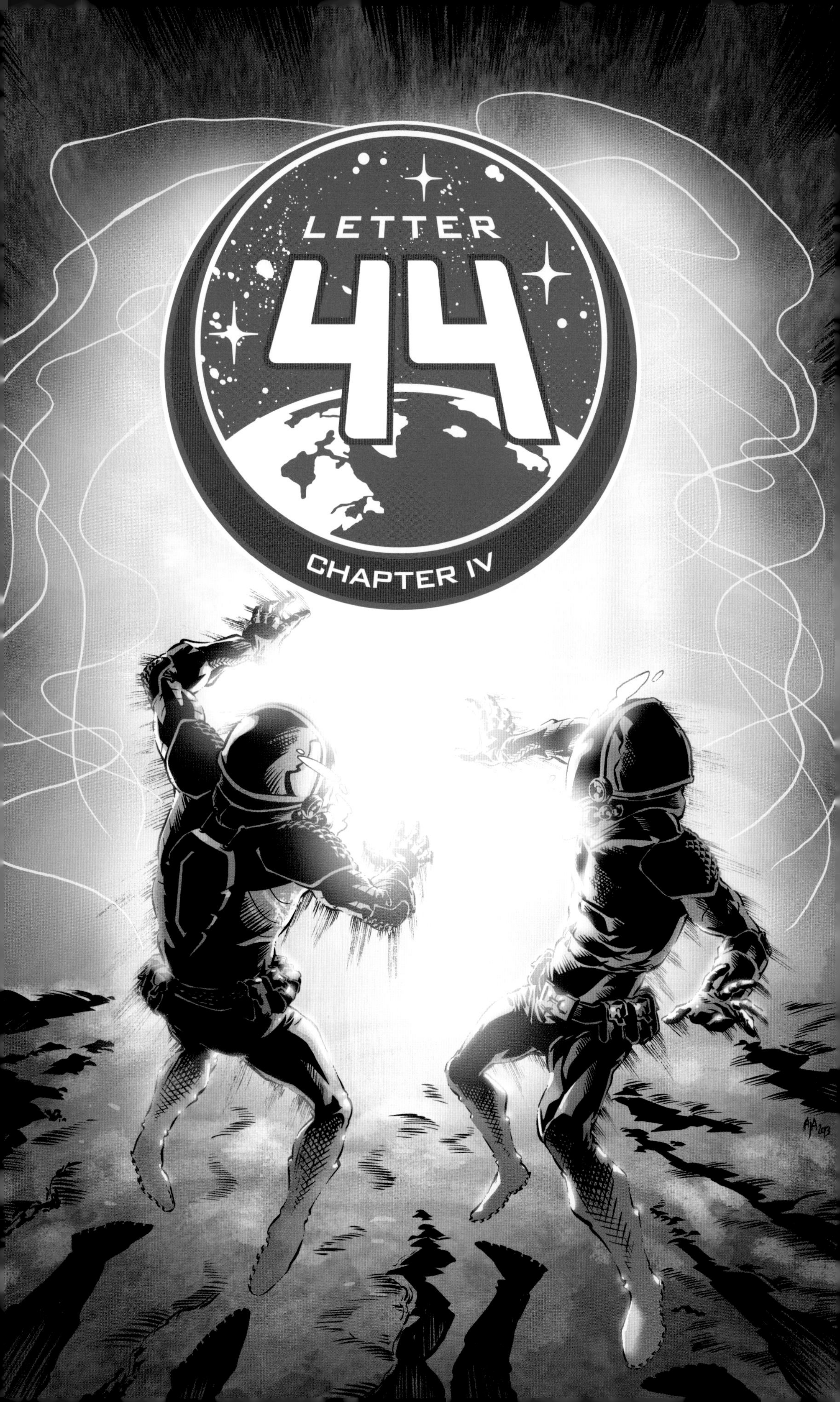
LETTER
44
CHAPTER IV

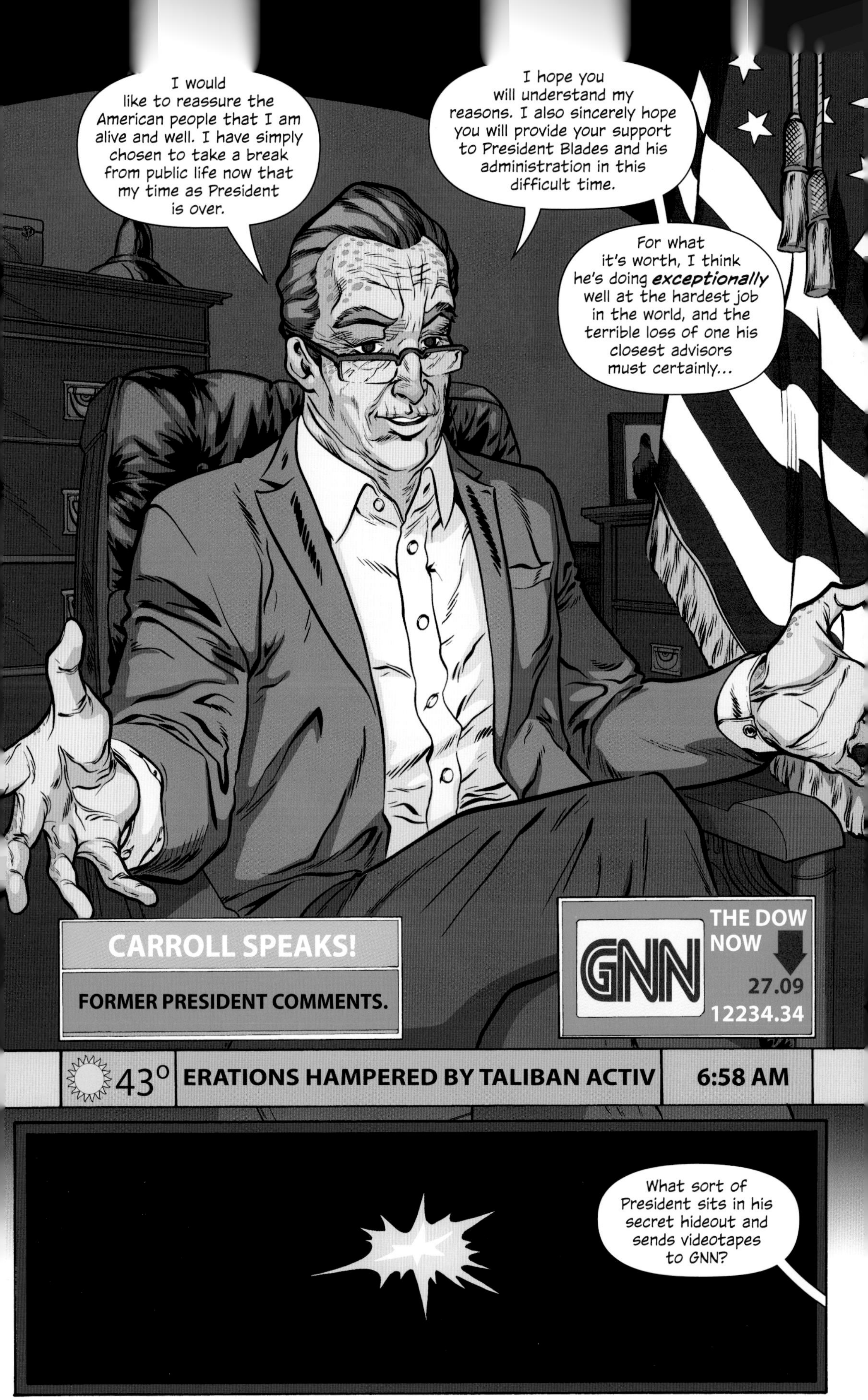
I would like to reassure the American people that I am alive and well. I have simply chosen to take a break from public life now that my time as President is over.
I hope you will understand my reasons. I also sincerely hope you will provide your support to President Blades and his administration in this difficult time.
For what it's worth, I think he's doing *exceptionally* well at the hardest job in the world, and the terrible loss of one his closest advisors must certainly...
CARROLL SPEAKS!
FORMER PRESIDENT COMMENTS.
GNN
THE DOW NOW
27.09
12234.34
43°
ERATIONS HAMPERED BY TALIBAN ACTIV
6:58 AM
What sort of President sits in his secret hideout and sends videotapes to GNN?

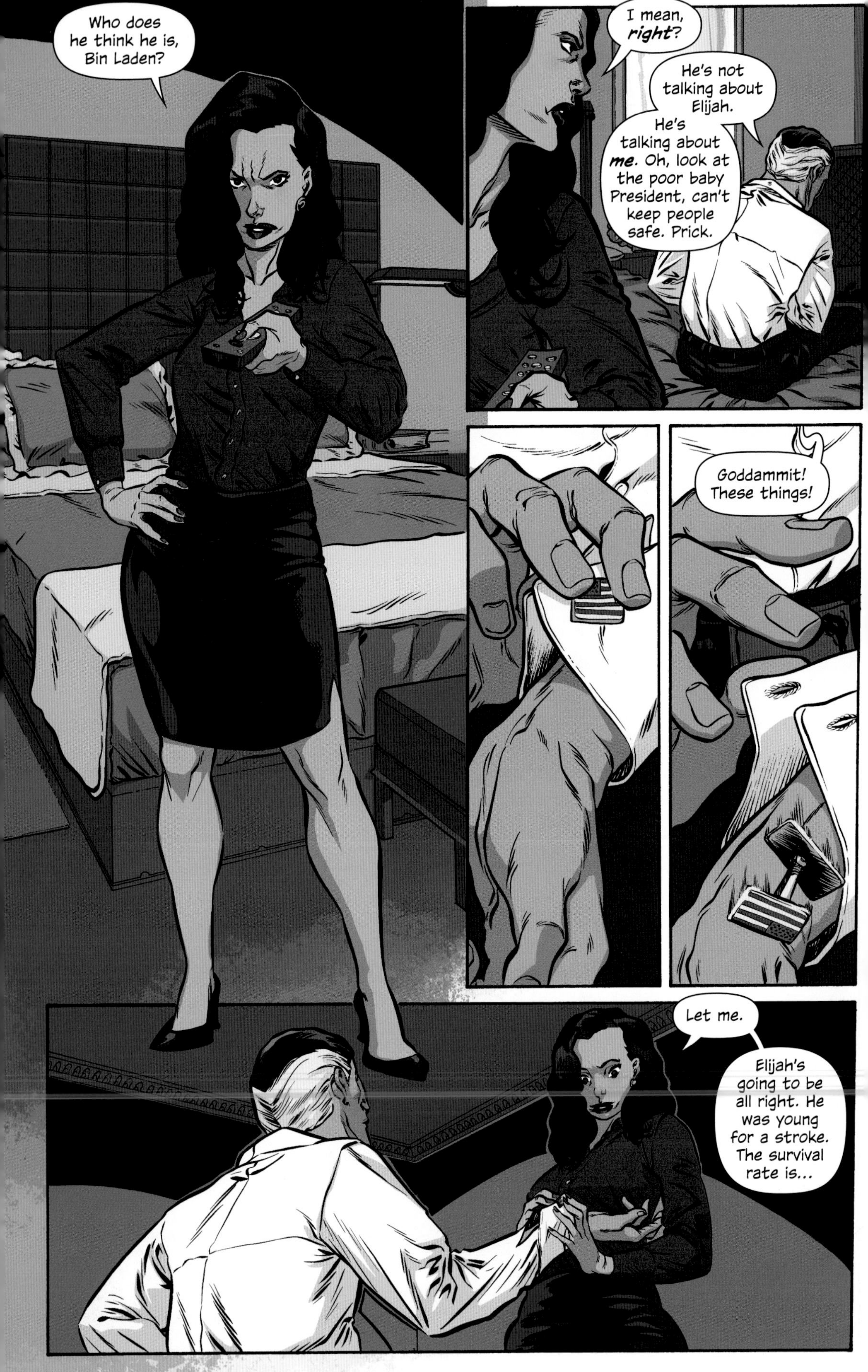

Who does he think he is, Bin Laden?
I mean, *right*?
He's not talking about Elijah.
He's talking about *me*. Oh, look at the poor baby President, can't keep people safe. Prick.
Goddammit! These things!
Let me.
Elijah's going to be all right. He was young for a stroke. The survival rate is...

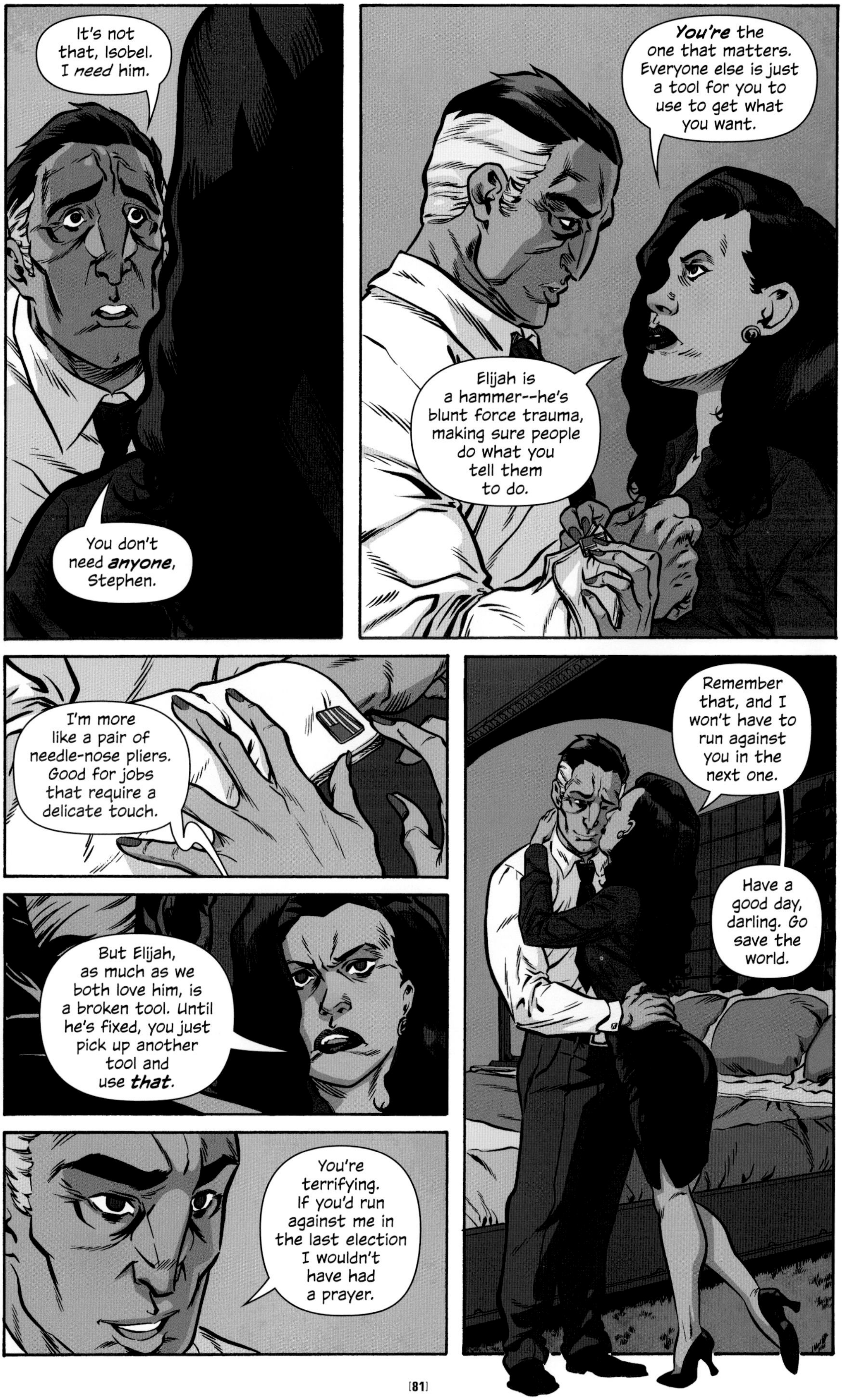
It's not that, Isobel. I *need* him.
You don't need ***anyone***, Stephen.
You're the one that matters. Everyone else is just a tool for you to use to get what you want.
Elijah is a hammer--he's blunt force trauma, making sure people do what you tell them to do.
I'm more like a pair of needle-nose pliers. Good for jobs that require a delicate touch.
But Elijah, as much as we both love him, is a broken tool. Until he's fixed, you just pick up another tool and use ***that***.
You're terrifying. If you'd run against me in the last election I wouldn't have had a prayer.
Remember that, and I won't have to run against you in the next one.
Have a good day, darling. Go save the world.

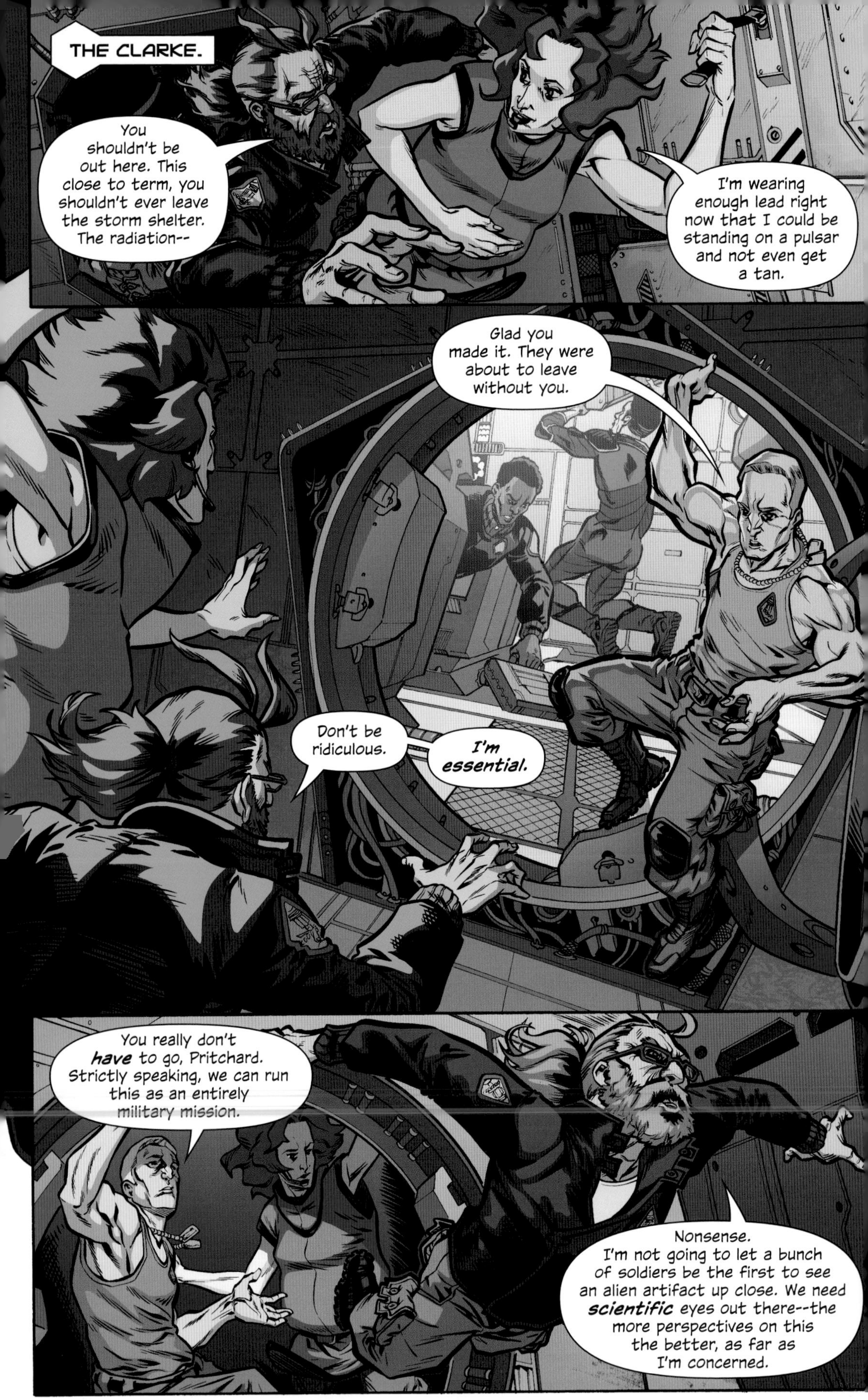
THE CLARKE.
You shouldn't be out here. This close to term, you shouldn't ever leave the storm shelter. The radiation--
I'm wearing enough lead right now that I could be standing on a pulsar and not even get a tan.
Glad you made it. They were about to leave without you.
Don't be ridiculous.
I'm essential.
You really don't ***have*** to go, Pritchard. Strictly speaking, we can run this as an entirely military mission.
Nonsense. I'm not going to let a bunch of soldiers be the first to see an alien artifact up close. We need ***scientific*** eyes out there--the more perspectives on this the better, as far as I'm concerned.

All right--four days there, four days back, plus two on the asteroid. You've got a little safety margin, but stay much longer and the trajectories won't work to get back to us.

We know, Colonel.

Not the sort of thing one forgets, when faced with the prospect of eternal space maroonment.

Never hurts to hear it again.

Major Drum, command of the *Bowman* is yours. Good luck, and get home safe.

Thank you, sir. We'll see you soon.

See you soon, darling. Stay in the storm shelter!

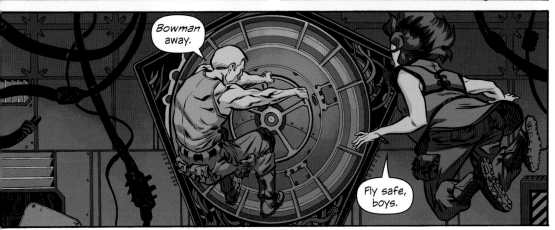

Bowman away.

Fly safe, boys.

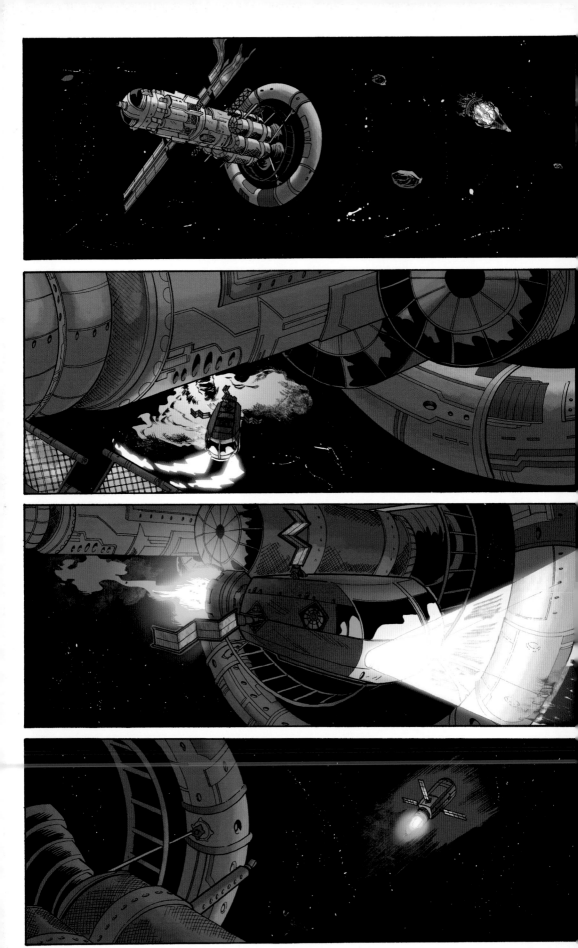

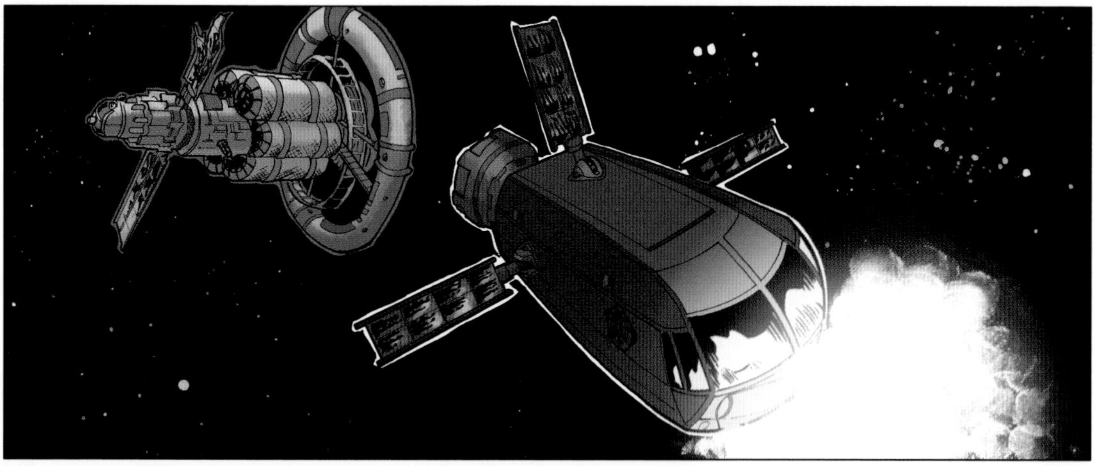
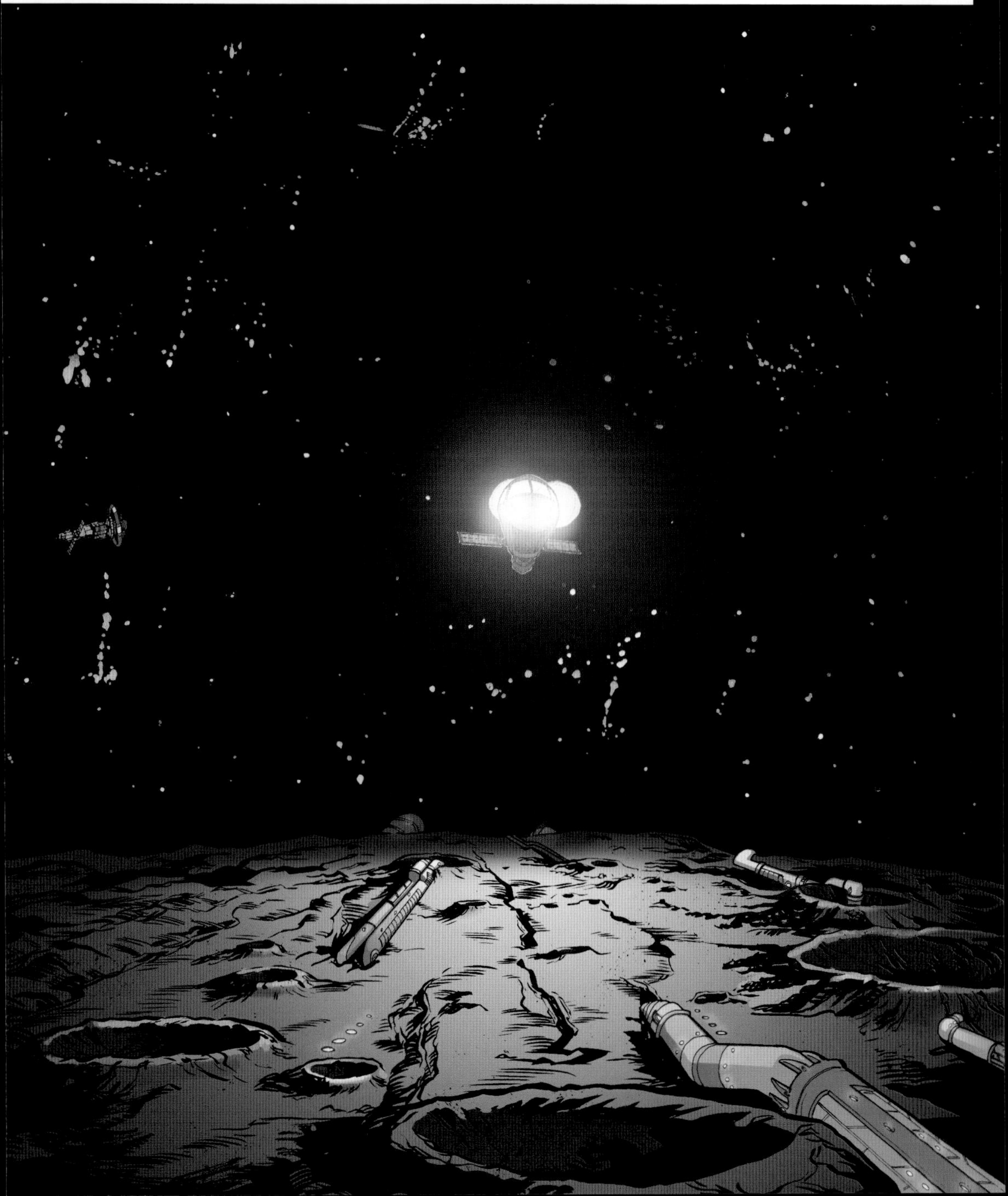

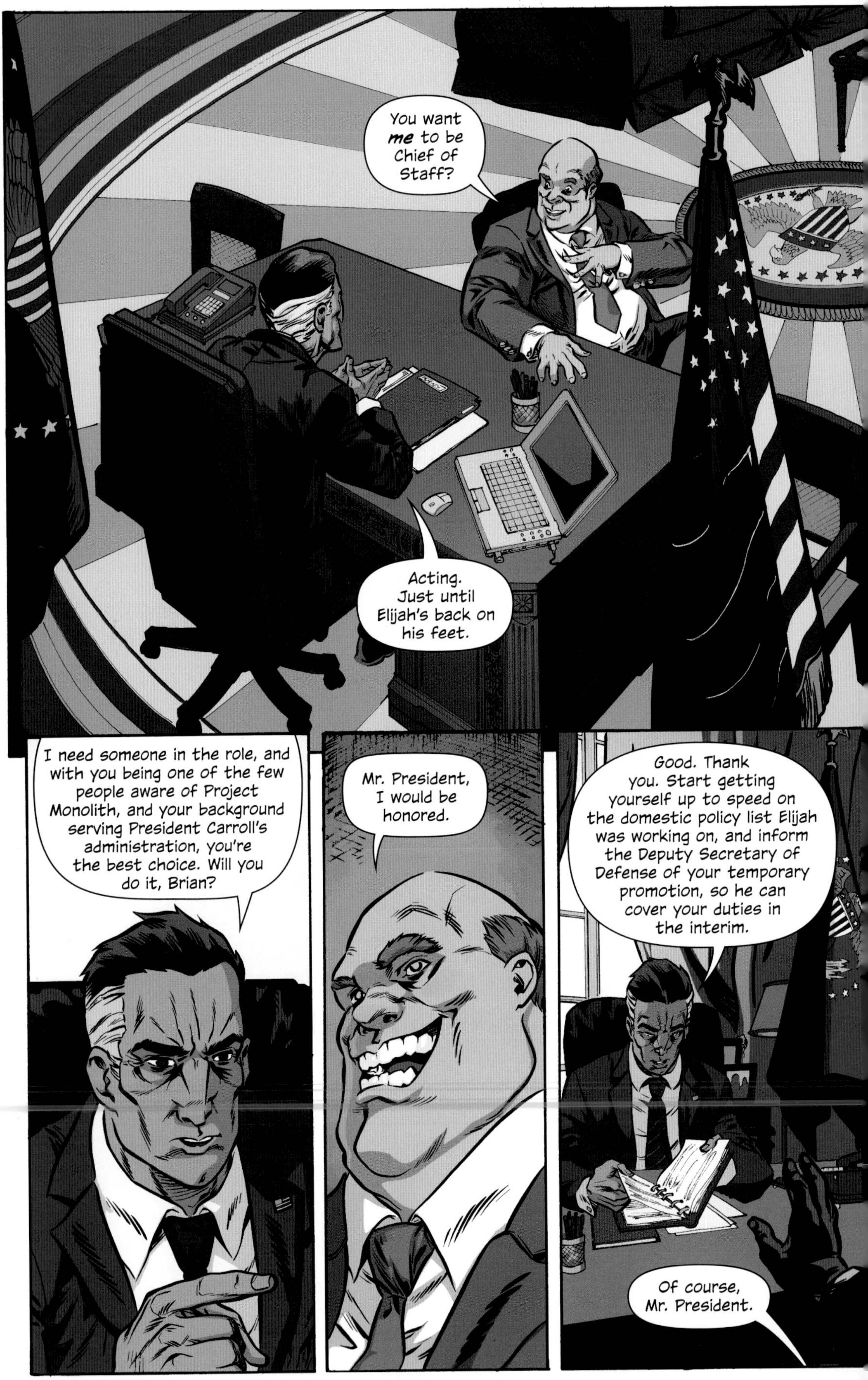

You want *me* to be Chief of Staff?
Acting. Just until Elijah's back on his feet.
I need someone in the role, and with you being one of the few people aware of Project Monolith, and your background serving President Carroll's administration, you're the best choice. Will you do it, Brian?
Mr. President, I would be honored.
Good. Thank you. Start getting yourself up to speed on the domestic policy list Elijah was working on, and inform the Deputy Secretary of Defense of your temporary promotion, so he can cover your duties in the interim.
Of course, Mr. President.

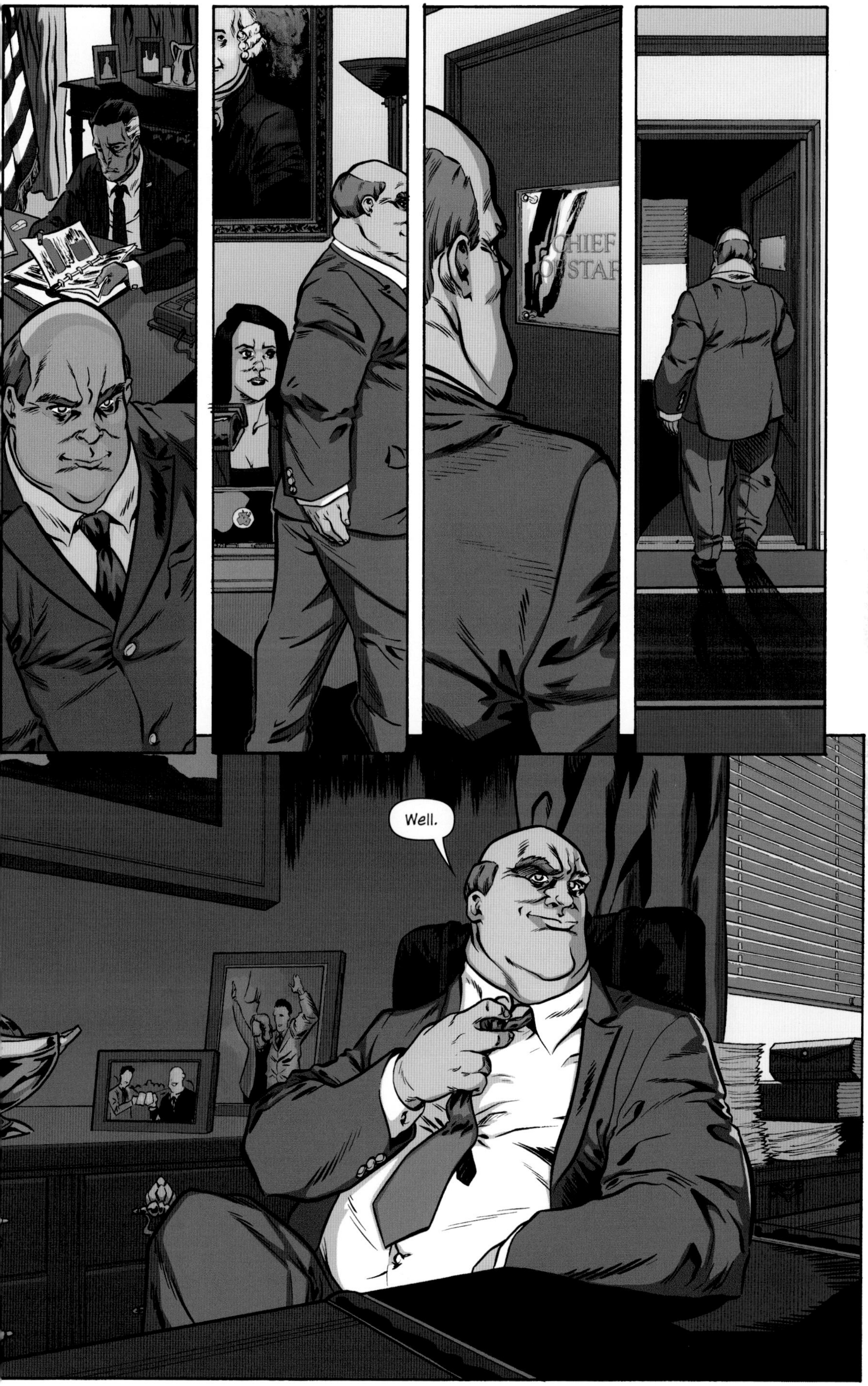

CHIEF OF STAFF
Well.

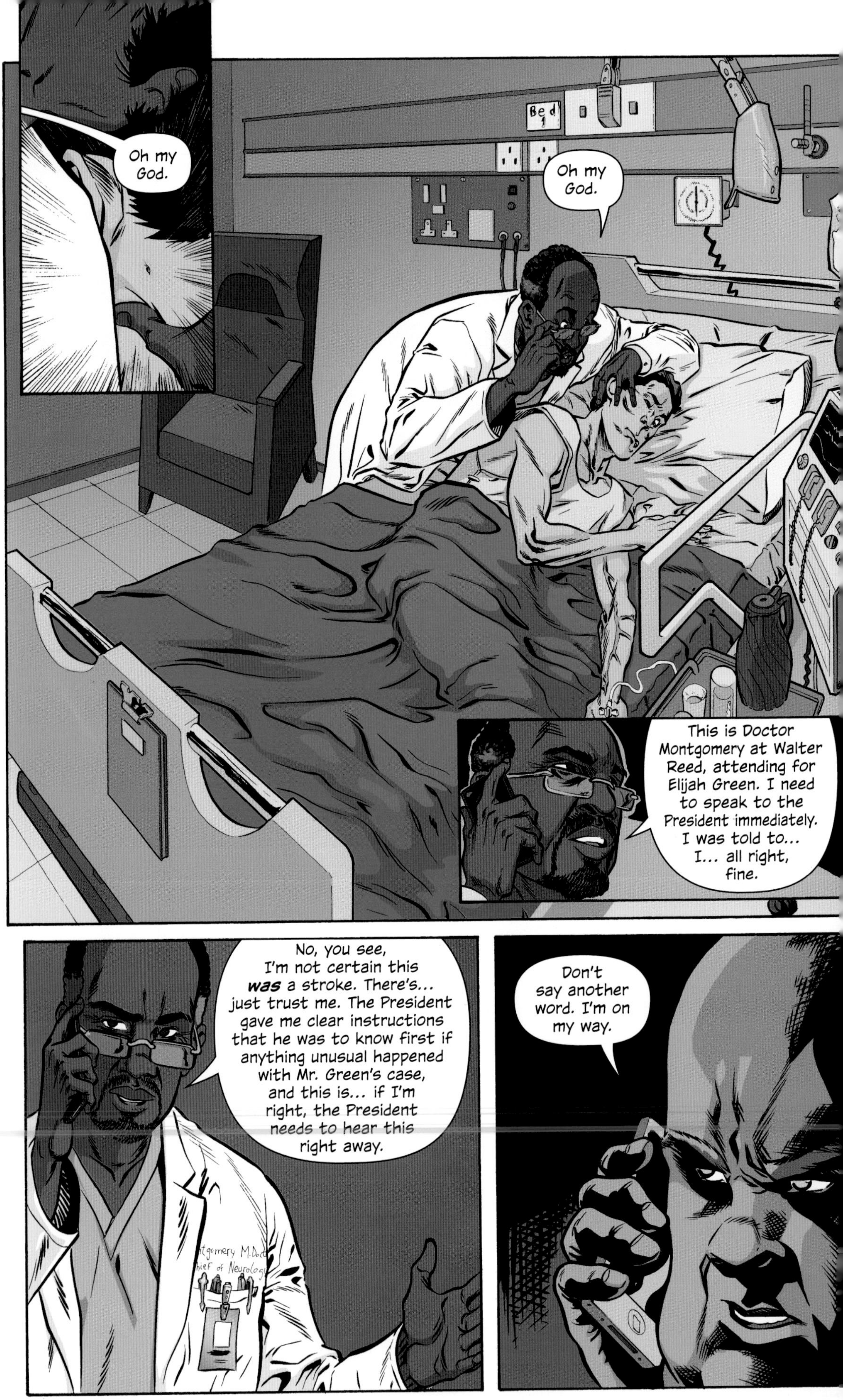
Oh my God.
Bed 1
Oh my God.
This is Doctor Montgomery at Walter Reed, attending for Elijah Green. I need to speak to the President immediately. I was told to... I... all right, fine.
No, you see, I'm not certain this *was* a stroke. There's... just trust me. The President gave me clear instructions that he was to know first if anything unusual happened with Mr. Green's case, and this is... if I'm right, the President needs to hear this right away.
Don't say another word. I'm on my way.

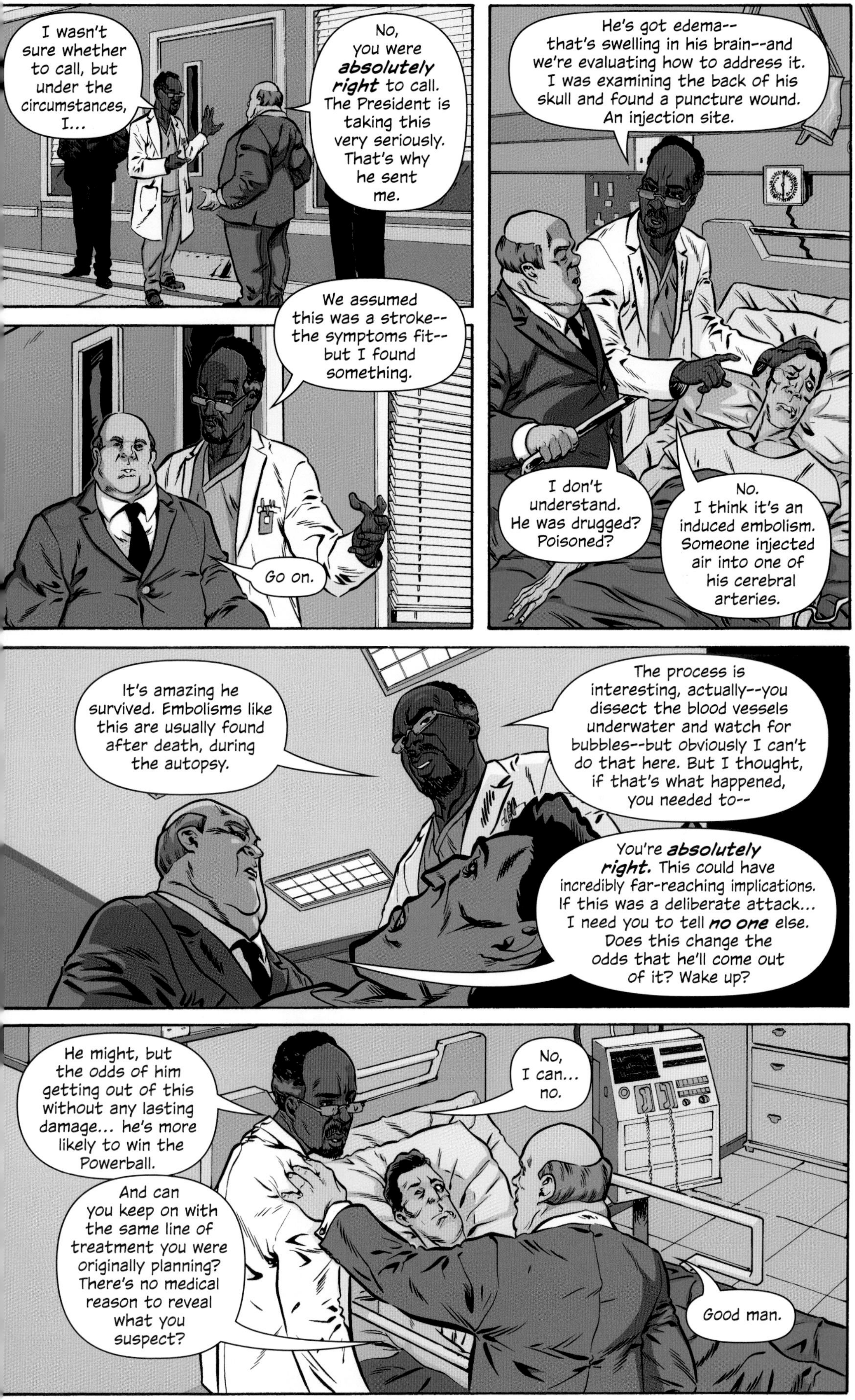

I wasn't sure whether to call, but under the circumstances, I...
No, you were ***absolutely right*** to call. The President is taking this very seriously. That's why he sent me.
We assumed this was a stroke--the symptoms fit--but I found something.
Go on.
He's got edema--that's swelling in his brain--and we're evaluating how to address it. I was examining the back of his skull and found a puncture wound. An injection site.
I don't understand. He was drugged? Poisoned?
No. I think it's an induced embolism. Someone injected air into one of his cerebral arteries.
It's amazing he survived. Embolisms like this are usually found after death, during the autopsy.
The process is interesting, actually--you dissect the blood vessels underwater and watch for bubbles--but obviously I can't do that here. But I thought, if that's what happened, you needed to--
You're ***absolutely right.*** This could have incredibly far-reaching implications. If this was a deliberate attack... I need you to tell ***no one*** else. Does this change the odds that he'll come out of it? Wake up?
He might, but the odds of him getting out of this without any lasting damage... he's more likely to win the Powerball.
No, I can... no.
And can you keep on with the same line of treatment you were originally planning? There's no medical reason to reveal what you suspect?
Good man.

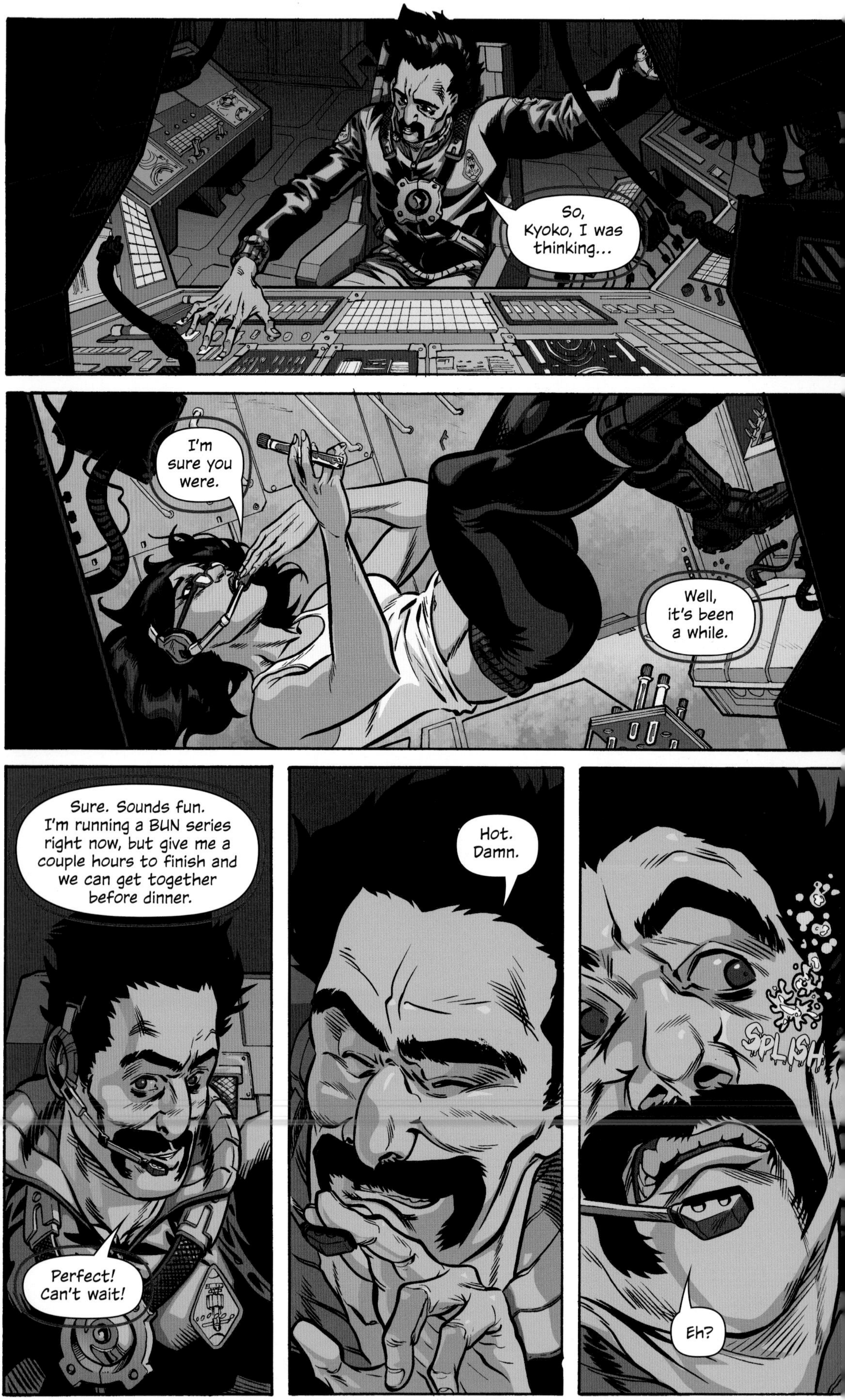
So, Kyoko, I was thinking...
I'm sure you were.
Well, it's been a while.
Sure. Sounds fun. I'm running a BUN series right now, but give me a couple hours to finish and we can get together before dinner.
Perfect! Can't wait!
Hot. Damn.
SPLISH
Eh?

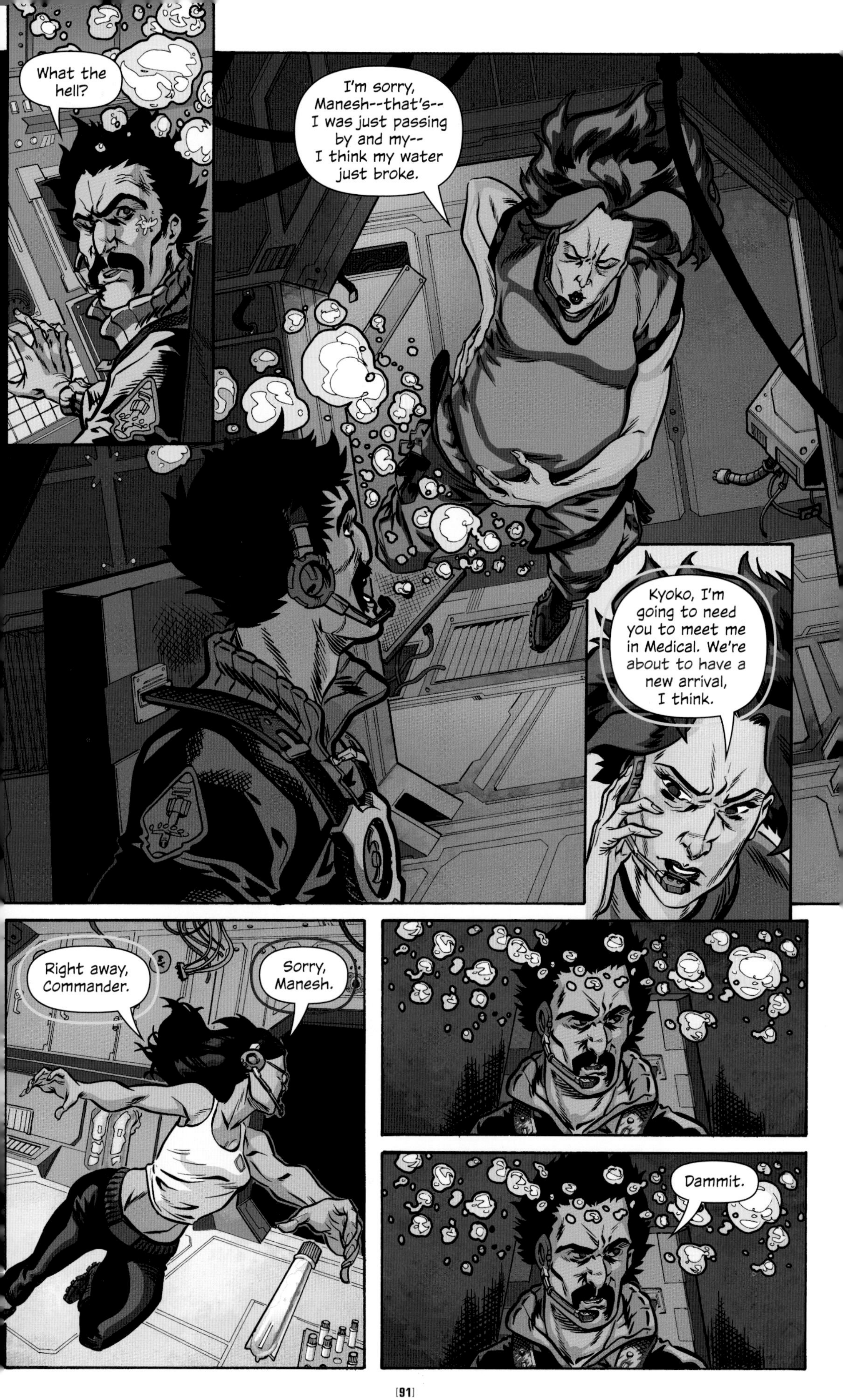
What the hell?
I'm sorry, Manesh--that's-- I was just passing by and my-- I think my water just broke.
Kyoko, I'm going to need you to meet me in Medical. We're about to have a new arrival, I think.
Right away, Commander.
Sorry, Manesh.
Dammit.

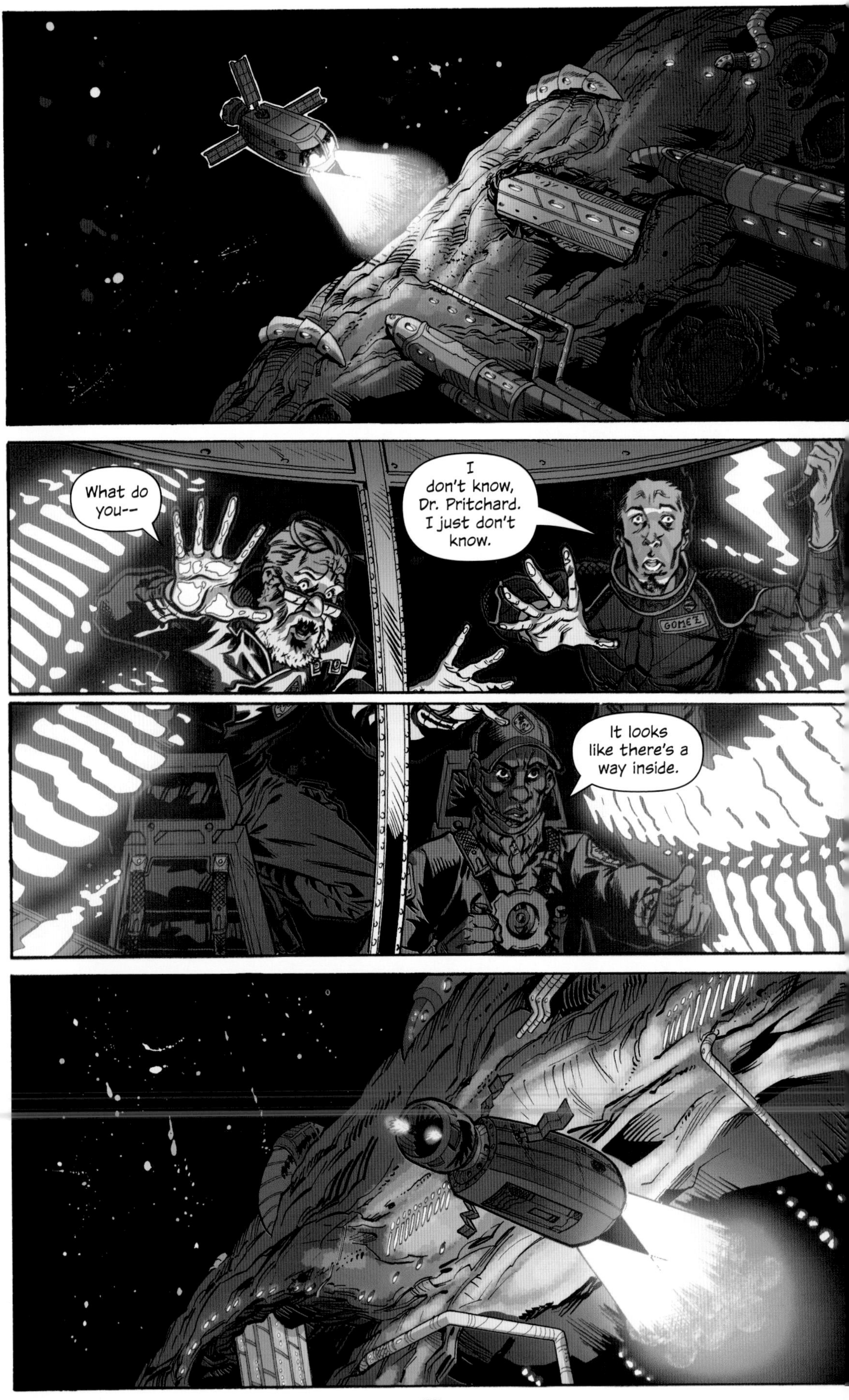
What do you--
I don't know, Dr. Pritchard. I just don't know.
It looks like there's a way inside.

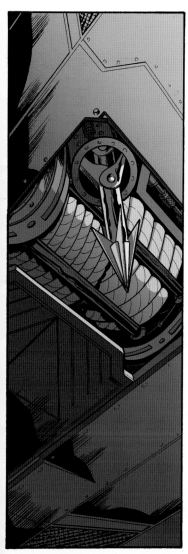

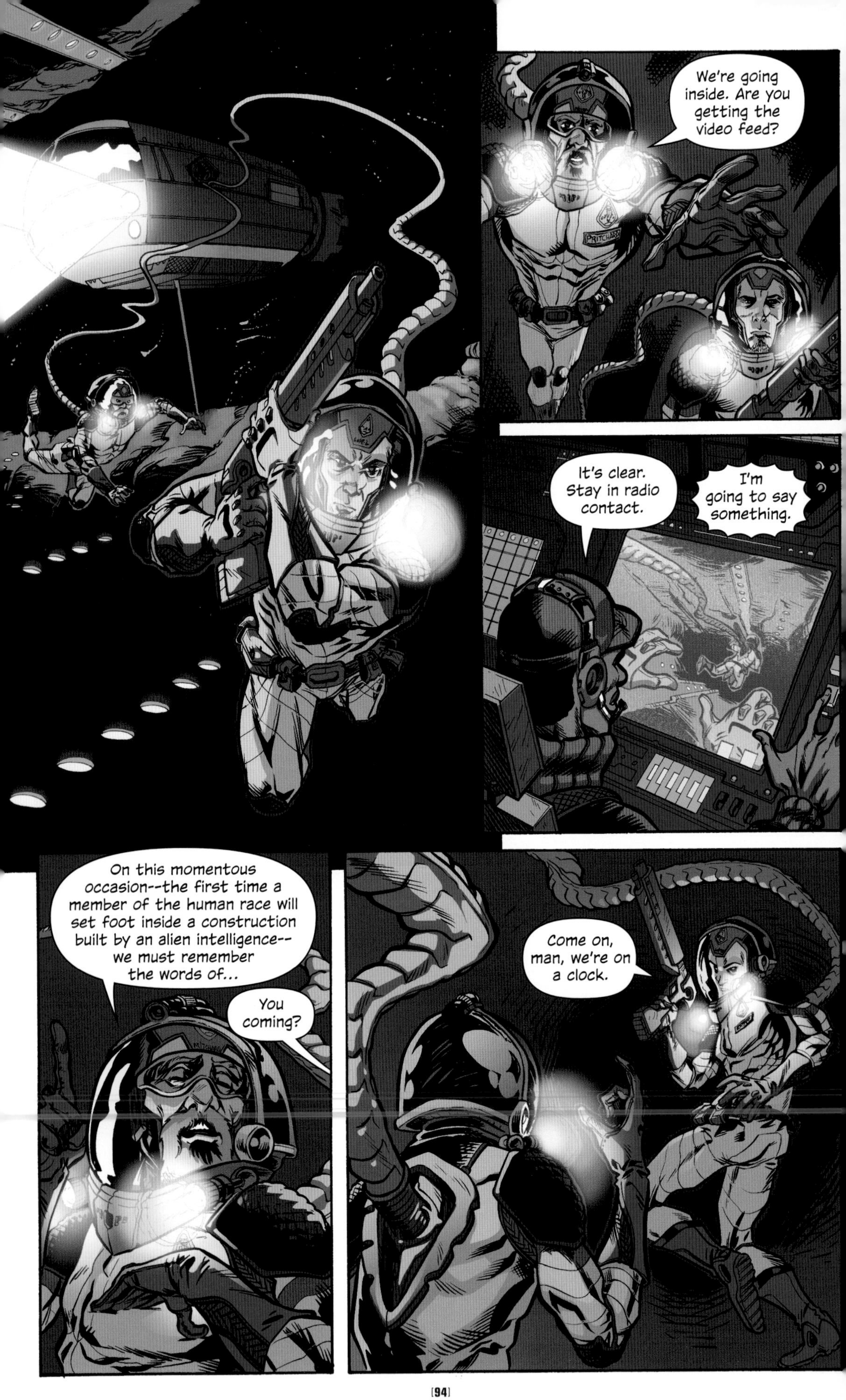

We're going inside. Are you getting the video feed?
It's clear. Stay in radio contact.
I'm going to say something.
On this momentous occasion--the first time a member of the human race will set foot inside a construction built by an alien intelligence--we must remember the words of...
You coming?
Come on, man, we're on a clock.

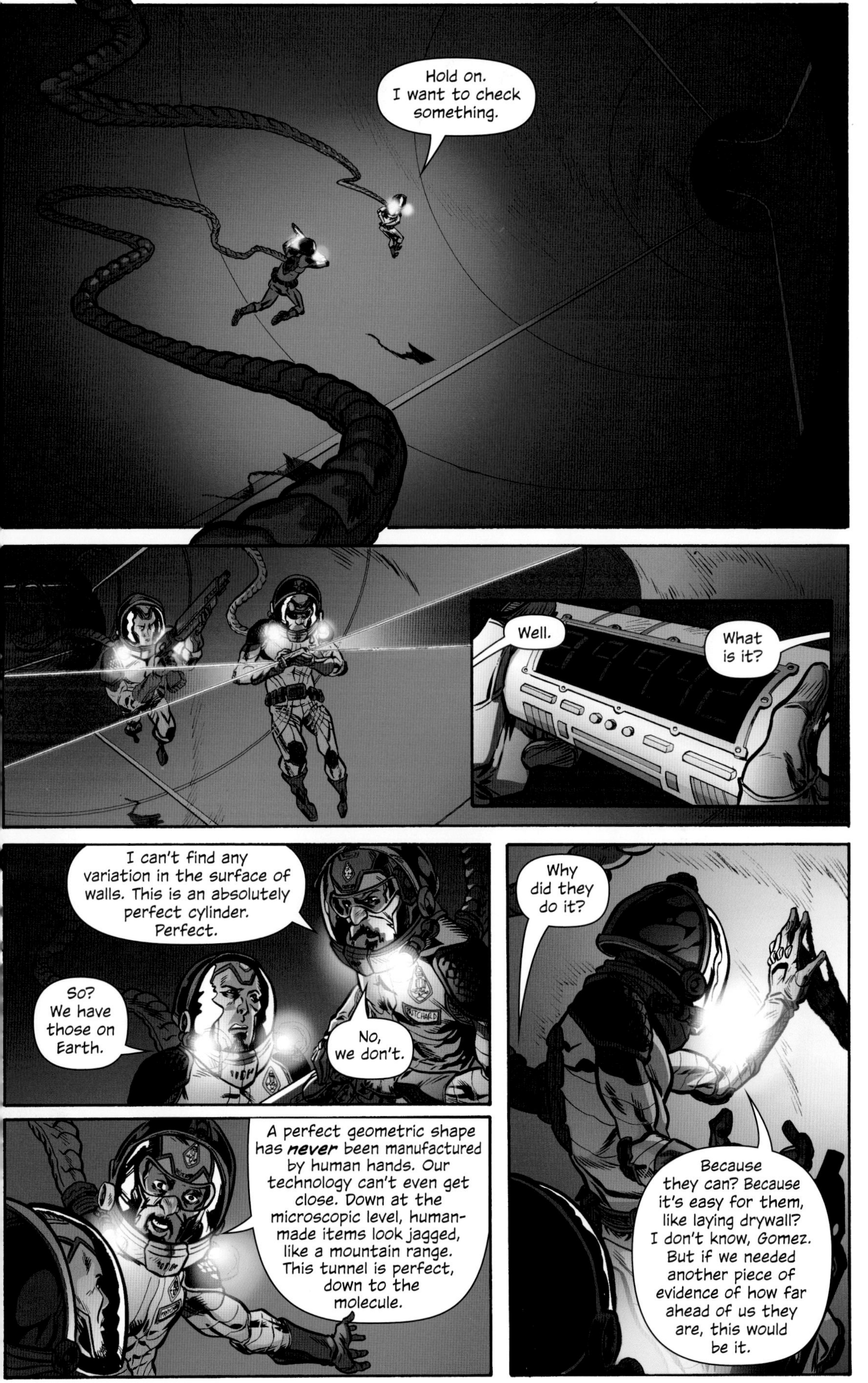
Hold on. I want to check something.
Well.
What is it?
I can't find any variation in the surface of walls. This is an absolutely perfect cylinder. Perfect.
So? We have those on Earth.
No, we don't.
Why did they do it?
A perfect geometric shape has ***never*** been manufactured by human hands. Our technology can't even get close. Down at the microscopic level, human-made items look jagged, like a mountain range. This tunnel is perfect, down to the molecule.
Because they can? Because it's easy for them, like laying drywall? I don't know, Gomez. But if we needed another piece of evidence of how far ahead of us they are, this would be it.

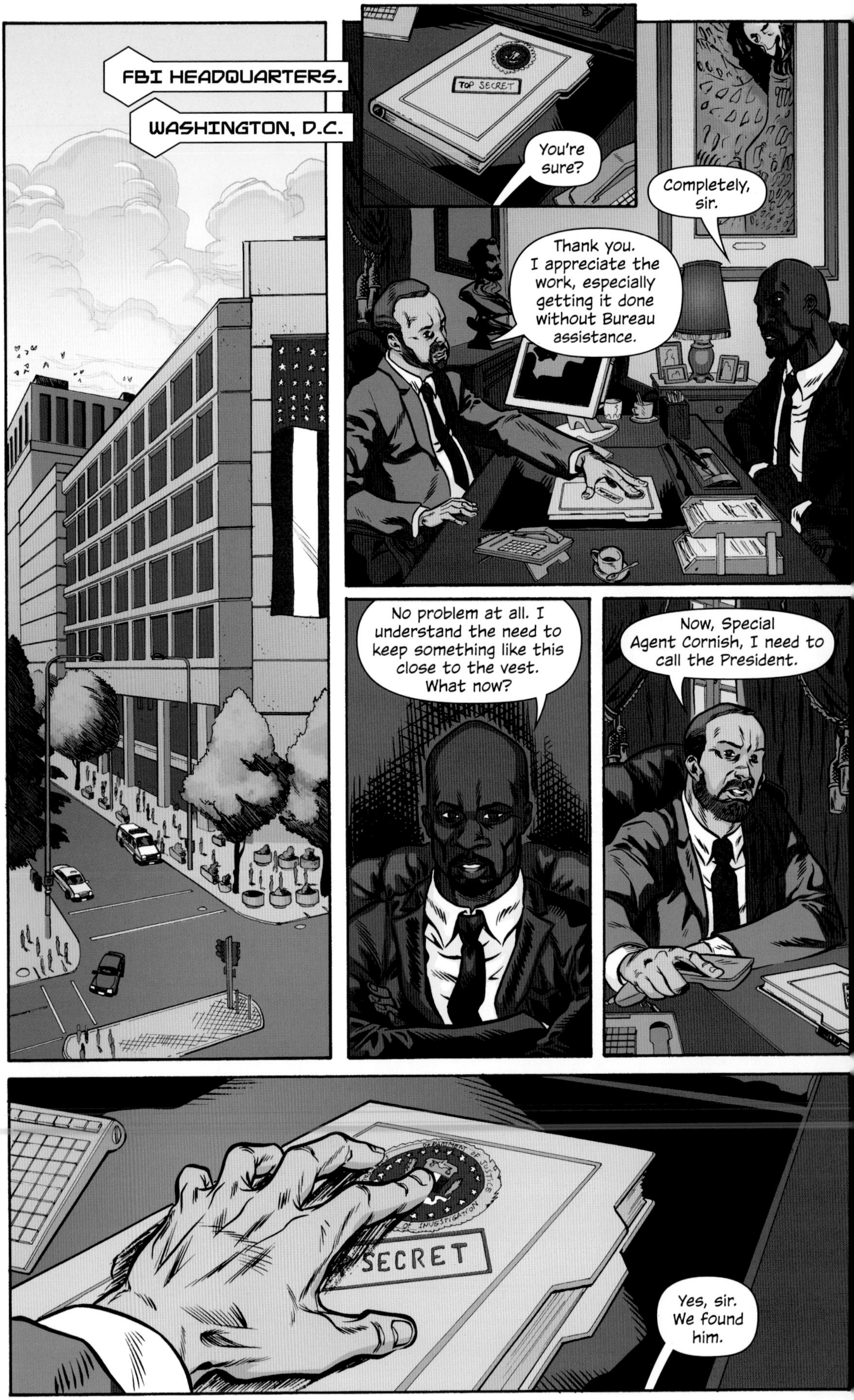

FBI HEADQUARTERS.
WASHINGTON, D.C.
TOP SECRET
You're sure?
Completely, sir.
Thank you. I appreciate the work, especially getting it done without Bureau assistance.
No problem at all. I understand the need to keep something like this close to the vest. What now?
Now, Special Agent Cornish, I need to call the President.
SECRET
Yes, sir. We found him.

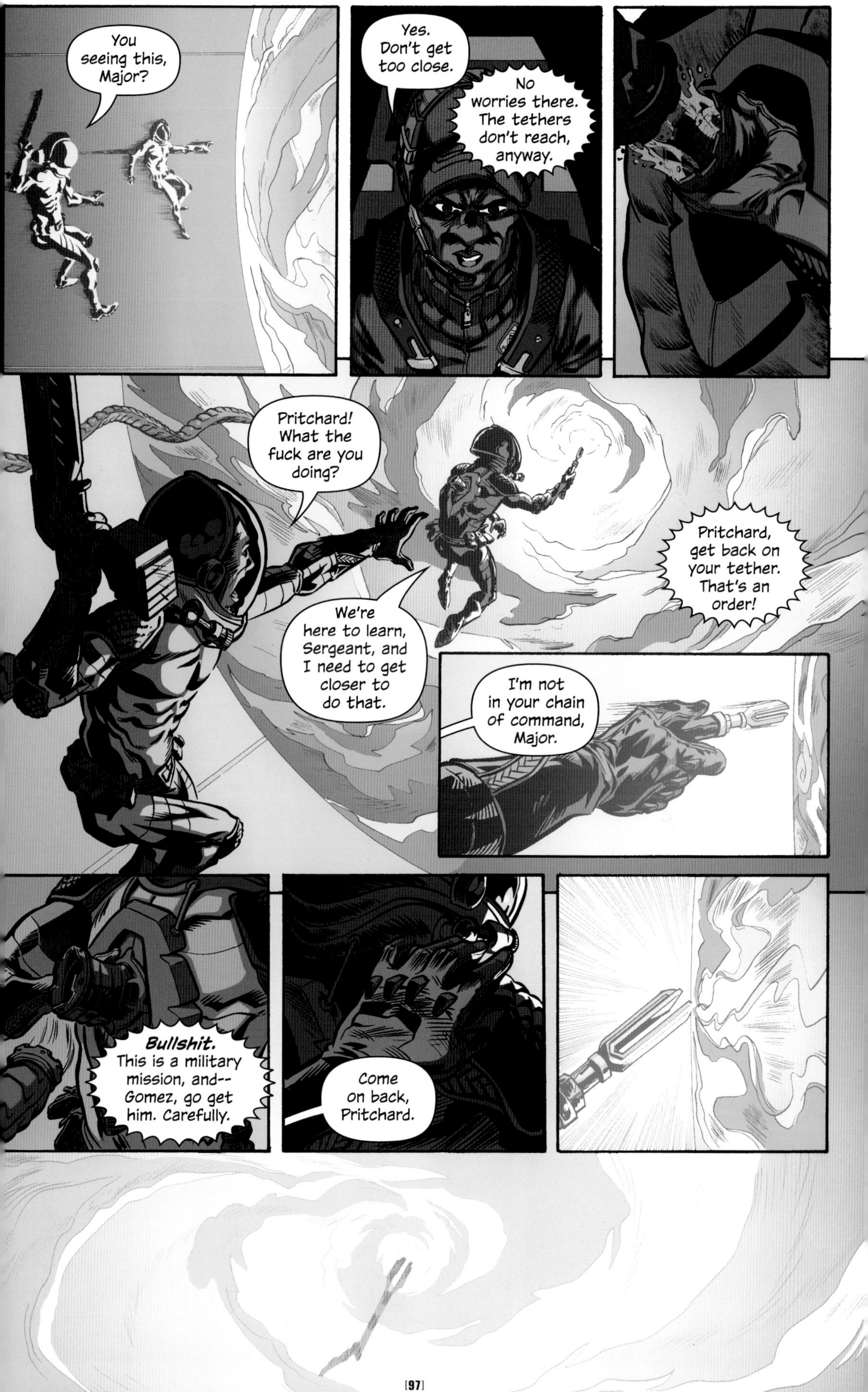
You seeing this, Major?
Yes. Don't get too close.
No worries there. The tethers don't reach, anyway.
Pritchard! What the fuck are you doing?
Pritchard, get back on your tether. That's an order!
We're here to learn, Sergeant, and I need to get closer to do that.
I'm not in your chain of command, Major.
Bullshit. This is a military mission, and-- Gomez, go get him. Carefully.
Come on back, Pritchard.

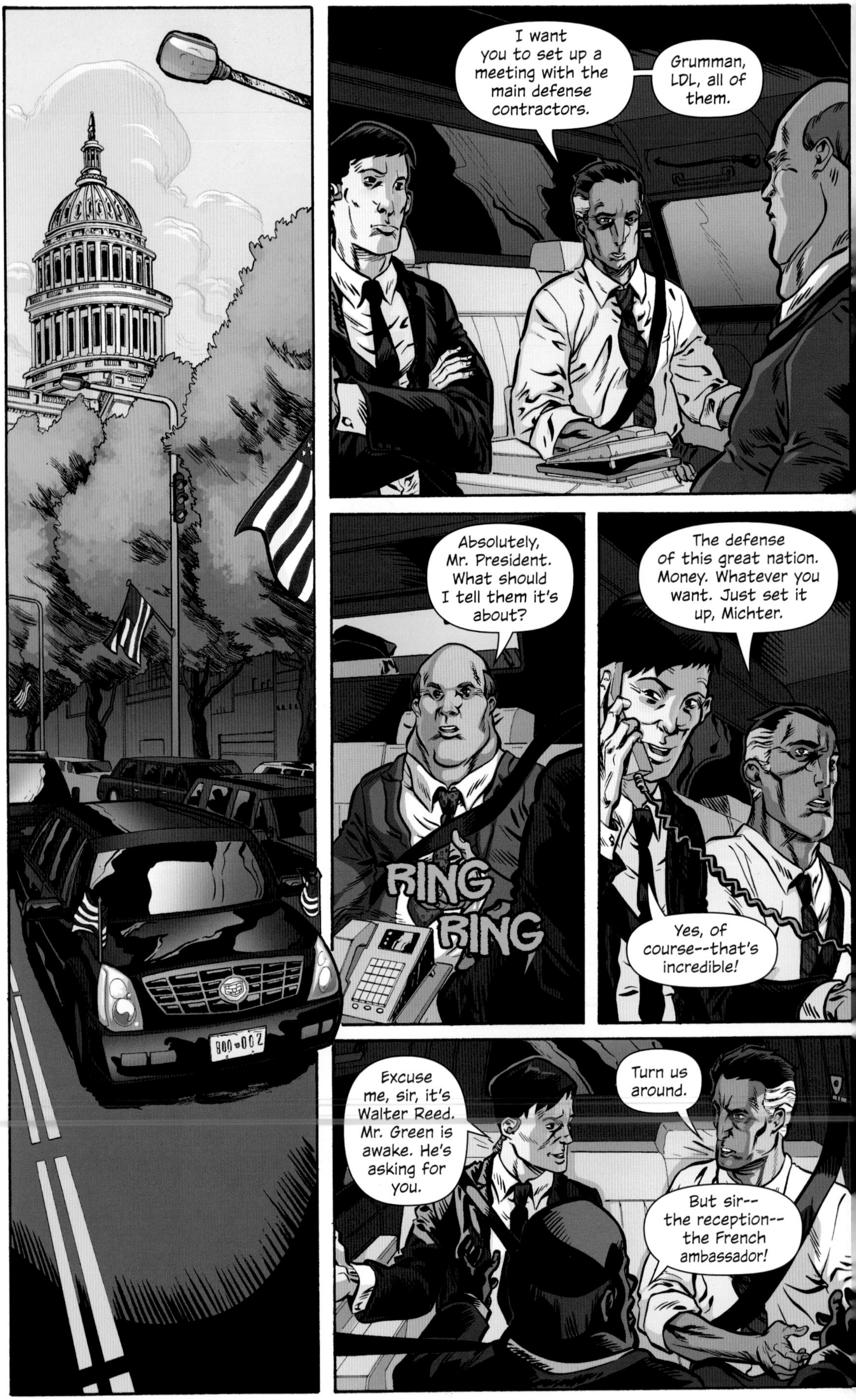
I want you to set up a meeting with the main defense contractors.
Grumman, LDL, all of them.
Absolutely, Mr. President. What should I tell them it's about?
RING
RING
The defense of this great nation. Money. Whatever you want. Just set it up, Michter.
Yes, of course--that's incredible!
Excuse me, sir, it's Walter Reed. Mr. Green is awake. He's asking for you.
Turn us around.
But sir-- the reception-- the French ambassador!

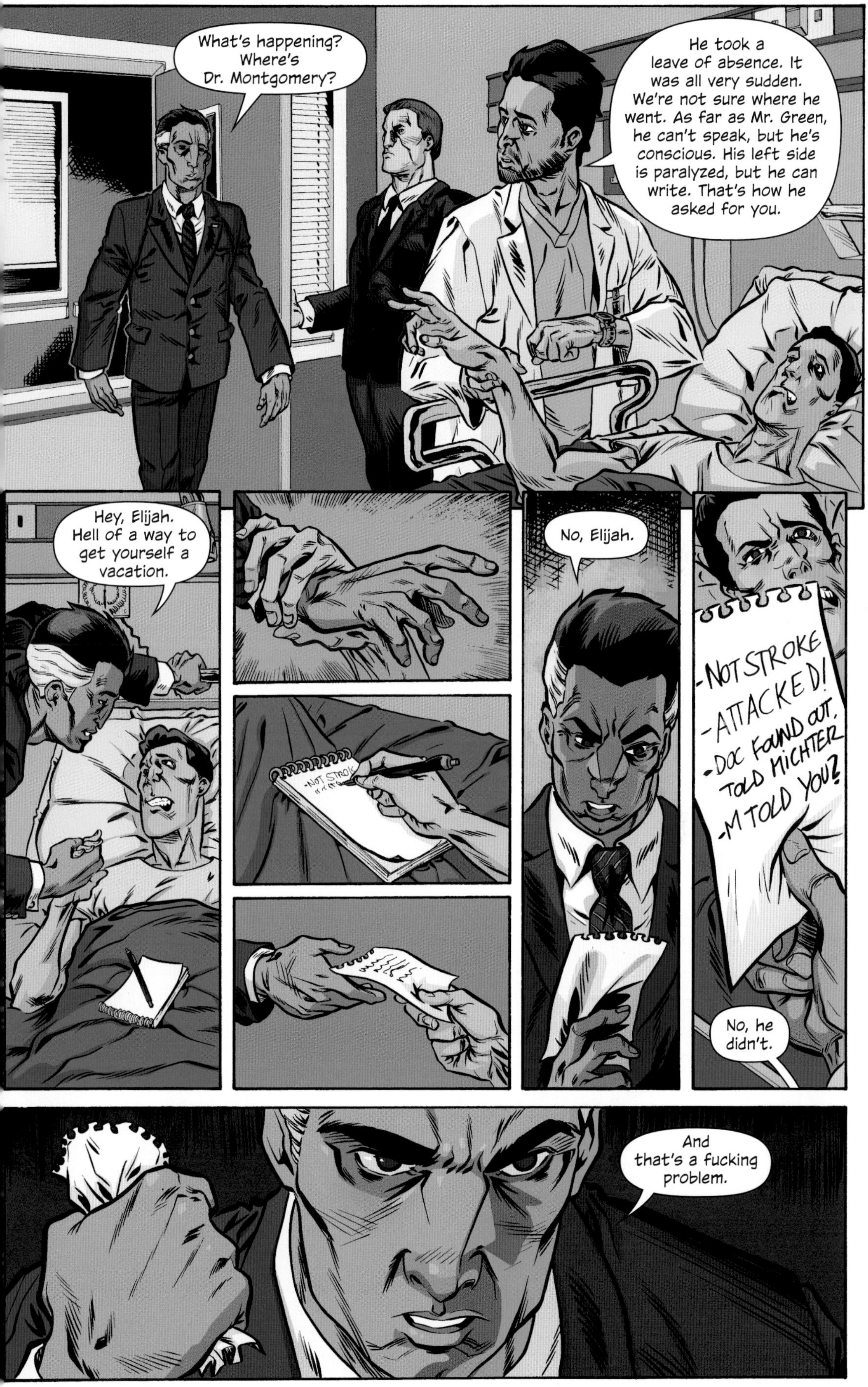

What's happening? Where's Dr. Montgomery?
He took a leave of absence. It was all very sudden. We're not sure where he went. As far as Mr. Green, he can't speak, but he's conscious. His left side is paralyzed, but he can write. That's how he asked for you.
Hey, Elijah. Hell of a way to get yourself a vacation.
No, Elijah.
-NOT STROKE
-ATTACKED!
-DOC FOUND OUT, TOLD MICHTER
-M TOLD YOU?
No, he didn't.
And that's a fucking problem.

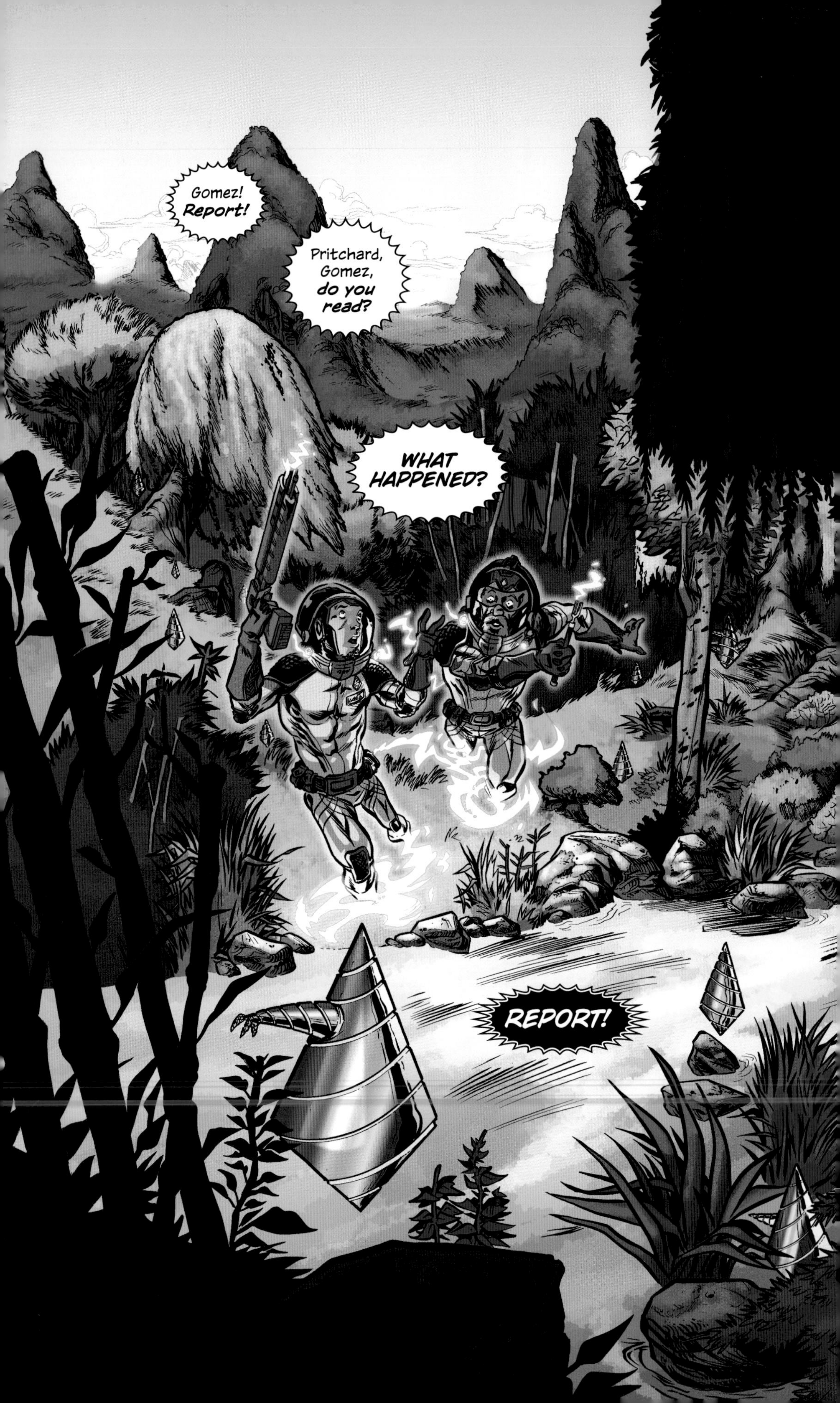

Gomez! Report!
Pritchard, Gomez, do you read?
WHAT HAPPENED?
REPORT!

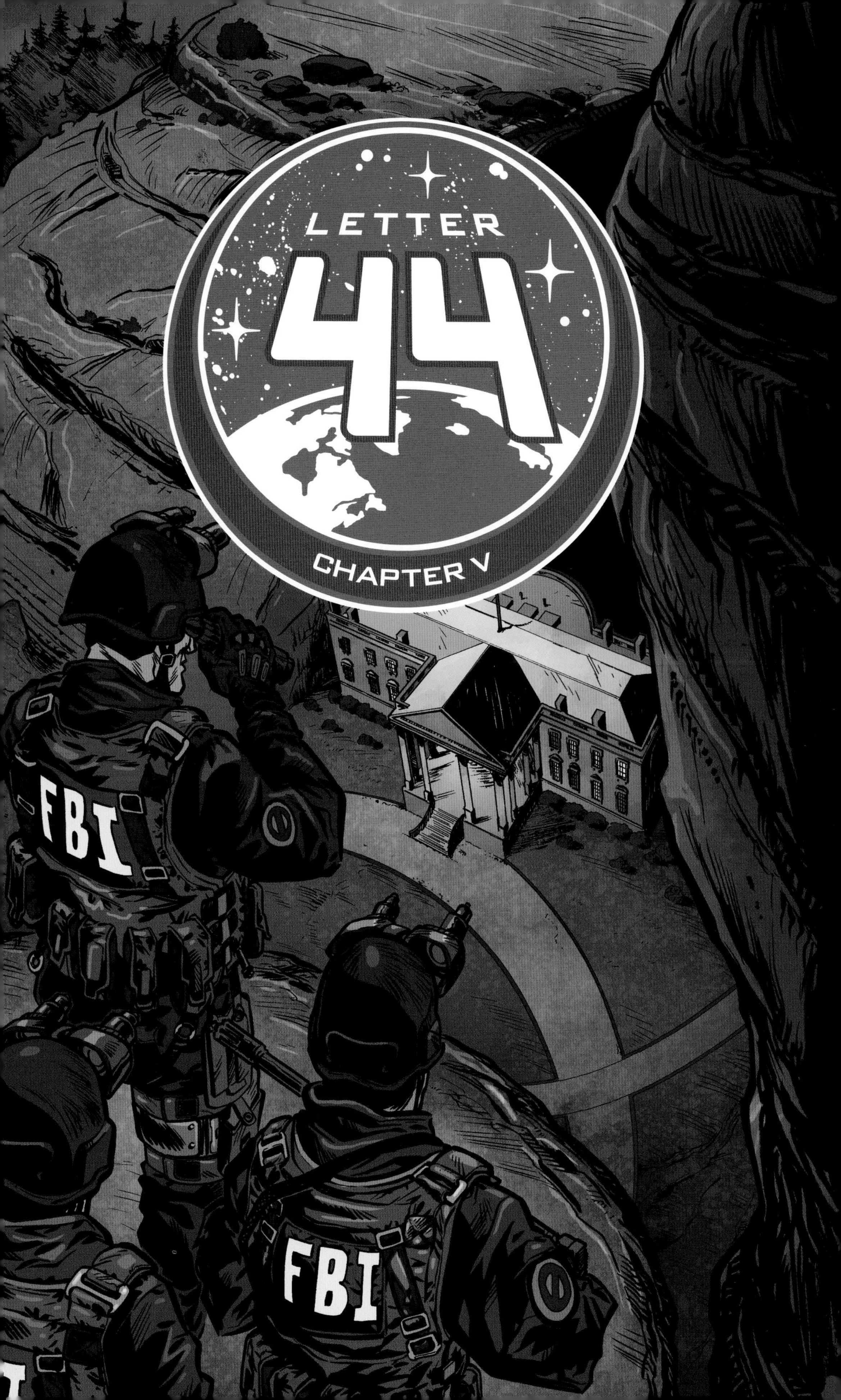
LETTER
44
CHAPTER V
FBI
FBI

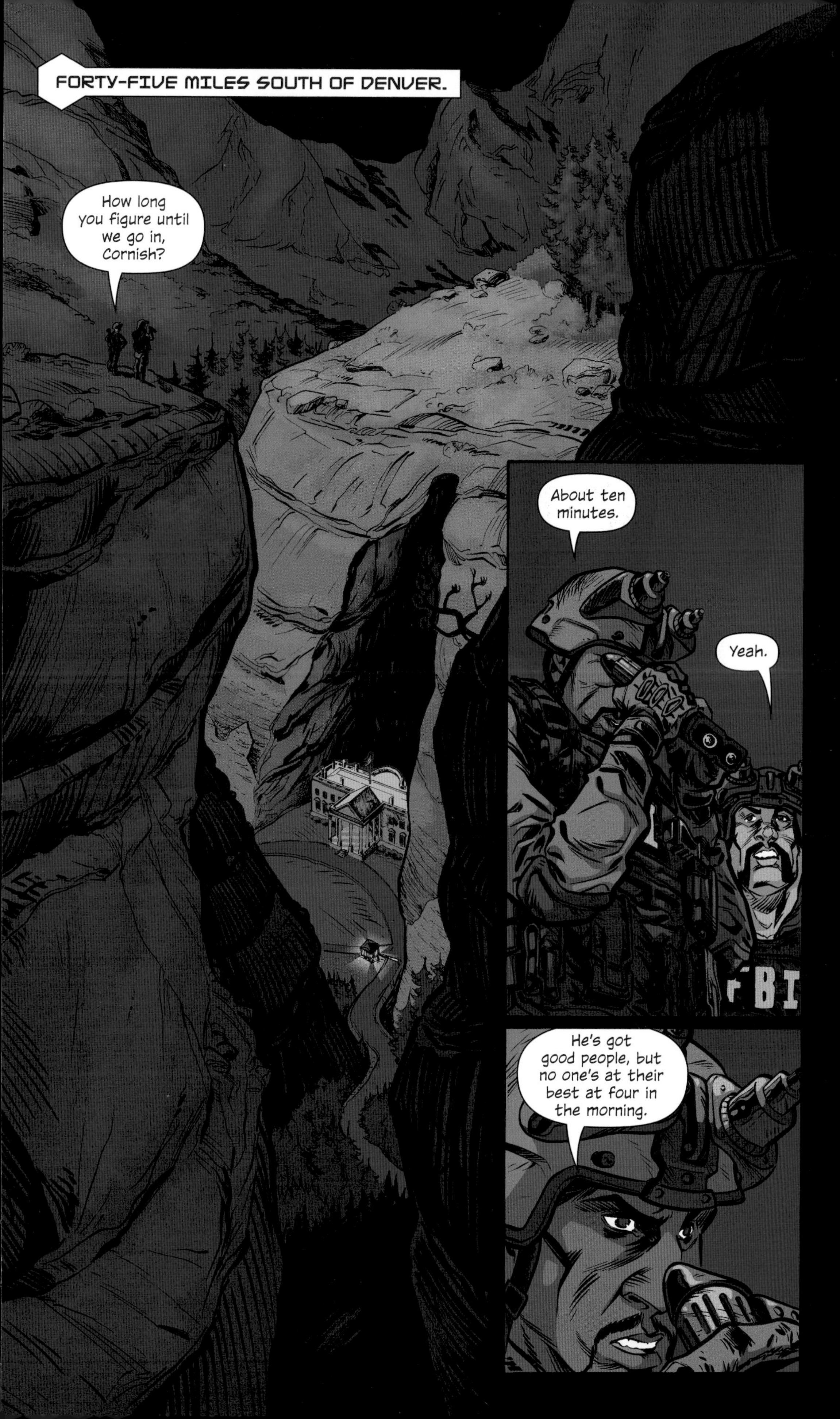
FORTY-FIVE MILES SOUTH OF DENVER.
How long you figure until we go in, Cornish?
About ten minutes.
Yeah.
FBI
He's got good people, but no one's at their best at four in the morning.

SEALs, though...

Ex-SEALs, and a bunch of other SpecOps guys. They've all been out for years, and they aren't training every day. Not like they used to.

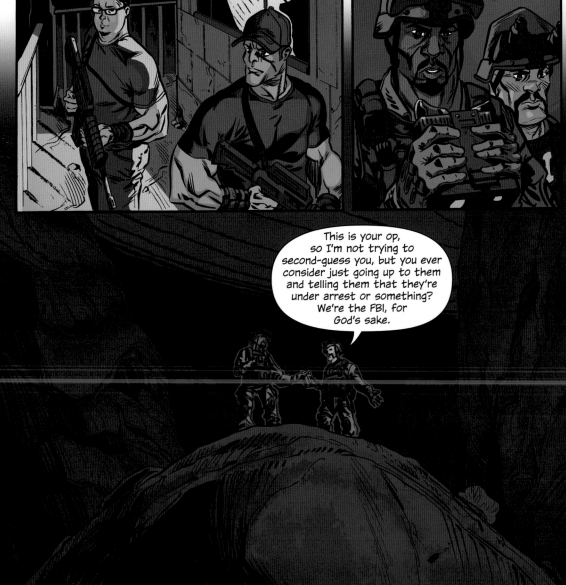

Easy pickings?

I wouldn't go *that* far.

This is your op, so I'm not trying to second-guess you, but you ever consider just going up to them and telling them that they're under arrest or something? We're the FBI, for God's sake.

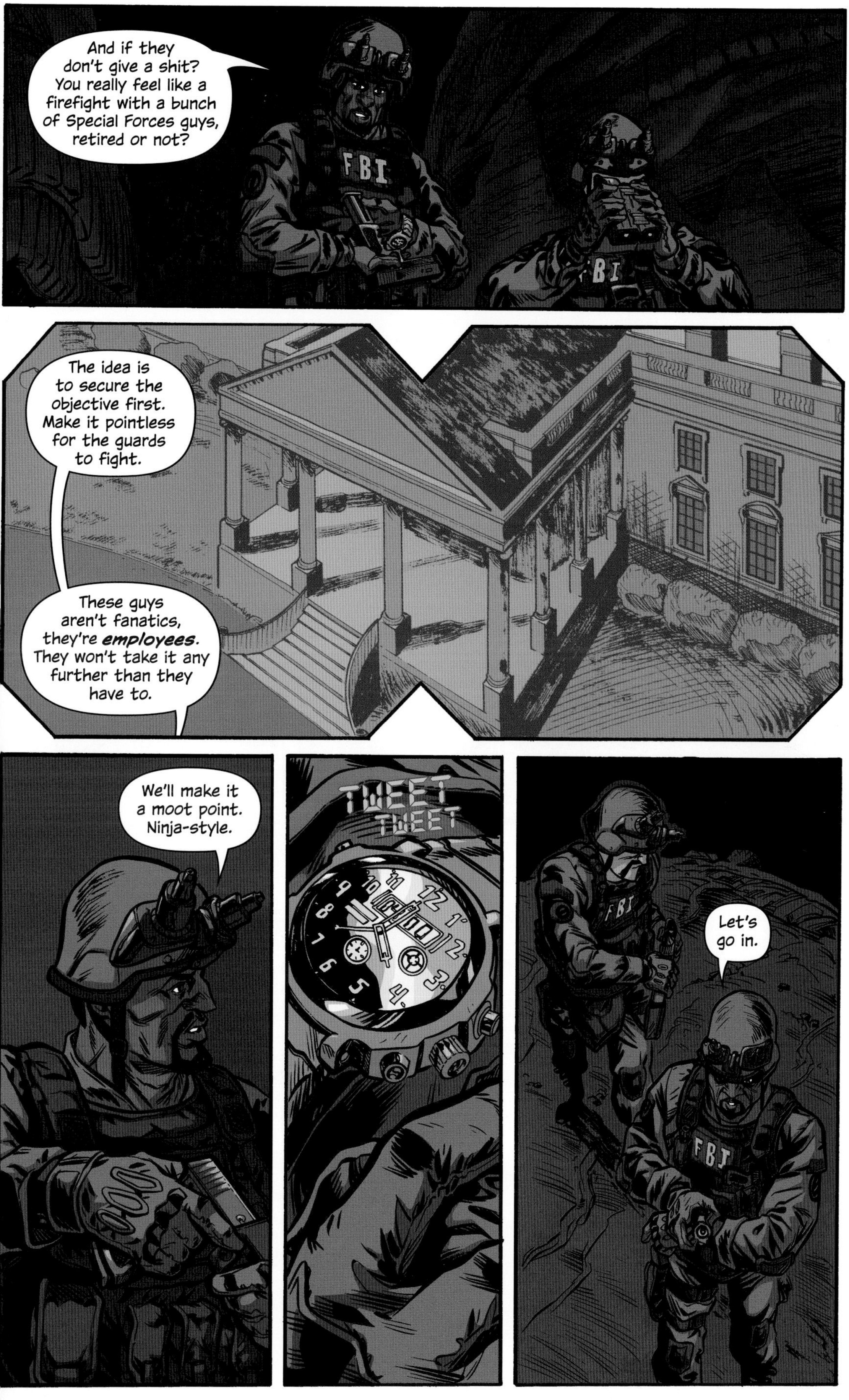

And if they don't give a shit? You really feel like a firefight with a bunch of Special Forces guys, retired or not?
FBI
FBI
The idea is to secure the objective first. Make it pointless for the guards to fight.
These guys aren't fanatics, they're ***employees***. They won't take it any further than they have to.
We'll make it a moot point. Ninja-style.
TWEET TWEET
FBI
Let's go in.
FBI

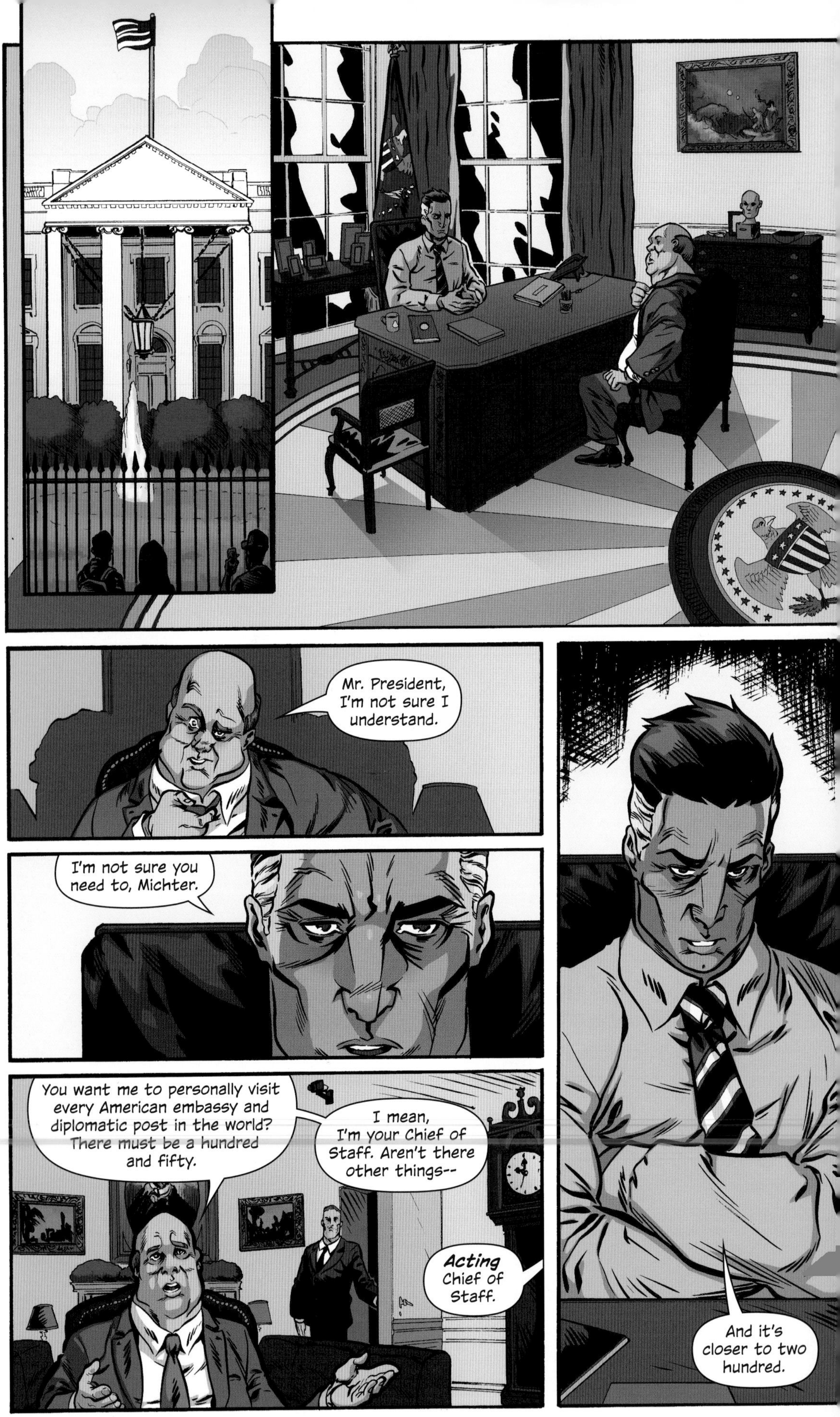
Mr. President, I'm not sure I understand.
I'm not sure you need to, Michter.
You want me to personally visit every American embassy and diplomatic post in the world? There must be a hundred and fifty.
I mean, I'm your Chief of Staff. Aren't there other things--
Acting Chief of Staff.
And it's closer to two hundred.

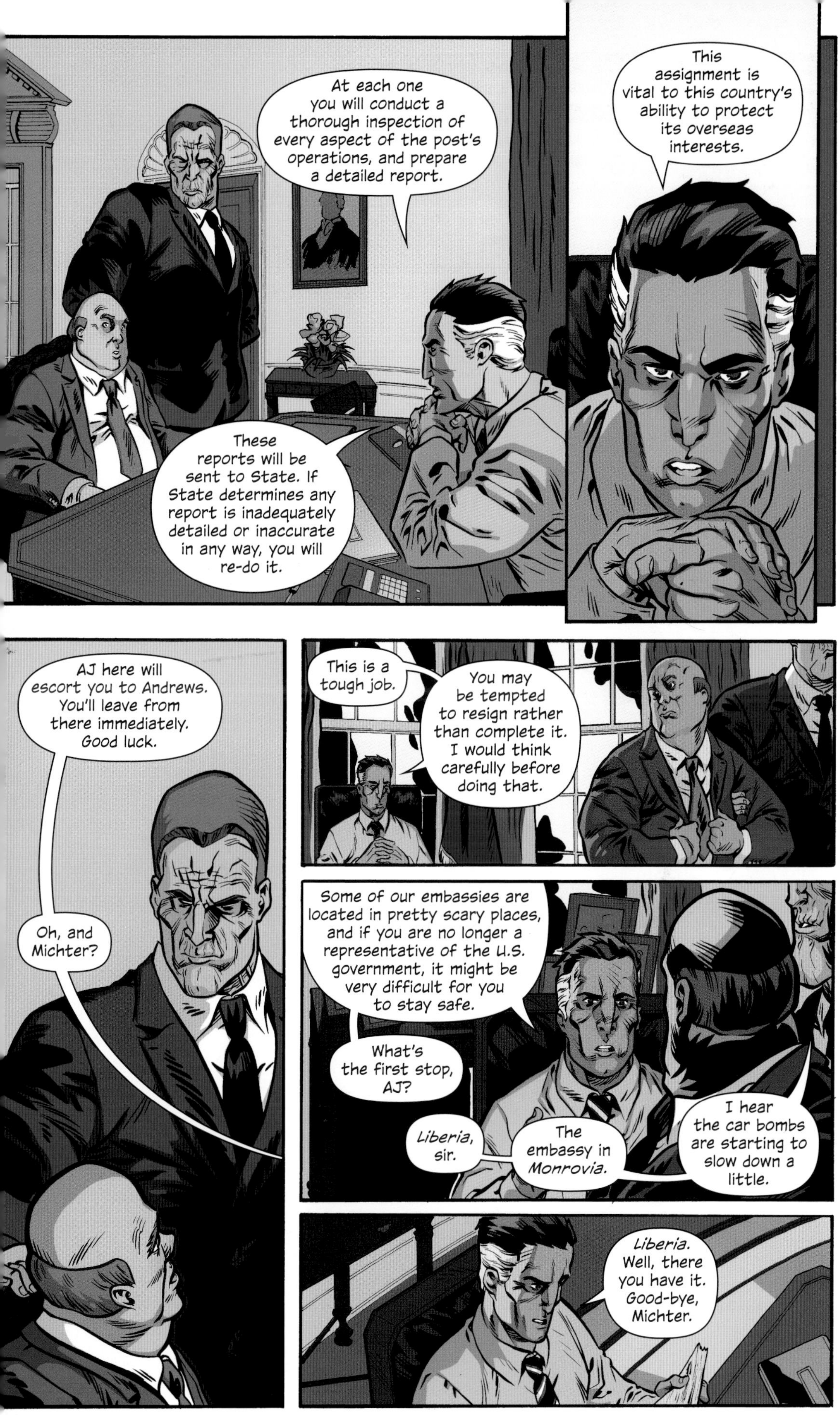
At each one you will conduct a thorough inspection of every aspect of the post's operations, and prepare a detailed report.
These reports will be sent to State. If State determines any report is inadequately detailed or inaccurate in any way, you will re-do it.
This assignment is vital to this country's ability to protect its overseas interests.
AJ here will escort you to Andrews. You'll leave from there immediately. Good luck.
Oh, and Michter?
This is a tough job.
You may be tempted to resign rather than complete it. I would think carefully before doing that.
Some of our embassies are located in pretty scary places, and if you are no longer a representative of the U.S. government, it might be very difficult for you to stay safe.
What's the first stop, AJ?
Liberia, sir.
The embassy in *Monrovia*.
I hear the car bombs are starting to slow down a little.
Liberia. Well, there you have it. Good-bye, Michter.

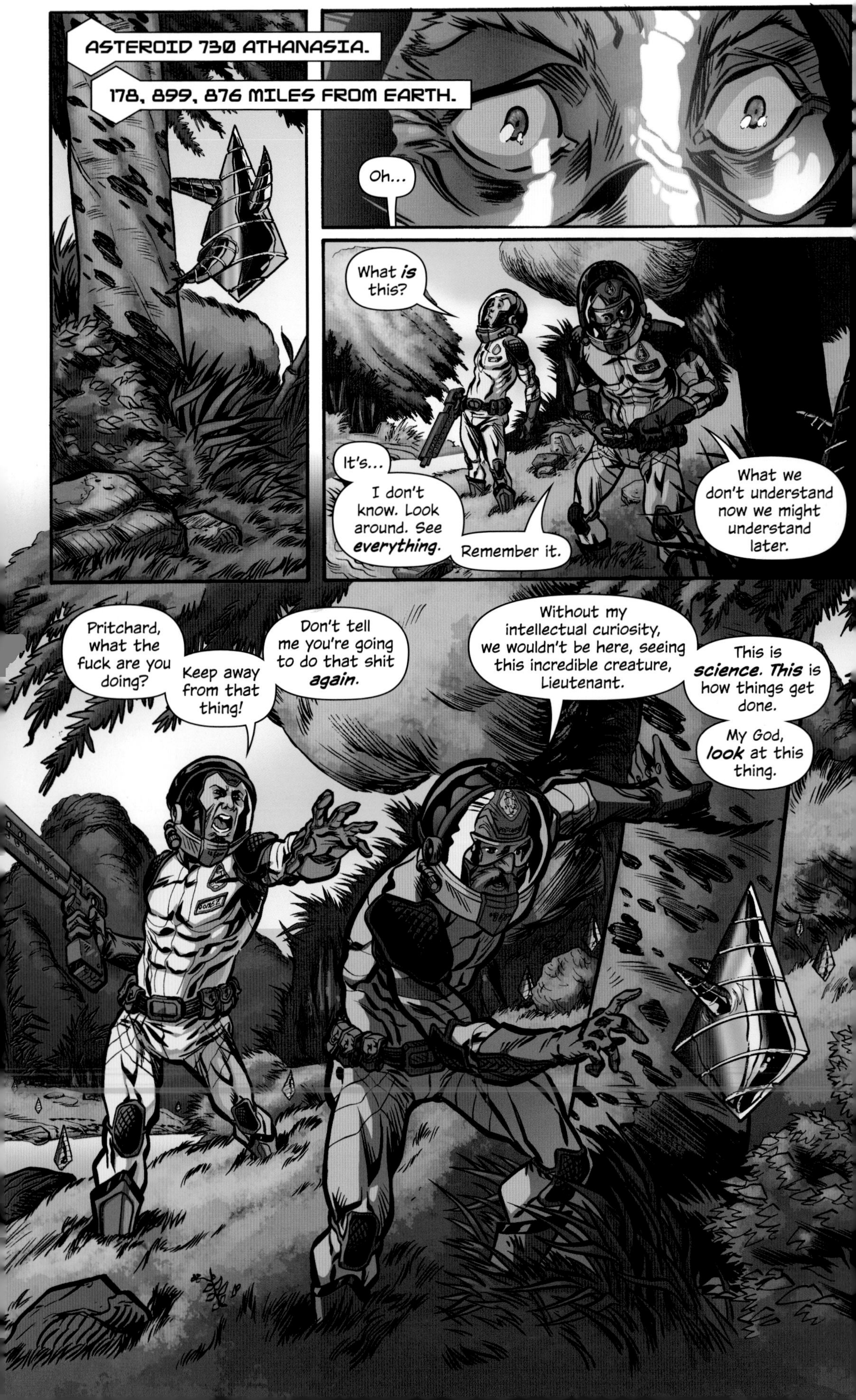
ASTEROID 730 ATHANASIA.
178, 899, 876 MILES FROM EARTH.
Oh...
What *is* this?
It's...
I don't know. Look around. See *everything*.
Remember it.
What we don't understand now we might understand later.
Pritchard, what the fuck are you doing?
Keep away from that thing!
Don't tell me you're going to do that shit *again*.
Without my intellectual curiosity, we wouldn't be here, seeing this incredible creature, Lieutenant.
This is *science*. *This* is how things get done.
My God, *look* at this thing.

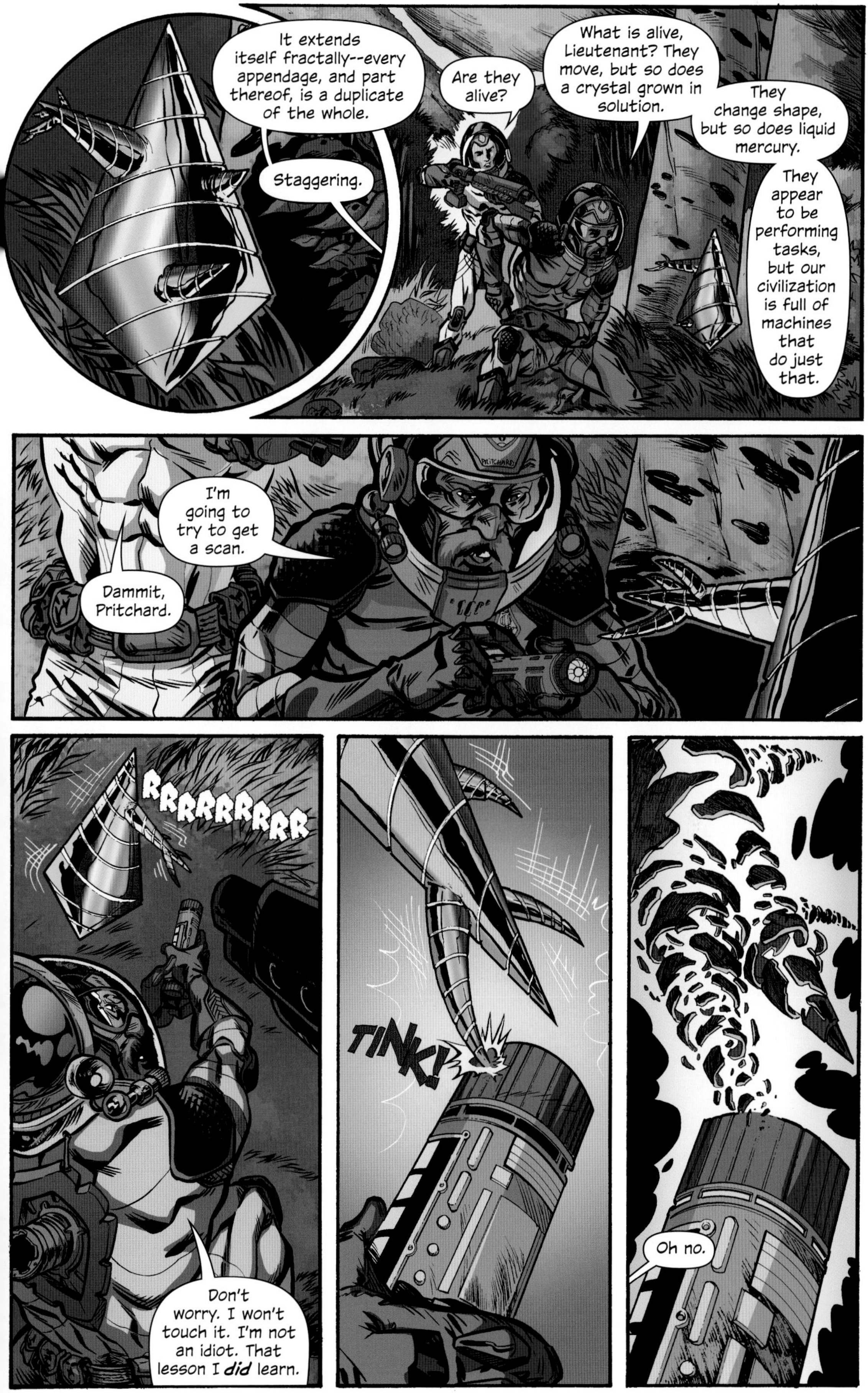
It extends itself fractally--every appendage, and part thereof, is a duplicate of the whole.
Staggering.
Are they alive?
What is alive, Lieutenant? They move, but so does a crystal grown in solution.
They change shape, but so does liquid mercury.
They appear to be performing tasks, but our civilization is full of machines that do just that.
PRITCHARD
I'm going to try to get a scan.
Dammit, Pritchard.
RRRRRRRRRR
Don't worry. I won't touch it. I'm not an idiot. That lesson I *did* learn.
TINK!
Oh no.

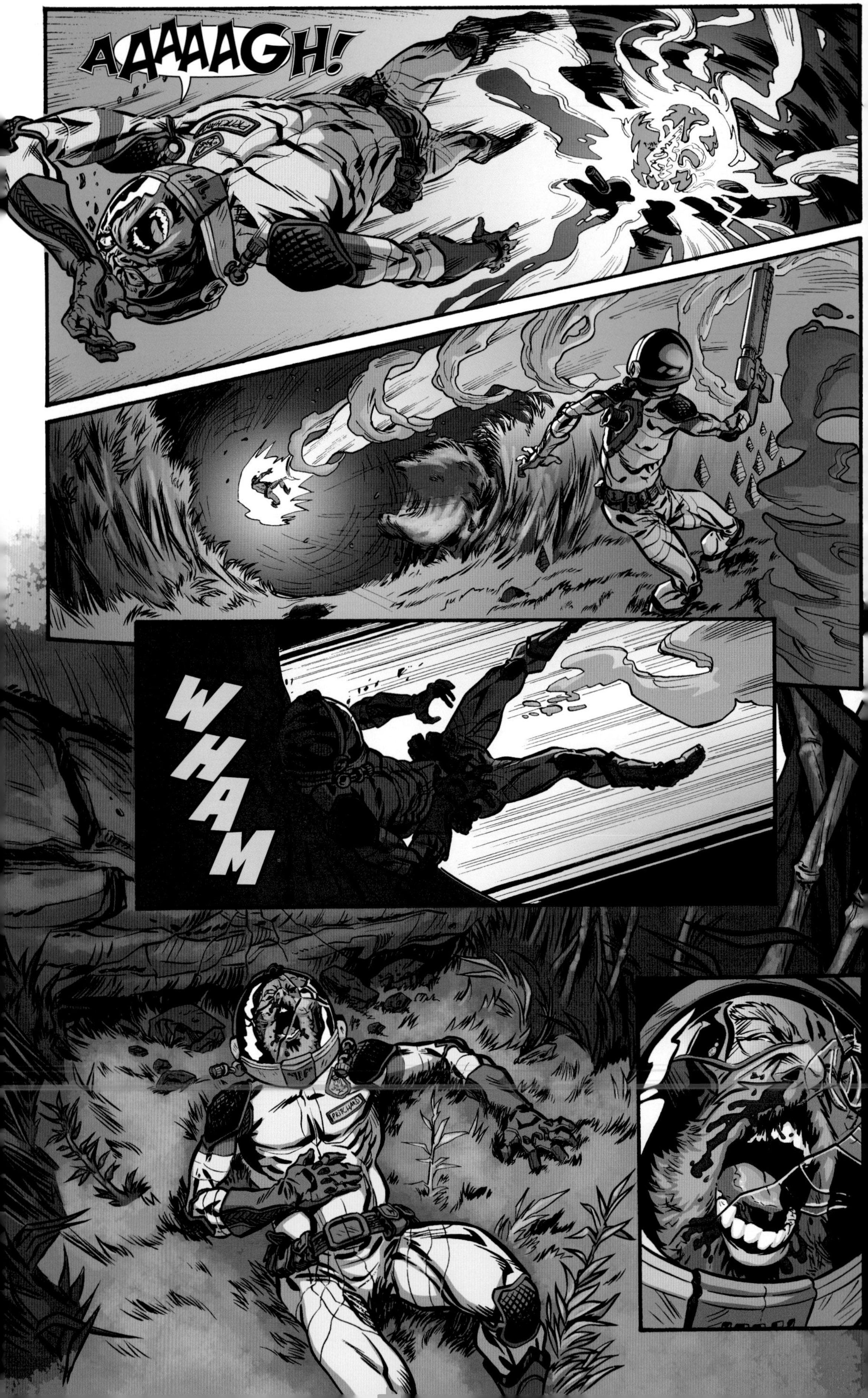
AAAAAGH!
WHAM
PRITCHARD

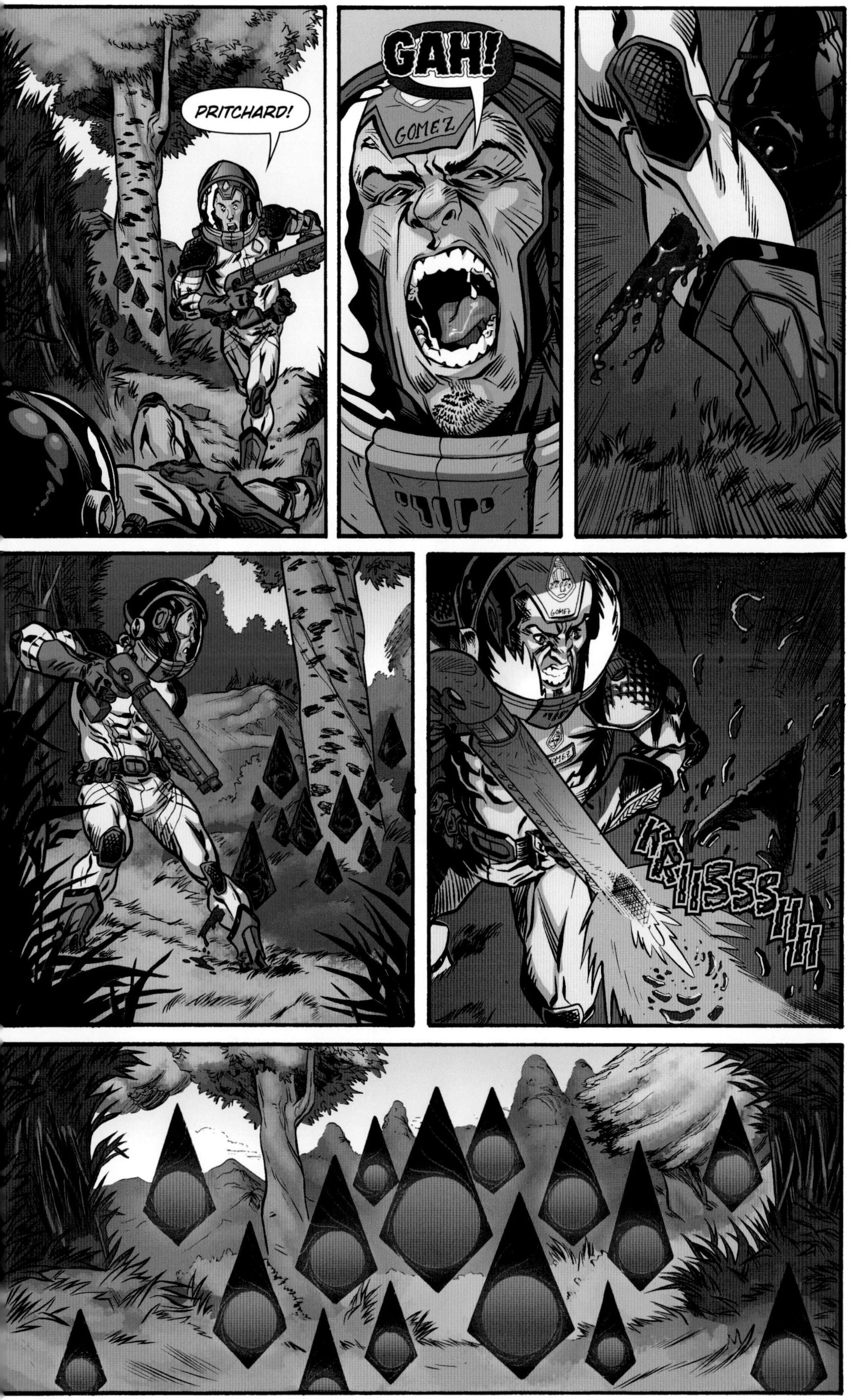
PRITCHARD!
GAH!
GOMEZ
GOMEZ
GOMEZ
KRIISSSHH

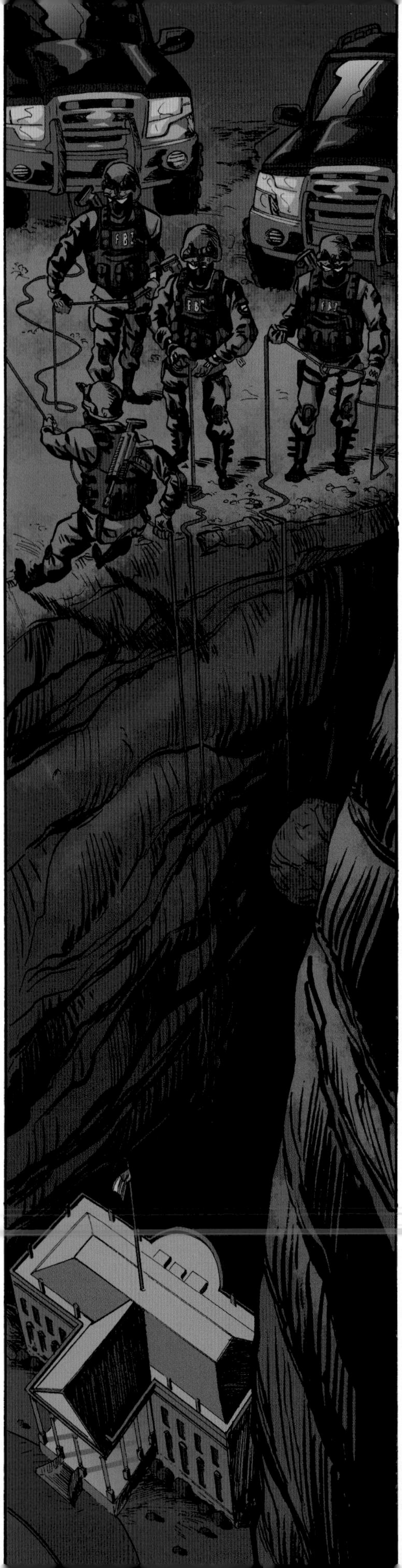
FBI

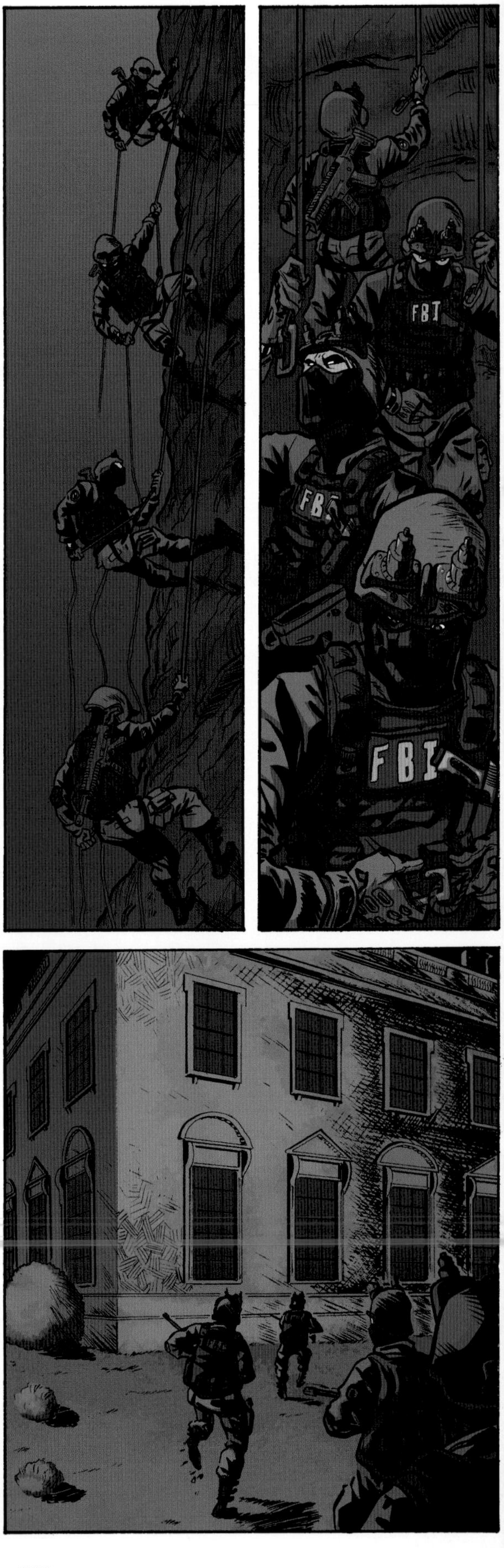
FBI
FBI

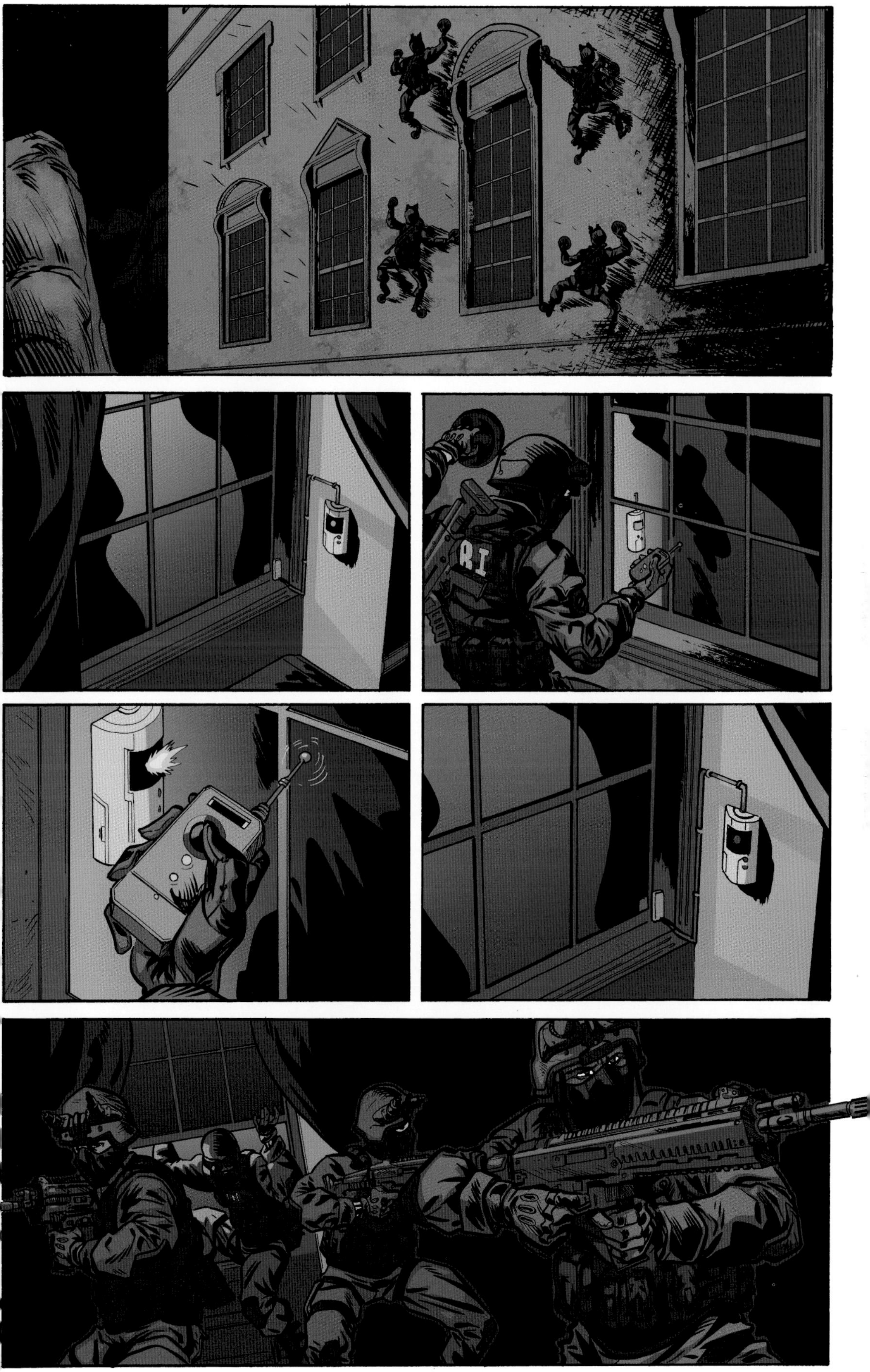

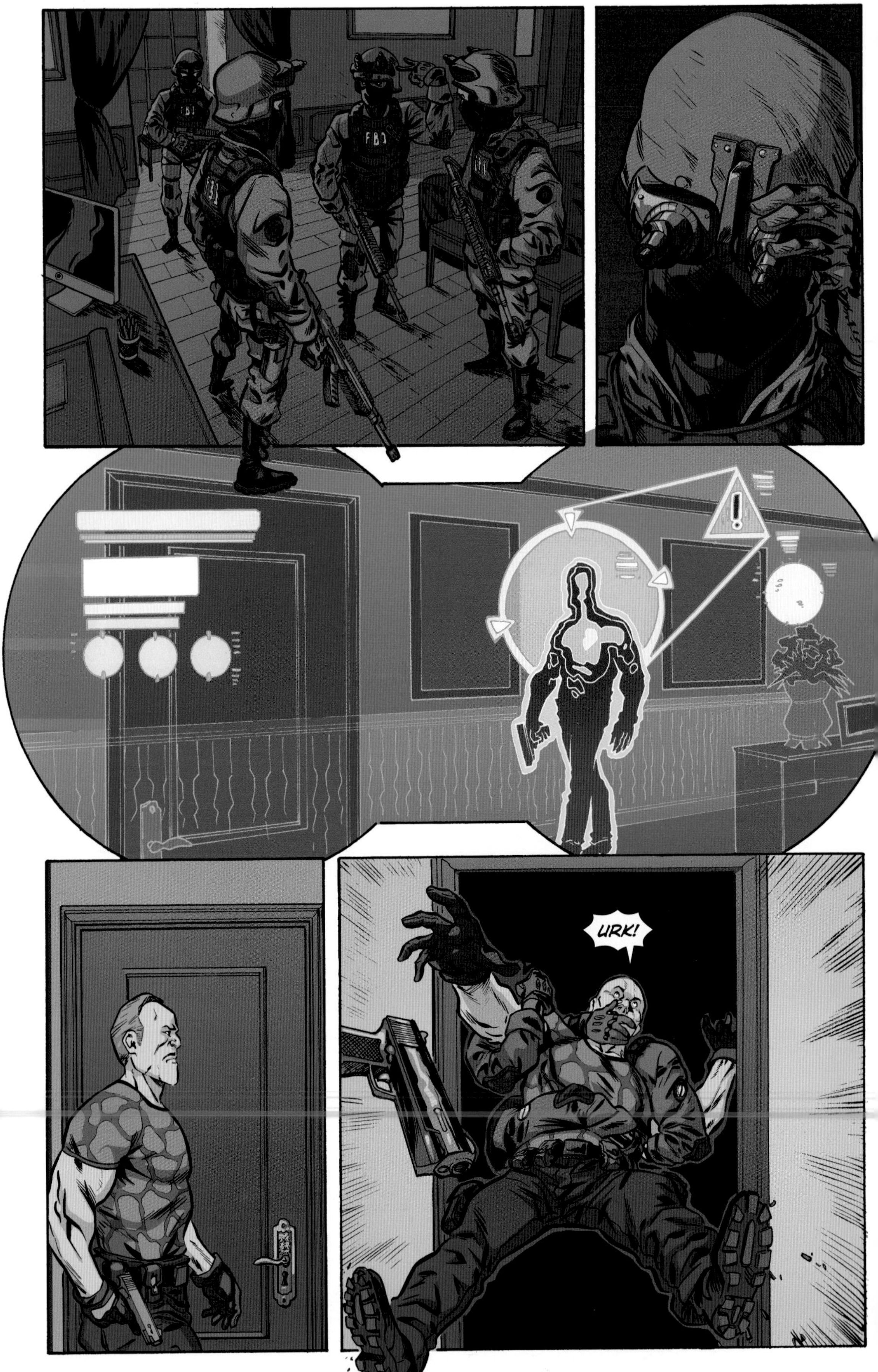
FBI
FBI
FBI
FBI
URK!

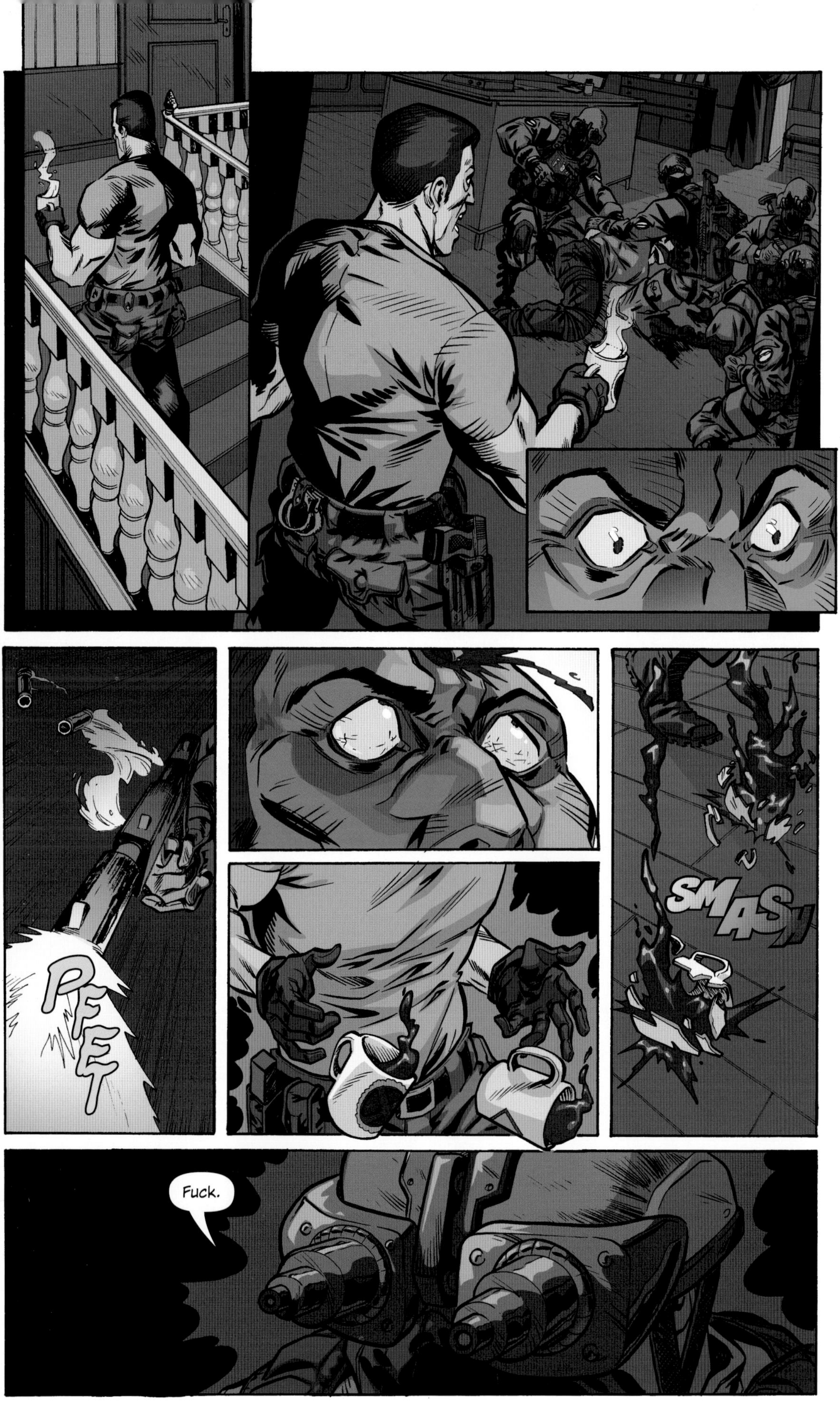
PFFT
SMASH
Fuck.

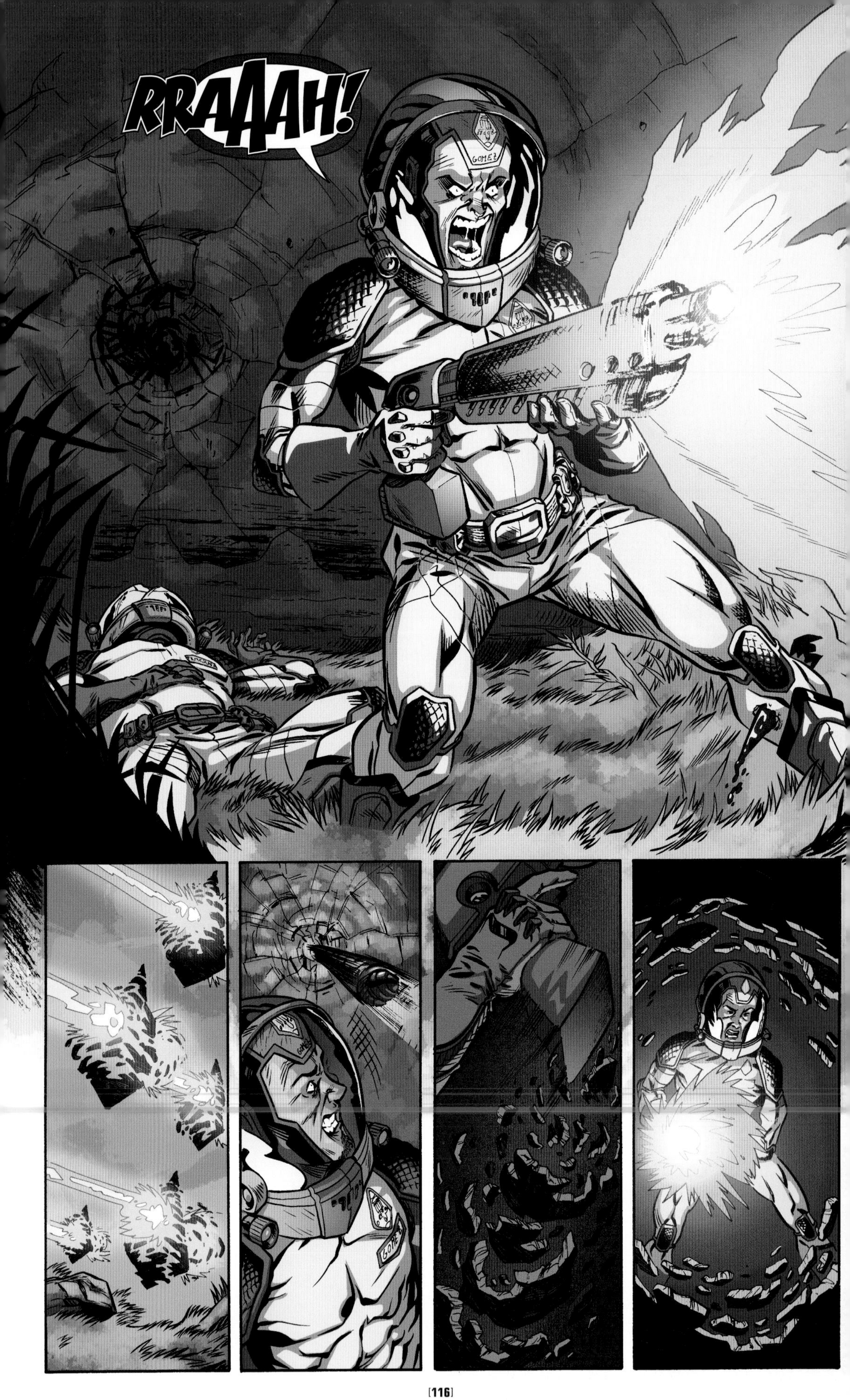
RRAAAH!

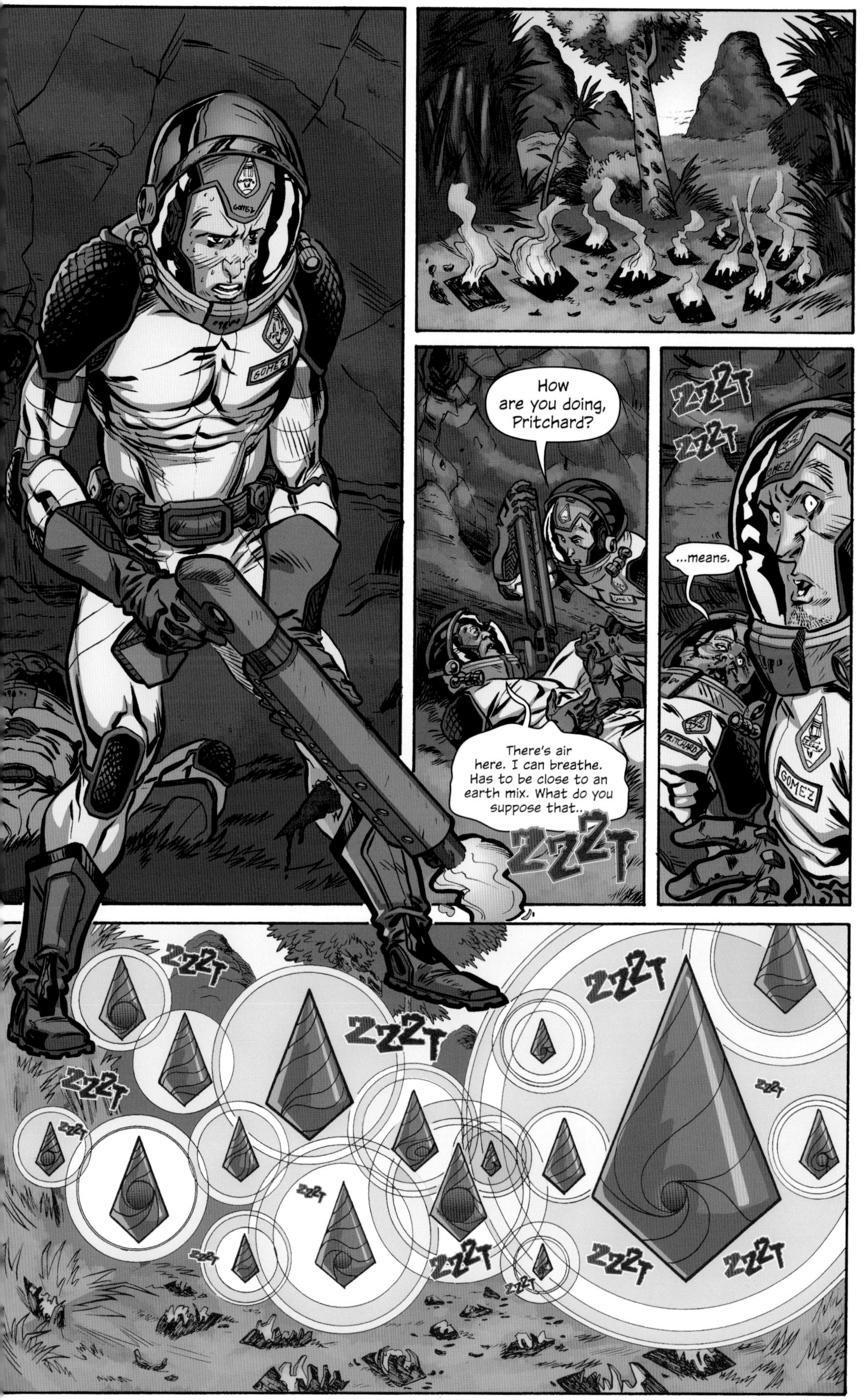

How are you doing, Pritchard?
There's air here. I can breathe. Has to be close to an earth mix. What do you suppose that..
ZZZT
ZZZT
ZZZT
...means.
ZZZT
ZZZT
ZZZT
ZZZT
ZZZT
ZZZT

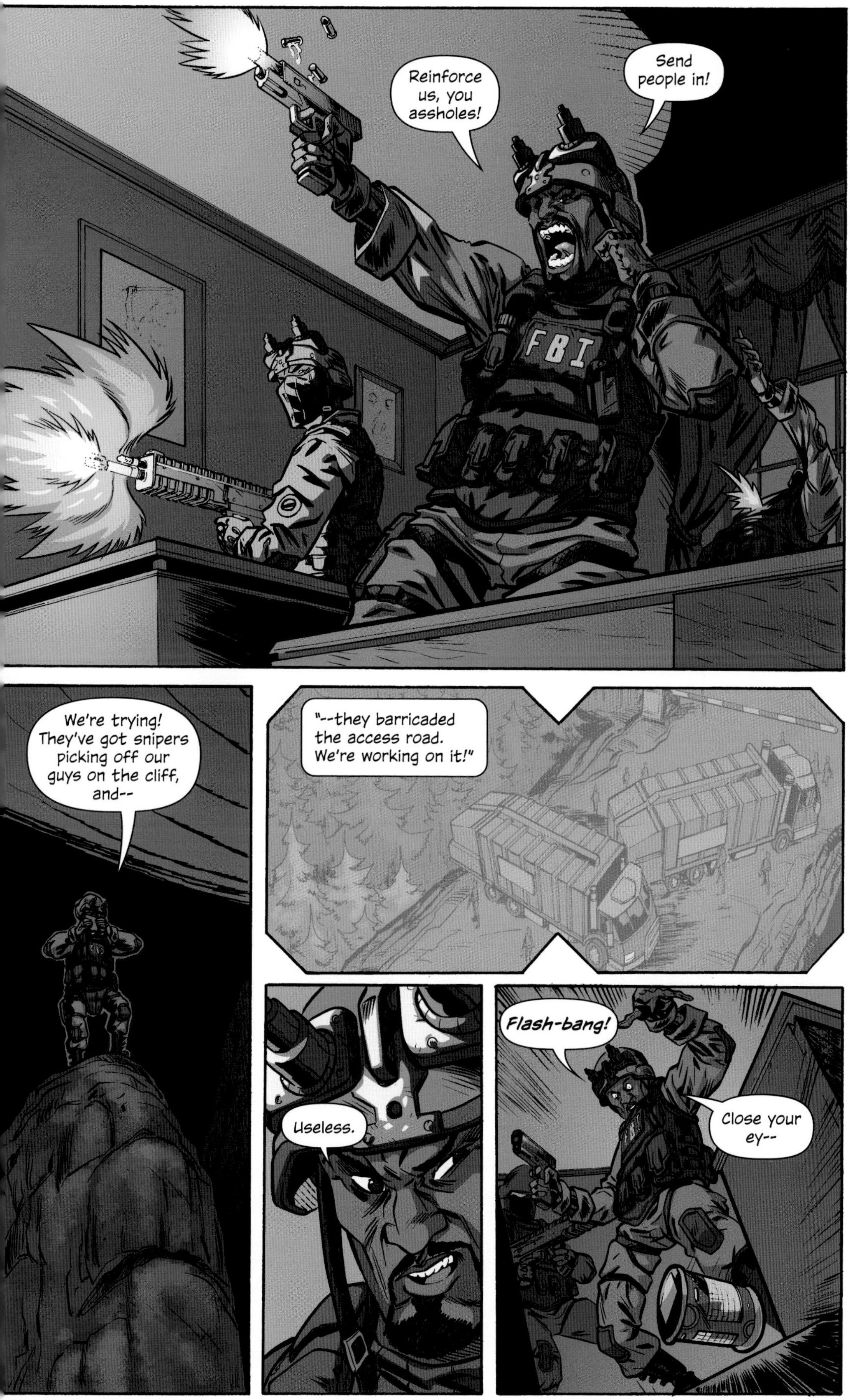
Reinforce us, you assholes!
Send people in!
We're trying! They've got snipers picking off our guys on the cliff, and--
"--they barricaded the access road. We're working on it!"
Useless.
Flash-bang!
Close your ey--

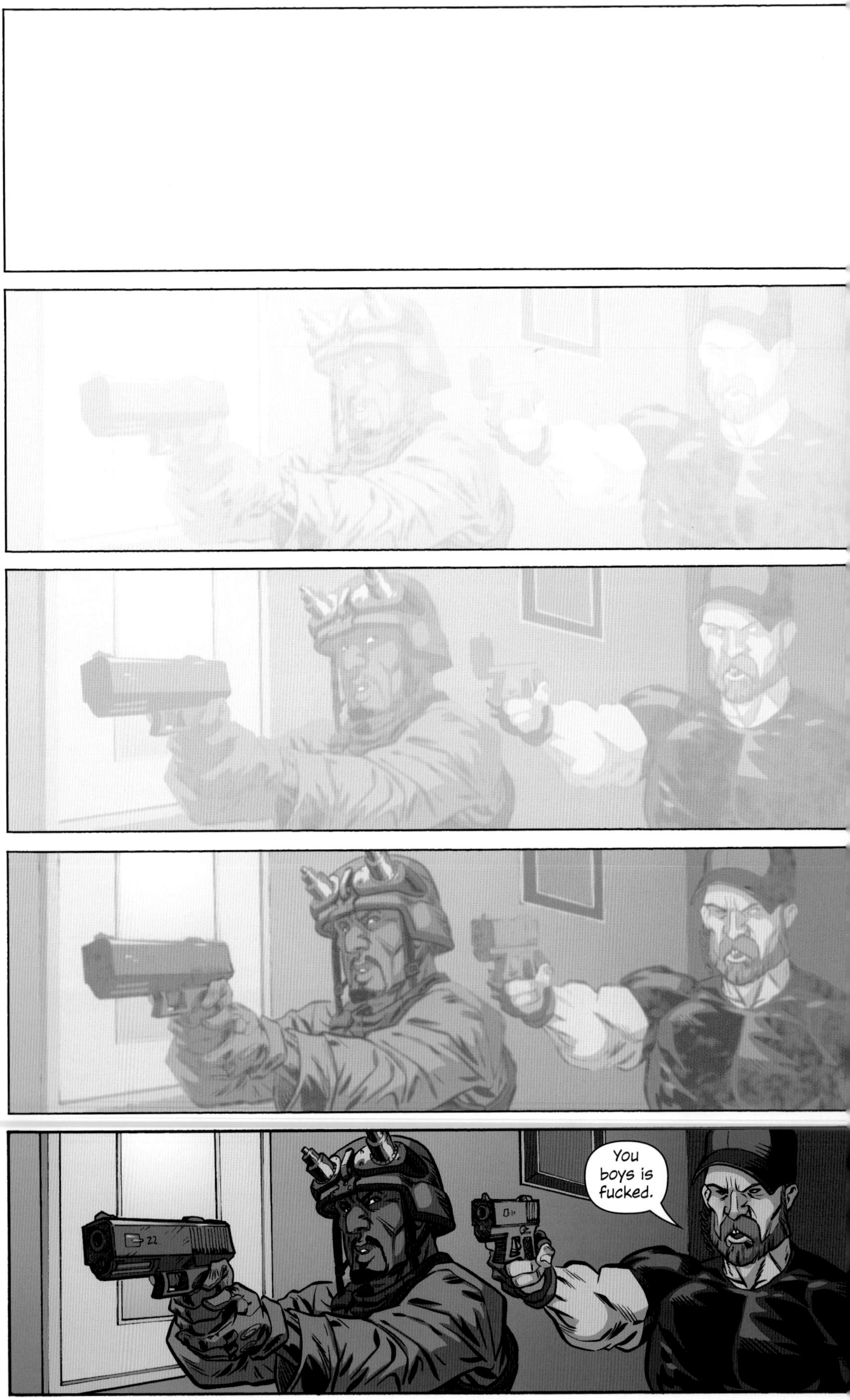
You boys is fucked.

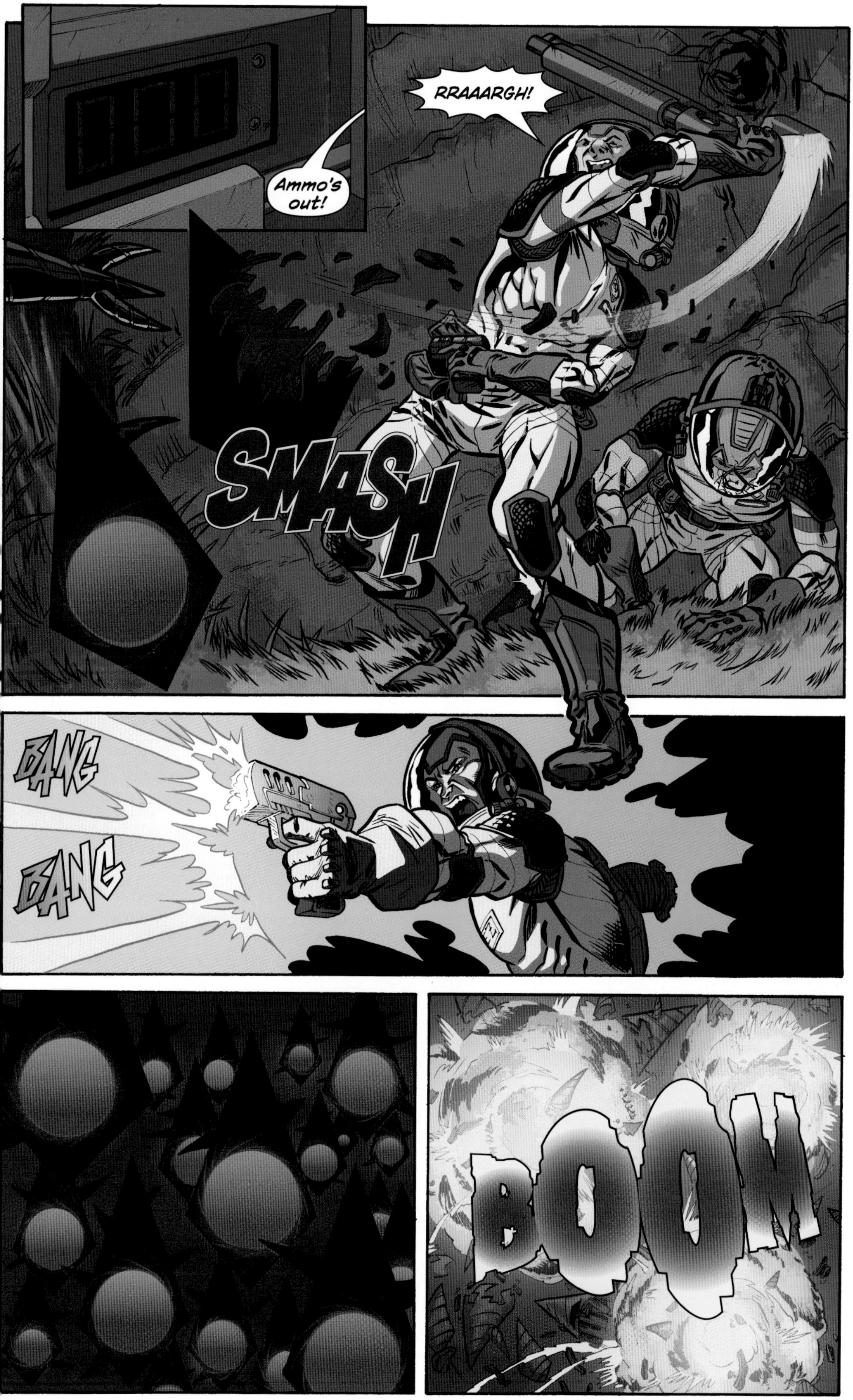

Ammo's out!
RRAAARGH!
SMASH
BANG
BANG
BOOM

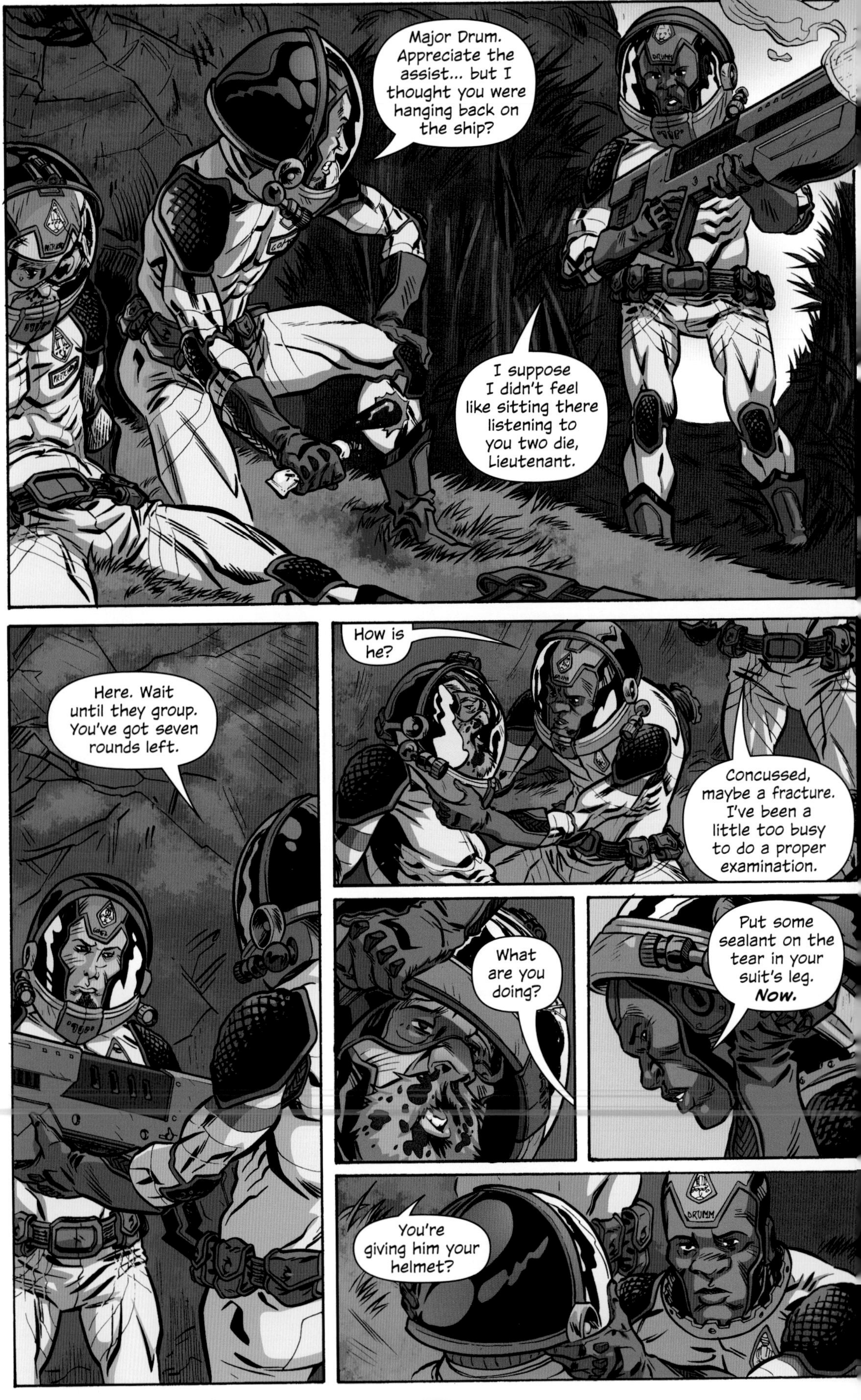

Major Drum. Appreciate the assist... but I thought you were hanging back on the ship?
I suppose I didn't feel like sitting there listening to you two die, Lieutenant.
Here. Wait until they group. You've got seven rounds left.
How is he?
Concussed, maybe a fracture. I've been a little too busy to do a proper examination.
What are you doing?
Put some sealant on the tear in your suit's leg. **Now.**
You're giving him your helmet?

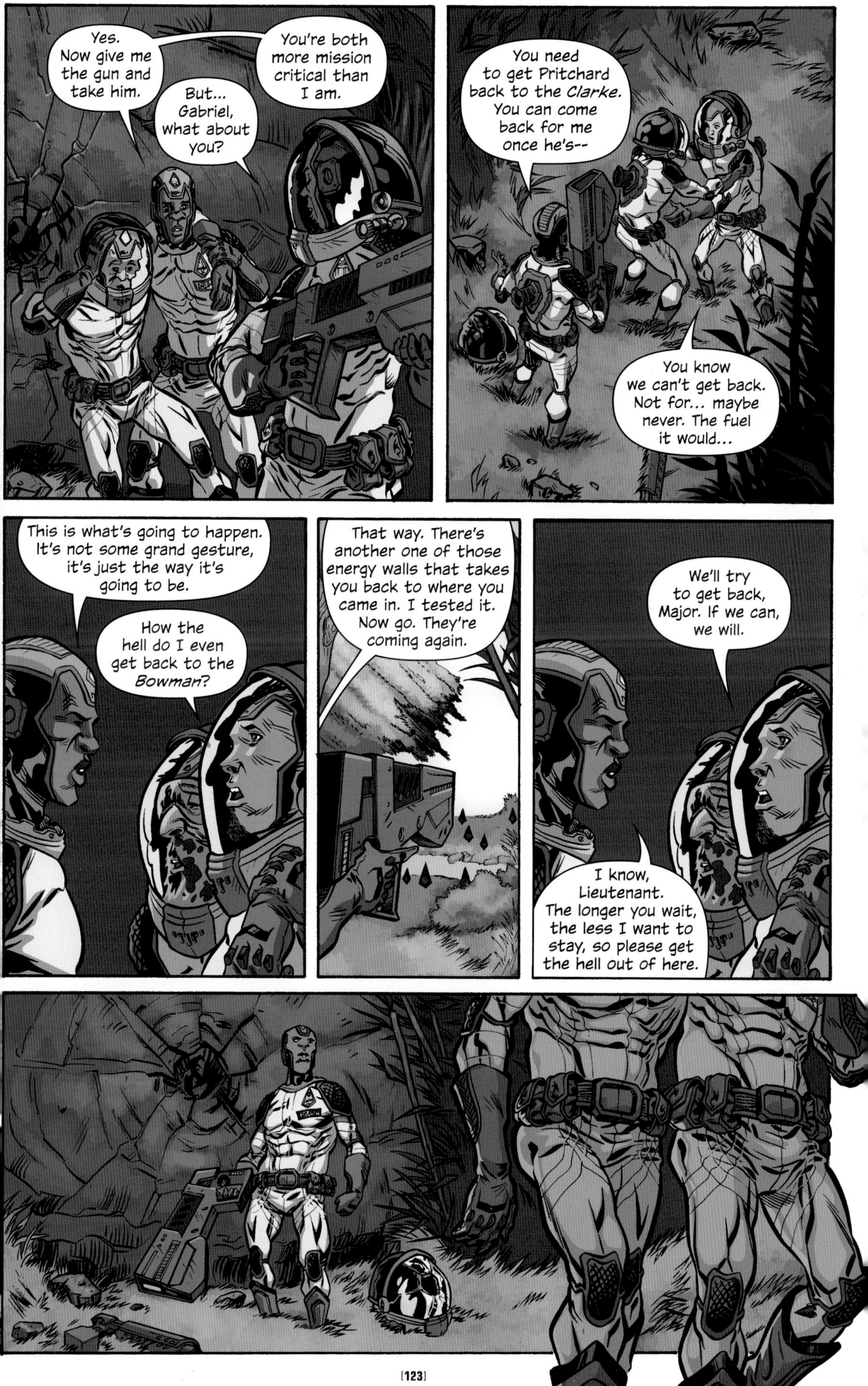
Yes. Now give me the gun and take him.
You're both more mission critical than I am.
But... Gabriel, what about you?
You need to get Pritchard back to the *Clarke*. You can come back for me once he's--
You know we can't get back. Not for... maybe never. The fuel it would...
This is what's going to happen. It's not some grand gesture, it's just the way it's going to be.
How the hell do I even get back to the *Bowman*?
That way. There's another one of those energy walls that takes you back to where you came in. I tested it. Now go. They're coming again.
We'll try to get back, Major. If we can, we will.
I know, Lieutenant. The longer you wait, the less I want to stay, so please get the hell out of here.

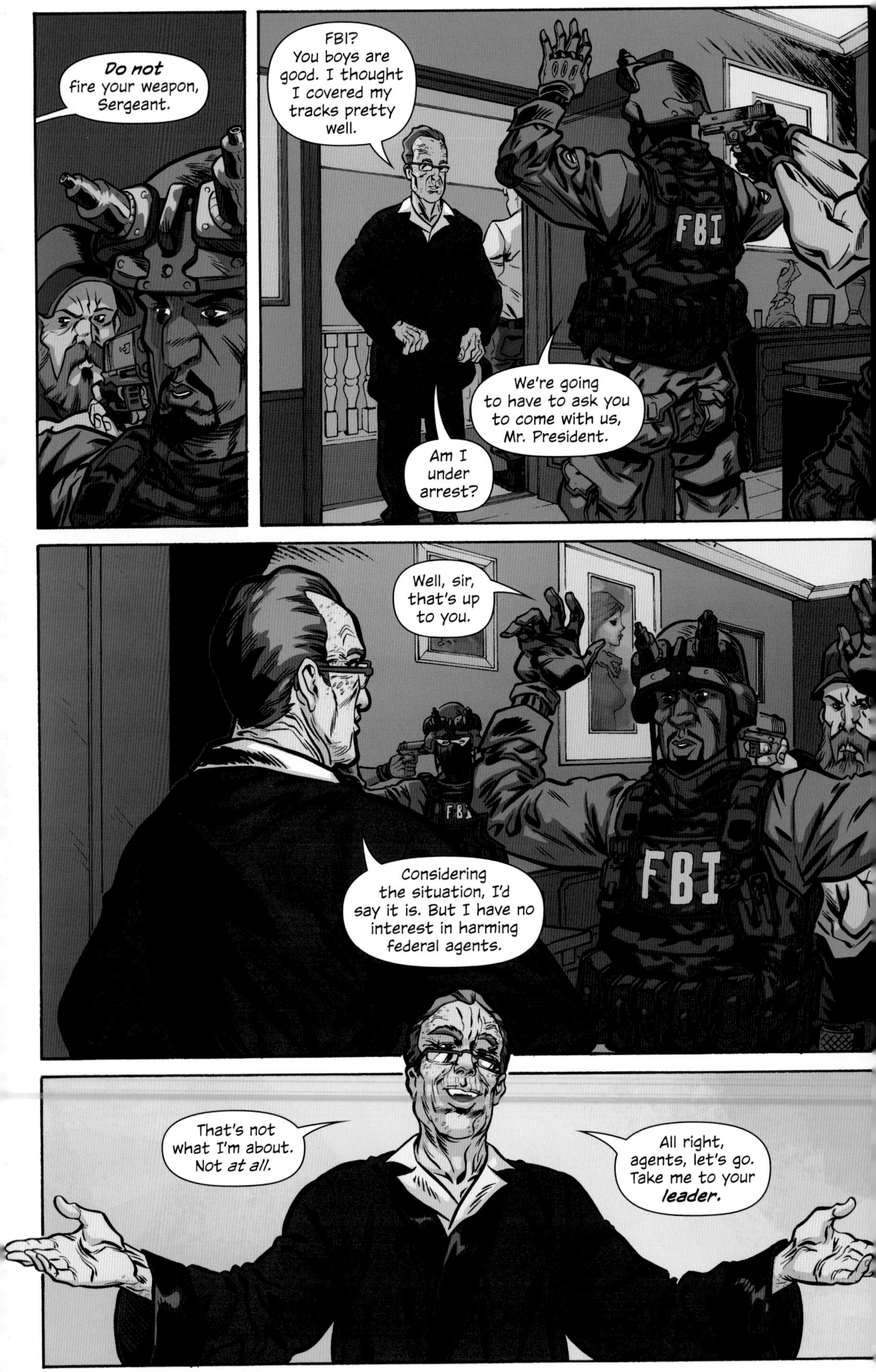
Do not fire your weapon, Sergeant.
FBI? You boys are good. I thought I covered my tracks pretty well.
FBI
We're going to have to ask you to come with us, Mr. President.
Am I under arrest?
Well, sir, that's up to you.
FBI
FBI
Considering the situation, I'd say it is. But I have no interest in harming federal agents.
That's not what I'm about. Not *at all*.
All right, agents, let's go. Take me to your ***leader.***

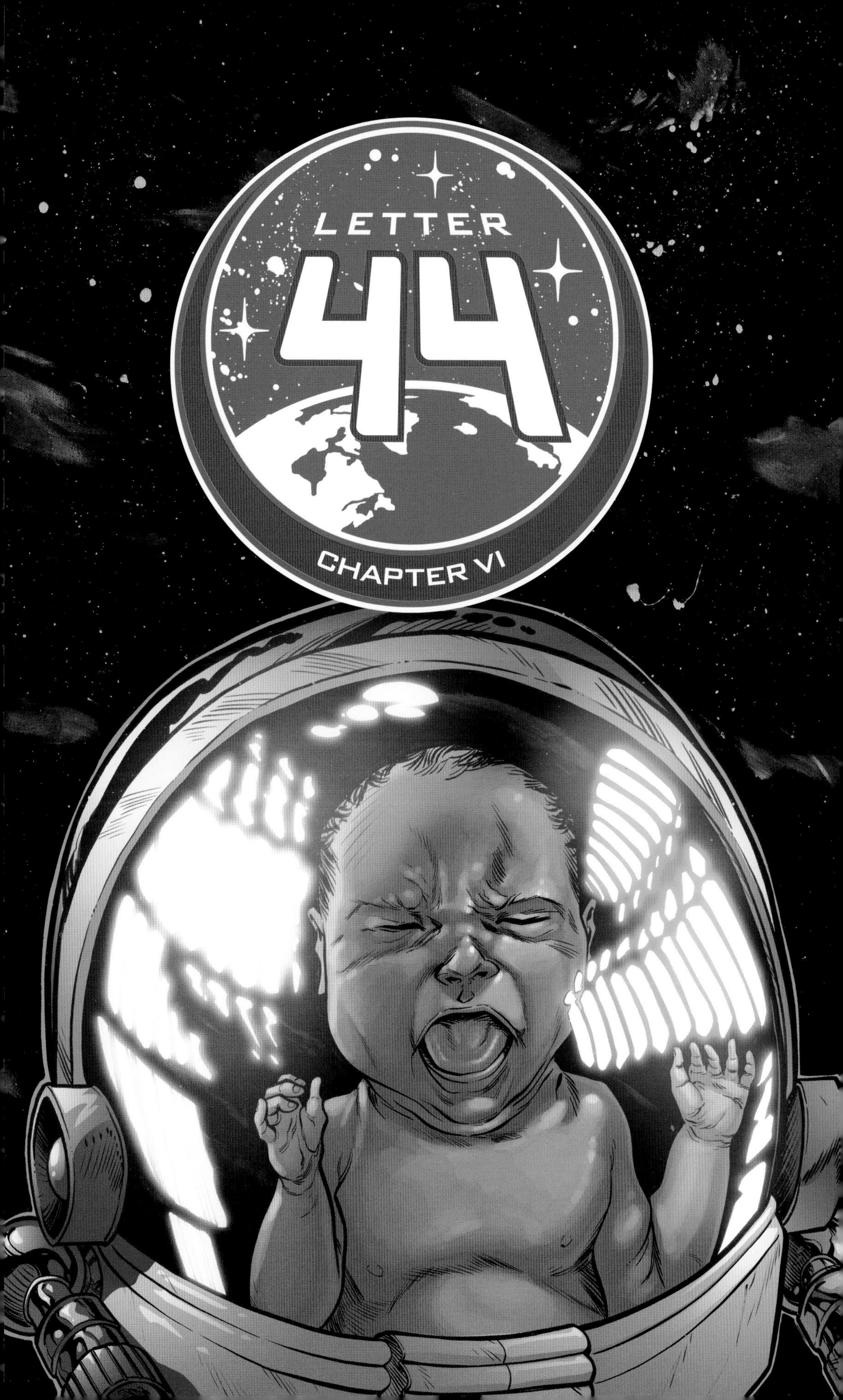
LETTER
44
CHAPTER VI

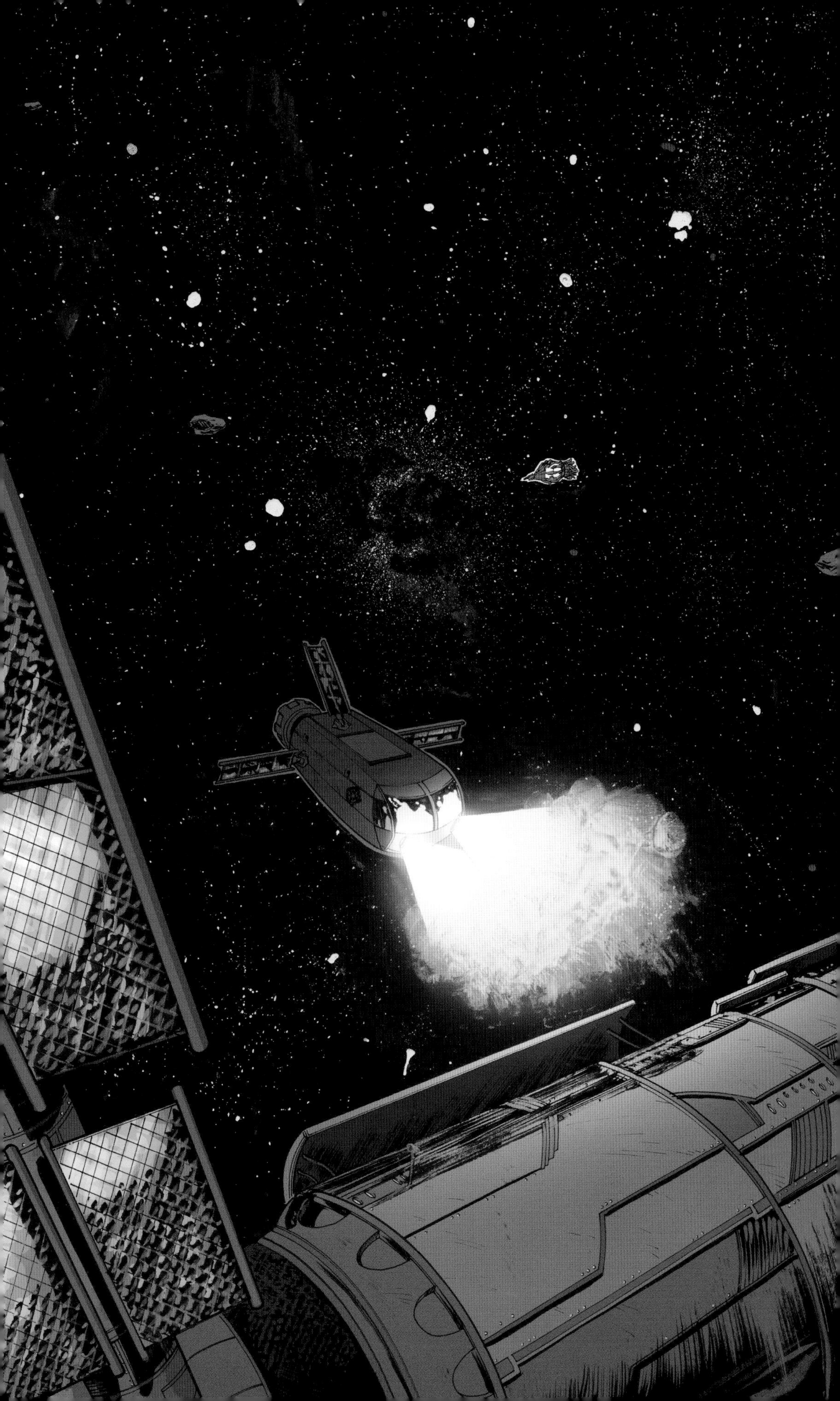

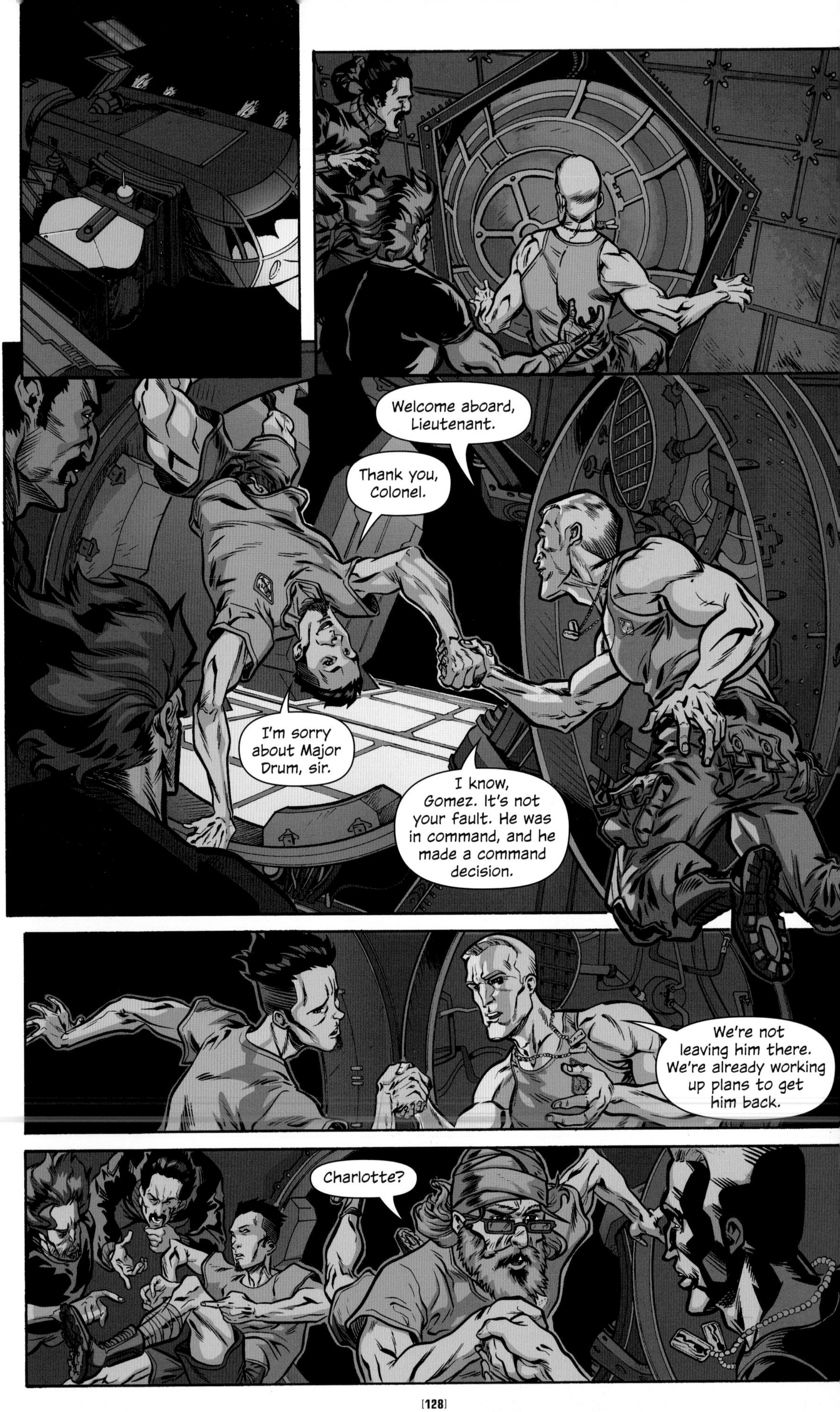
Welcome aboard, Lieutenant.
Thank you, Colonel.
I'm sorry about Major Drum, sir.
I know, Gomez. It's not your fault. He was in command, and he made a command decision.
We're not leaving him there. We're already working up plans to get him back.
Charlotte?

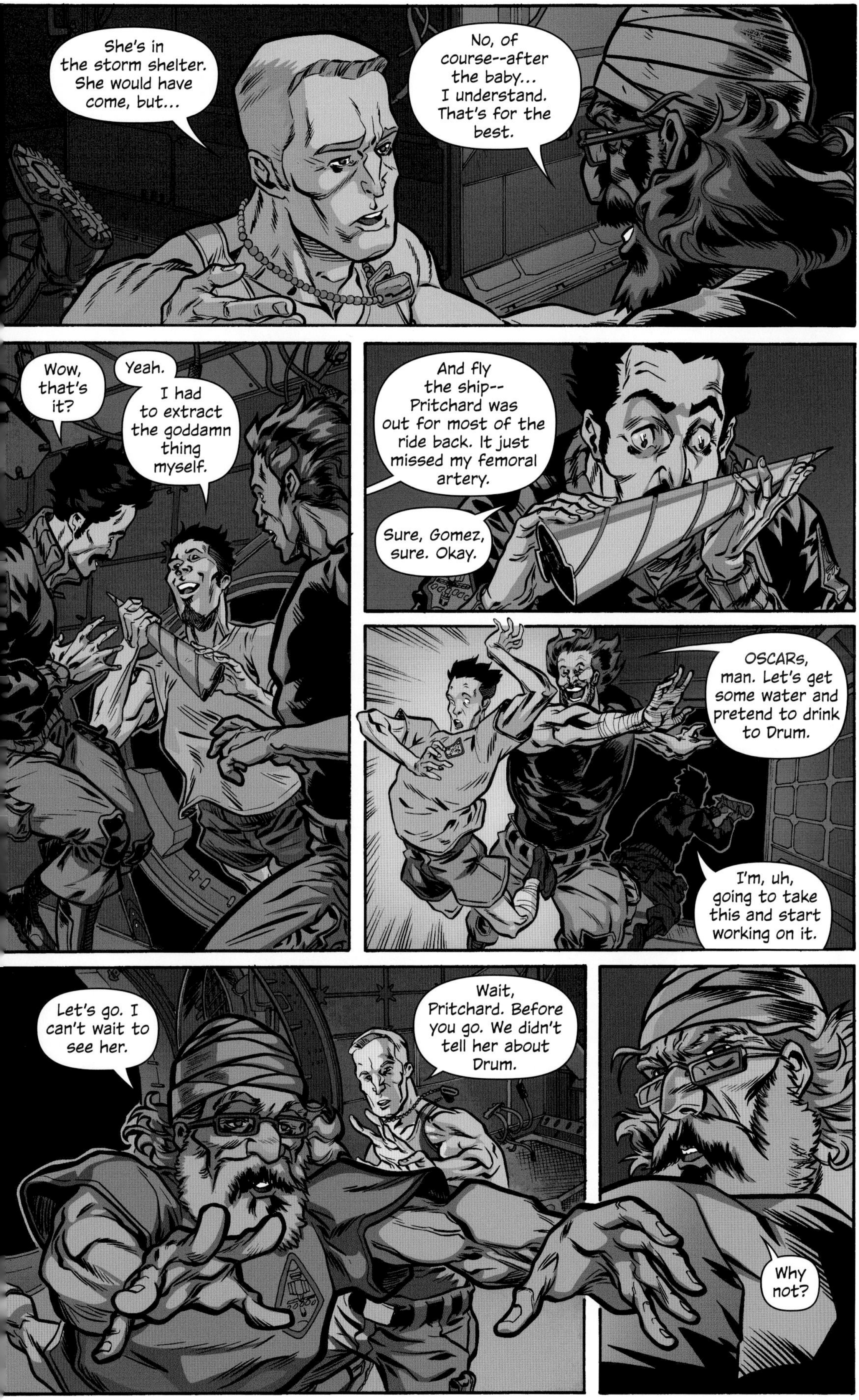
She's in the storm shelter. She would have come, but...
No, of course--after the baby... I understand. That's for the best.
Wow, that's it?
Yeah.
I had to extract the goddamn thing myself.
And fly the ship-- Pritchard was out for most of the ride back. It just missed my femoral artery.
Sure, Gomez, sure. Okay.
OSCARs, man. Let's get some water and pretend to drink to Drum.
I'm, uh, going to take this and start working on it.
Let's go. I can't wait to see her.
Wait, Pritchard. Before you go. We didn't tell her about Drum.
Why not?

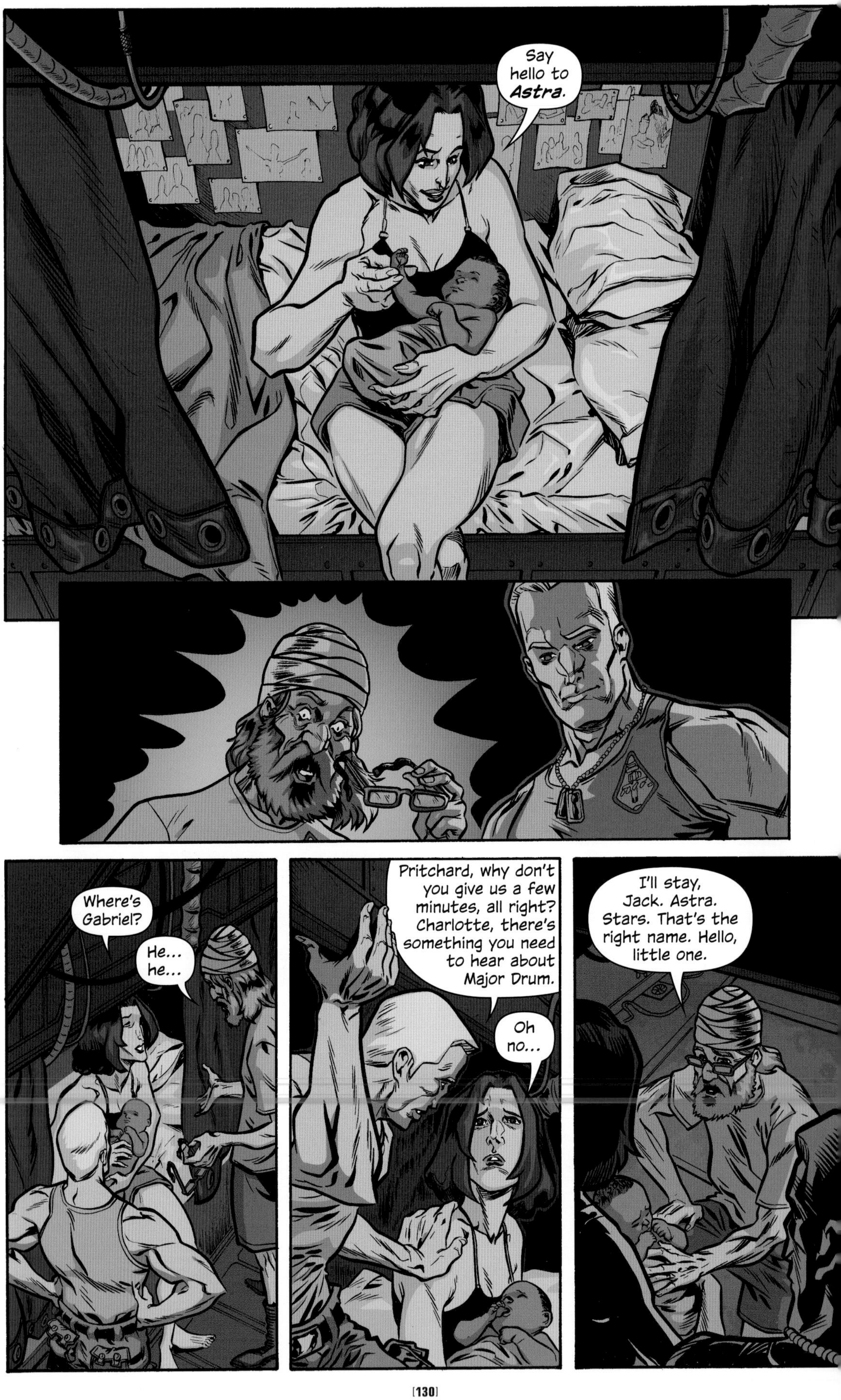
Say hello to **Astra**.
Where's Gabriel?
He... he...
Pritchard, why don't you give us a few minutes, all right? Charlotte, there's something you need to hear about Major Drum.
Oh no...
I'll stay, Jack. Astra. Stars. That's the right name. Hello, little one.

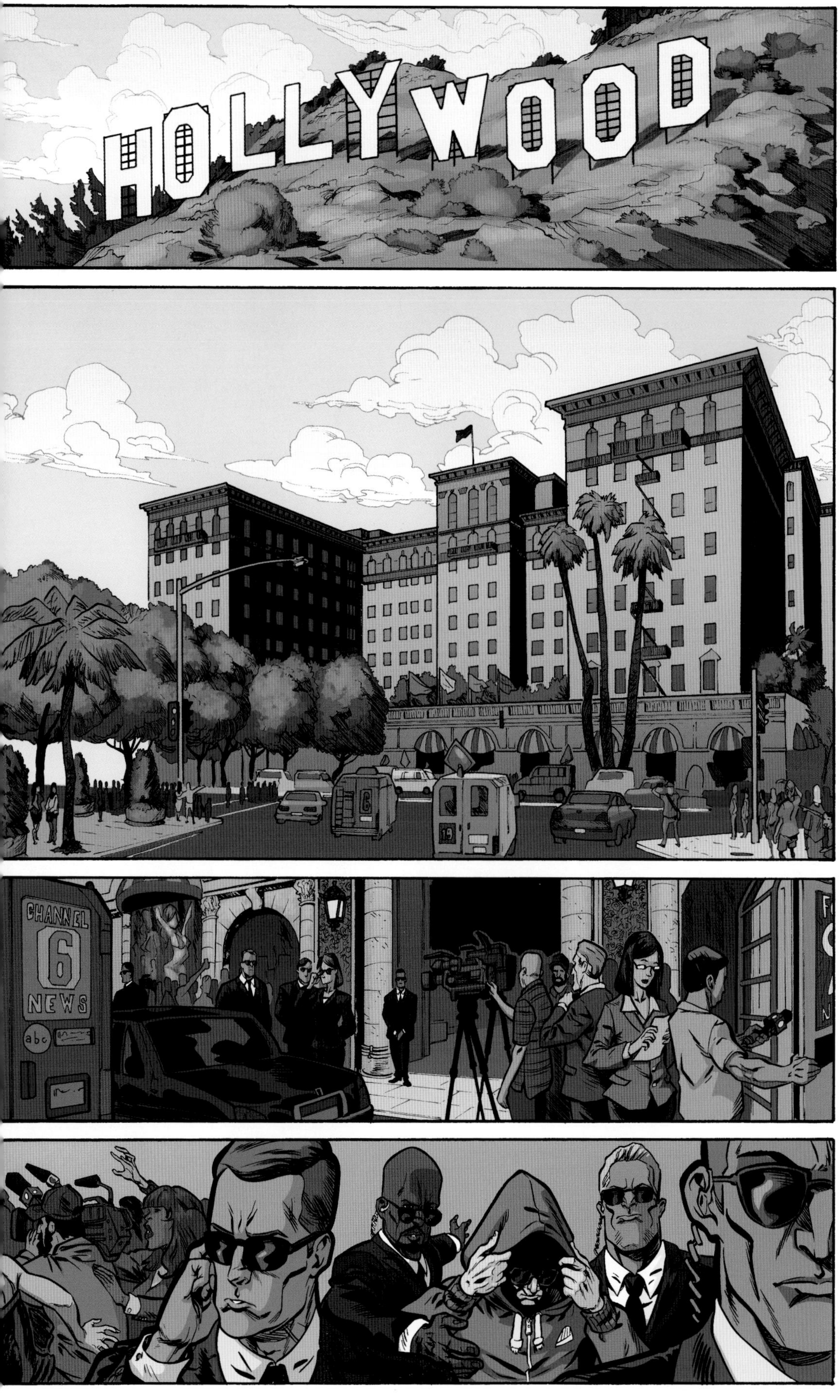
HOLLYWOOD
CHANNEL 6 NEWS
abc

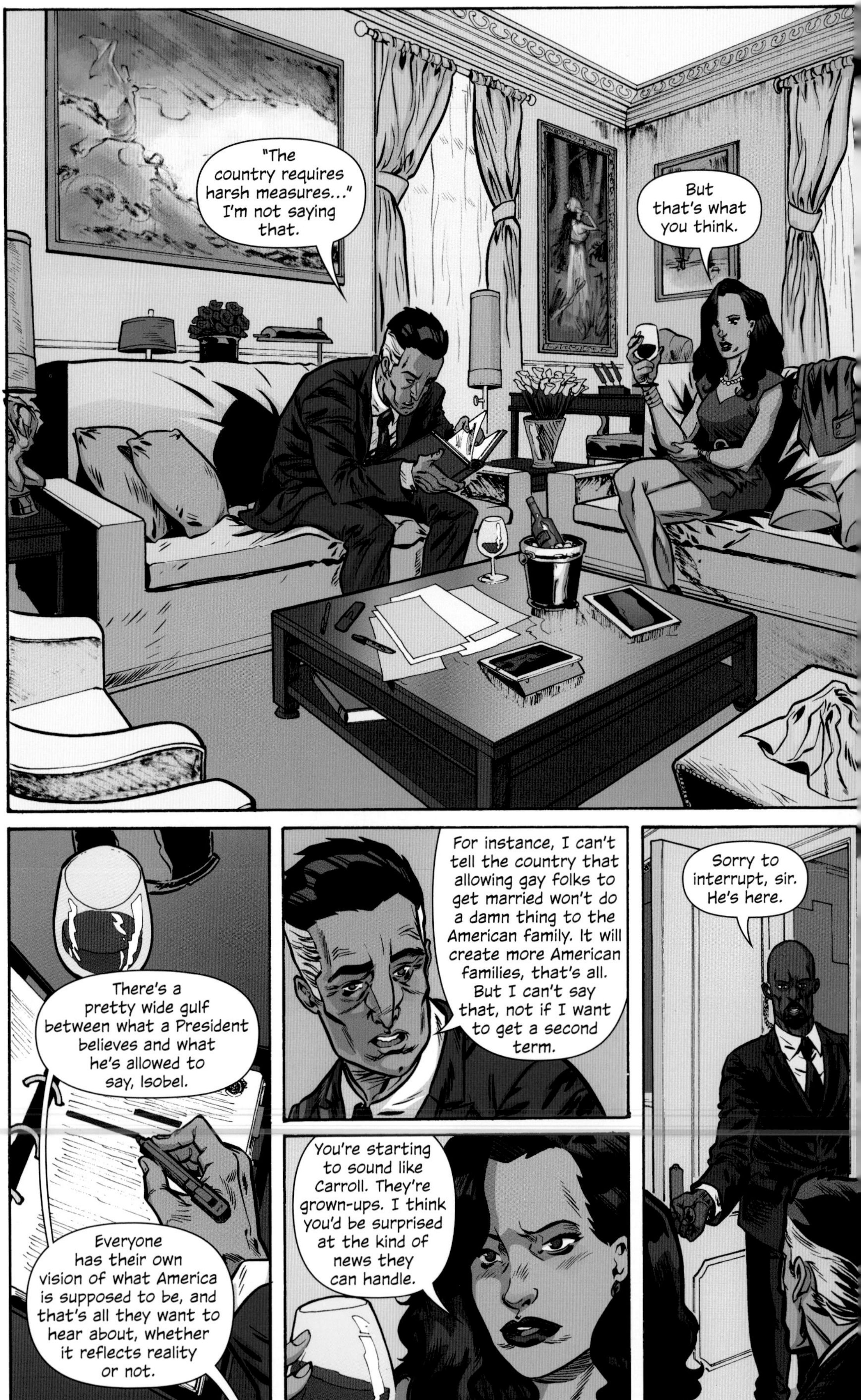
"The country requires harsh measures..." I'm not saying that.
But that's what you think.
There's a pretty wide gulf between what a President believes and what he's allowed to say, Isobel.
Everyone has their own vision of what America is supposed to be, and that's all they want to hear about, whether it reflects reality or not.
For instance, I can't tell the country that allowing gay folks to get married won't do a damn thing to the American family. It will create more American families, that's all. But I can't say that, not if I want to get a second term.
You're starting to sound like Carroll. They're grown-ups. I think you'd be surprised at the kind of news they can handle.
Sorry to interrupt, sir. He's here.

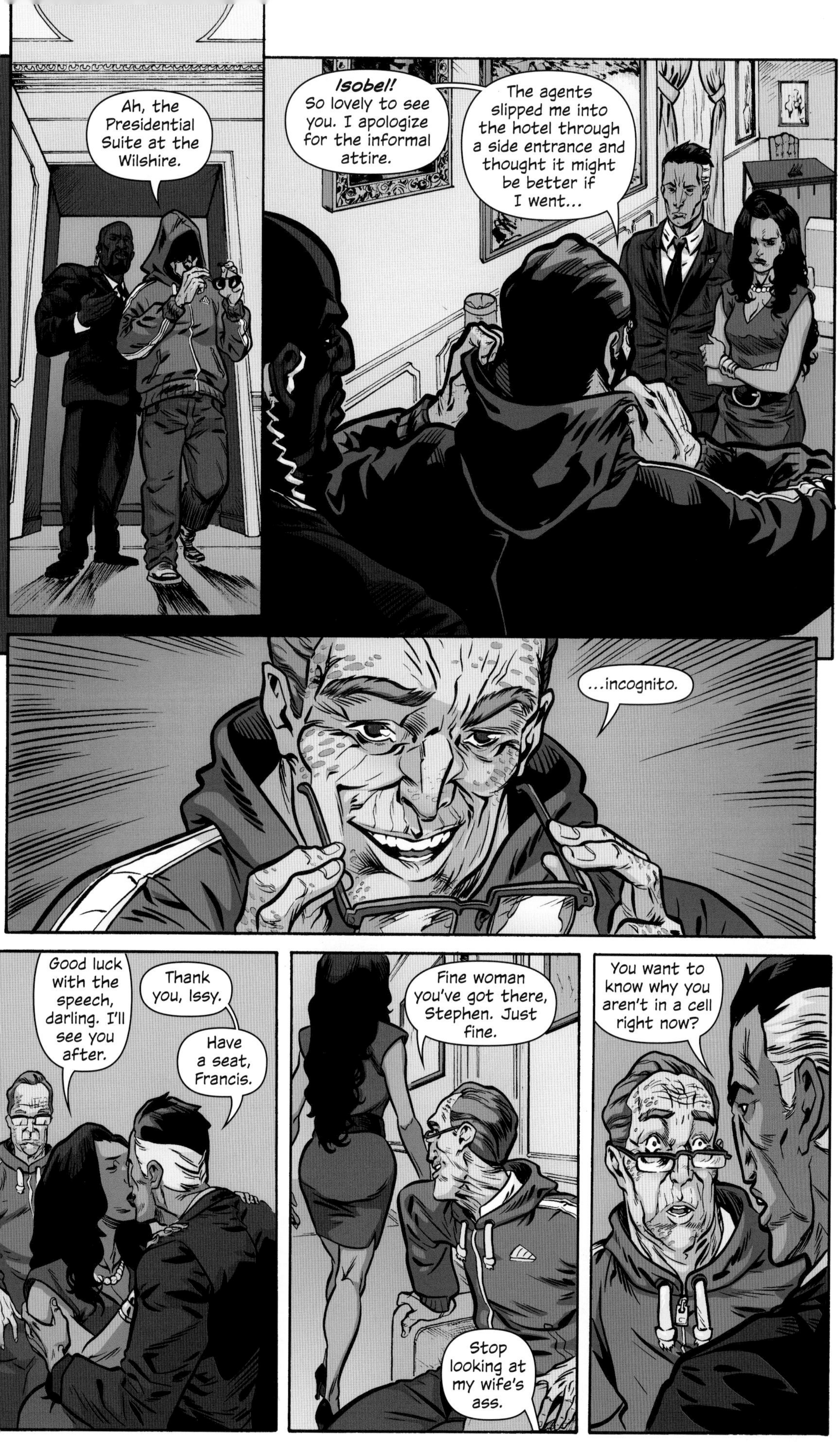
Ah, the Presidential Suite at the Wilshire.
Isobel! So lovely to see you. I apologize for the informal attire.
The agents slipped me into the hotel through a side entrance and thought it might be better if I went...
...incognito.
Good luck with the speech, darling. I'll see you after.
Thank you, Issy.
Have a seat, Francis.
Fine woman you've got there, Stephen. Just fine.
Stop looking at my wife's ass.
You want to know why you aren't in a cell right now?

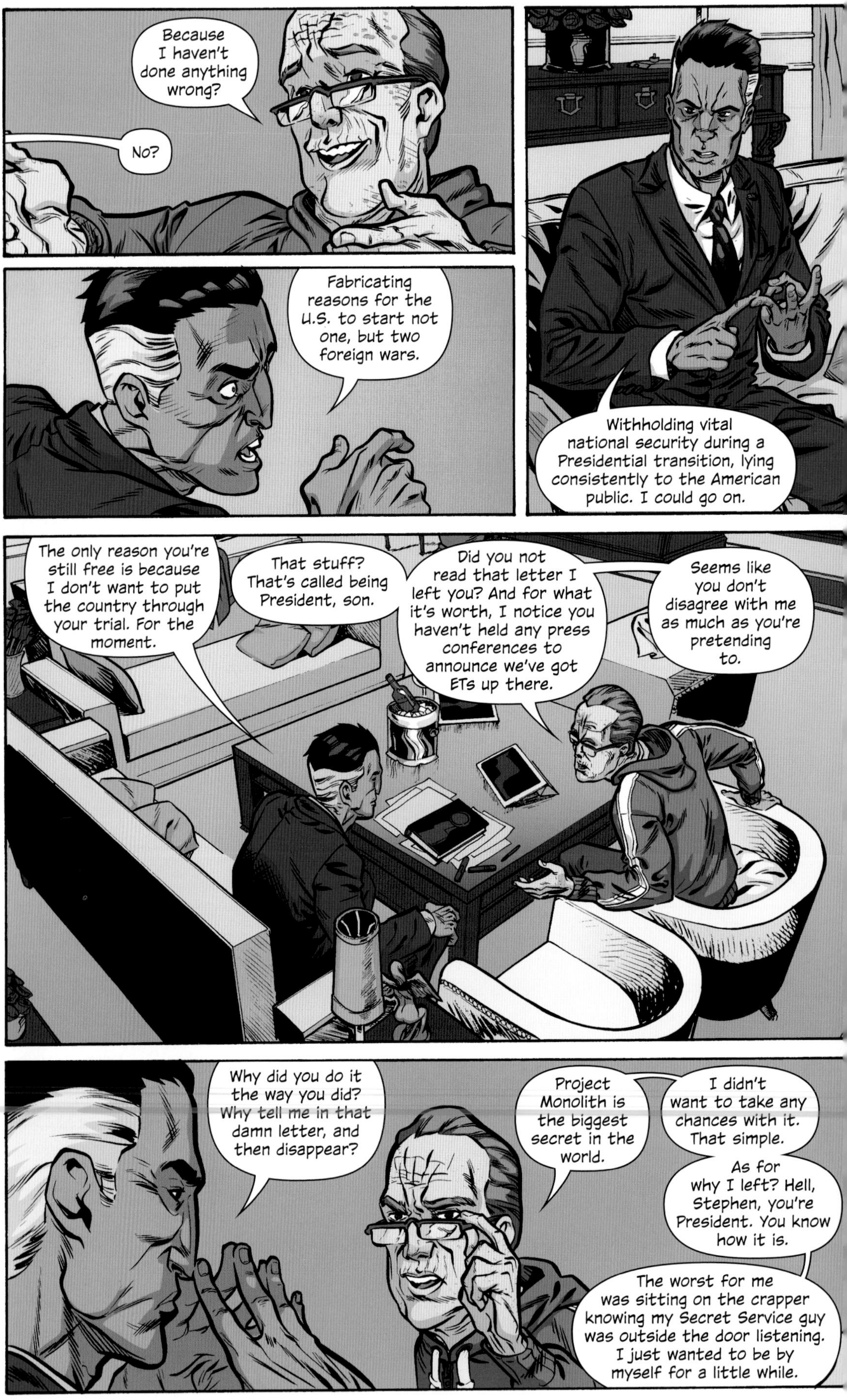
Because I haven't done anything wrong?
No?
Fabricating reasons for the U.S. to start not one, but two foreign wars.
Withholding vital national security during a Presidential transition, lying consistently to the American public. I could go on.
That stuff? That's called being President, son.
Did you not read that letter I left you? And for what it's worth, I notice you haven't held any press conferences to announce we've got ETs up there.
Seems like you don't disagree with me as much as you're pretending to.
The only reason you're still free is because I don't want to put the country through your trial. For the moment.
Why did you do it the way you did? Why tell me in that damn letter, and then disappear?
Project Monolith is the biggest secret in the world.
I didn't want to take any chances with it. That simple.
As for why I left? Hell, Stephen, you're President. You know how it is.
The worst for me was sitting on the crapper knowing my Secret Service guy was outside the door listening. I just wanted to be by myself for a little while.

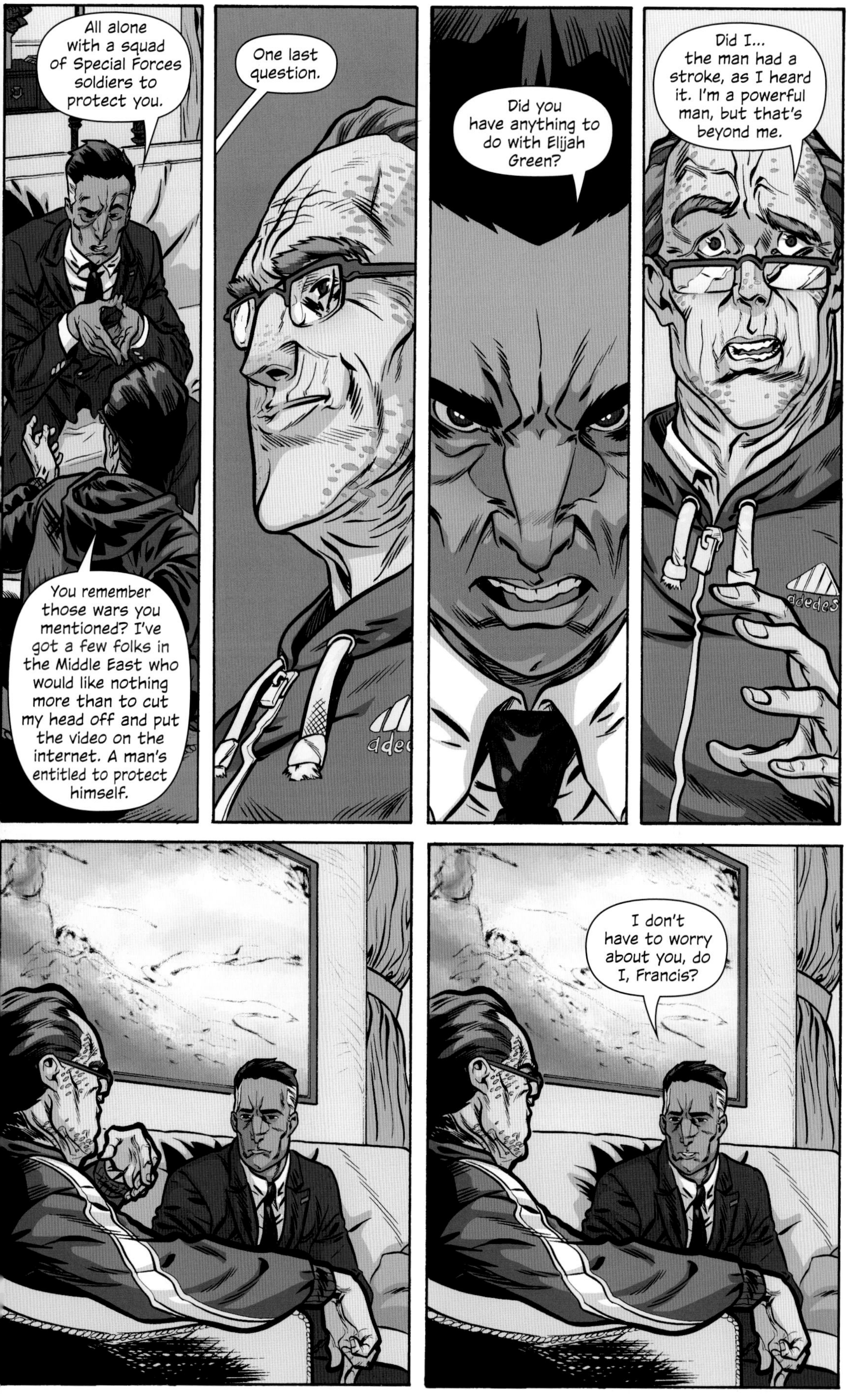
All alone with a squad of Special Forces soldiers to protect you.
You remember those wars you mentioned? I've got a few folks in the Middle East who would like nothing more than to cut my head off and put the video on the internet. A man's entitled to protect himself.
One last question.
adec
Did you have anything to do with Elijah Green?
Did I... the man had a stroke, as I heard it. I'm a powerful man, but that's beyond me.
adedes
I don't have to worry about you, do I, Francis?

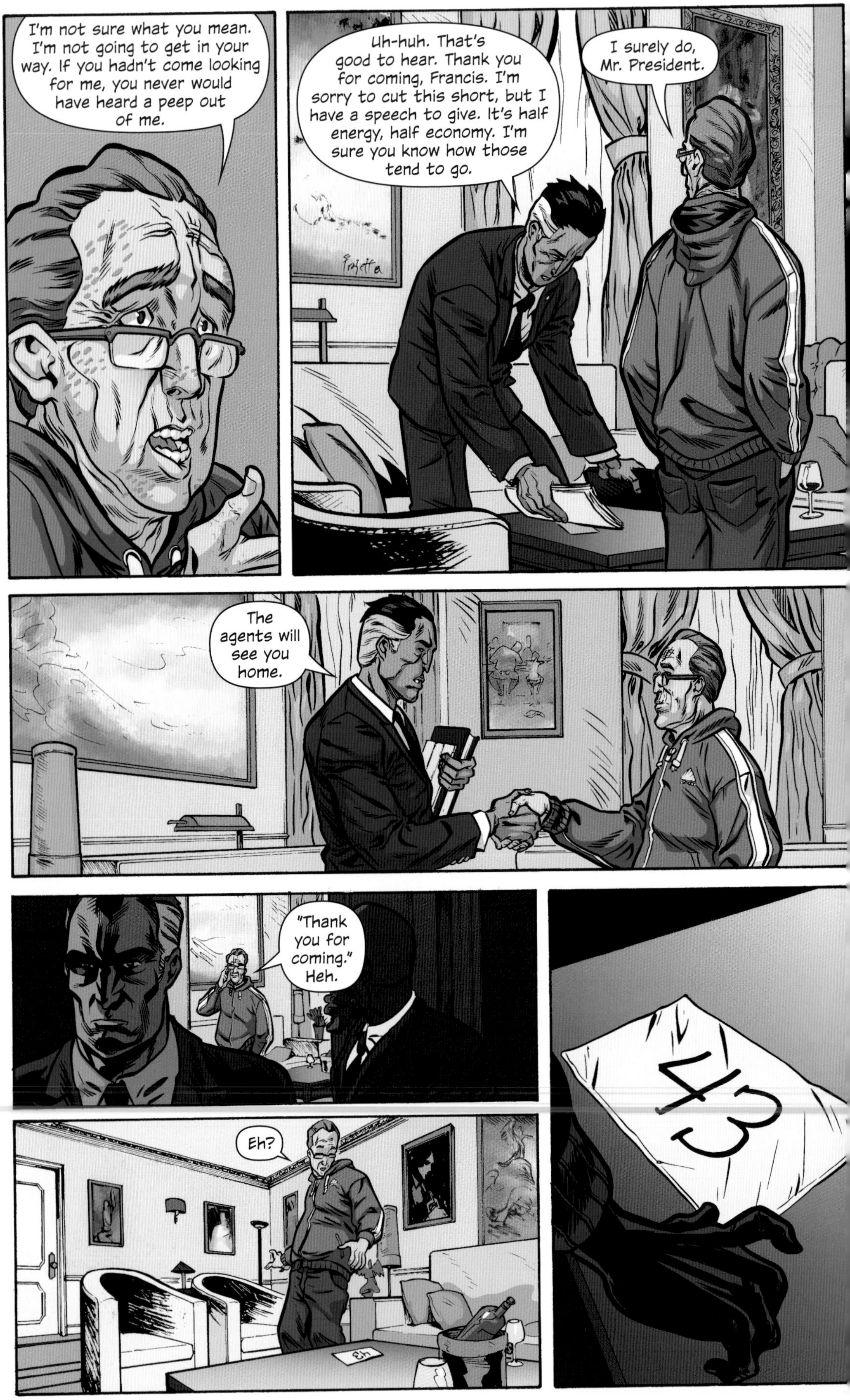
I'm not sure what you mean. I'm not going to get in your way. If you hadn't come looking for me, you never would have heard a peep out of me.
Uh-huh. That's good to hear. Thank you for coming, Francis. I'm sorry to cut this short, but I have a speech to give. It's half energy, half economy. I'm sure you know how those tend to go.
I surely do, Mr. President.
The agents will see you home.
"Thank you for coming." Heh.
Eh?
43

What the hell are we doing out here, Jack? We started with nine, now we're down to seven.

Eight. We're back up to eight.

You suppose he knew it was his?

No. He never would have stayed on that asteroid if he'd known. We both know why he stayed, but he'd have come back if he knew about Astra.

But that just underscores it--we're supposed to be learning something about these beings, trying to communicate, and the first time we encounter them we shoot at them?

Apparently you maimed one of them first. According to Gomez, anyway.

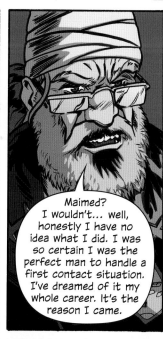

Maimed? I wouldn't... well, honestly I have no idea what I did. I was so certain I was the perfect man to handle a first contact situation. I've dreamed of it my whole career. It's the reason I came.

And then to come back and find out that the woman I... we... I mean, goddammit, Jack!

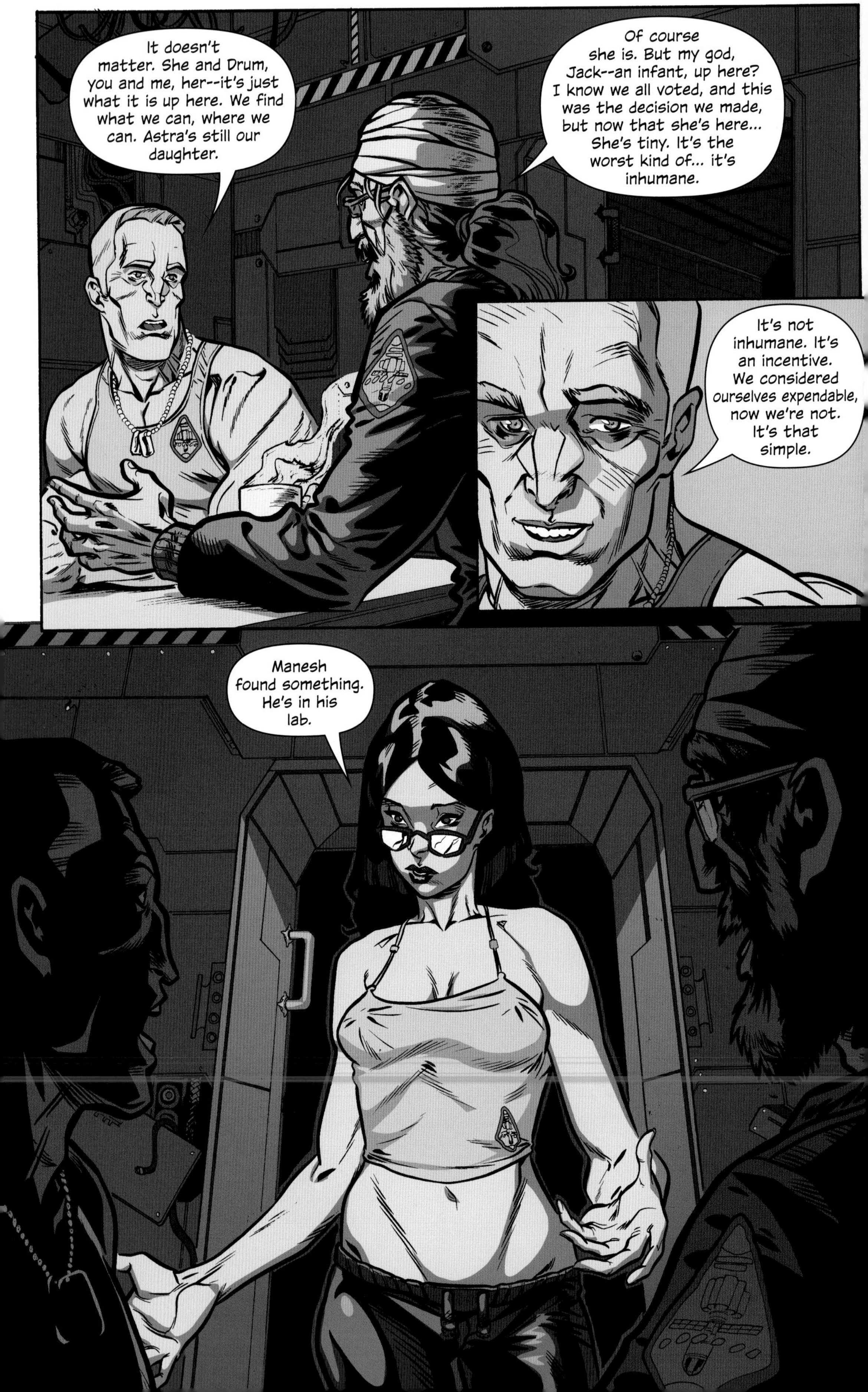
It doesn't matter. She and Drum, you and me, her--it's just what it is up here. We find what we can, where we can. Astra's still our daughter.
Of course she is. But my god, Jack--an infant, up here? I know we all voted, and this was the decision we made, but now that she's here... She's tiny. It's the worst kind of... it's inhumane.
It's not inhumane. It's an incentive. We considered ourselves expendable, now we're not. It's that simple.
Manesh found something. He's in his lab.

Hmph.
Dear Mr. President,
Please allow me to begin by saying that I didn't believe a single goddamn word you just said.
Dear Mr. President,
Please allow me to begin by saying that I didn't believe a single goddamn word you just said.
There's a term in boxing called the "rope-a-dope." Most people have heard of it, thanks to Muhammad Ali, but they have no idea what it actually means. I'll tell you: a rope-a-dope is when you let yourself get pushed back against the ropes. You stand there with your guard up, trying to slip punches, taking some, looking weak. What you're really doing is resting; letting the other guy get tired. Then, when you're ready, you bounce up off the ropes and start hitting back. Good stuff. I mention this for reasons that will be clear in a moment.
A rope-a-dope works because it's hard for the other guy to know whether you're actually about to fall over. But what can they do? Either they keep punching, or they back off. Either way, you get to plan, and quite literally come out swinging.
This is my country now, not yours. I'll handle it as I see fit. Stop fucking with me, Mr. President.
I've assigned the Joint Chiefs to use that wonderful Project Monolith tech to end your wars. I've got all the big defense contractors churning out the new stuff as fast as they can. I want us out of your messes. I'm done calling soldiers' mothers. Your boy Michter is in Somalia, last I heard. I don't expect he'll be influencing much policy from now on.
You were the most powerful person
could have done so much good
You're done.

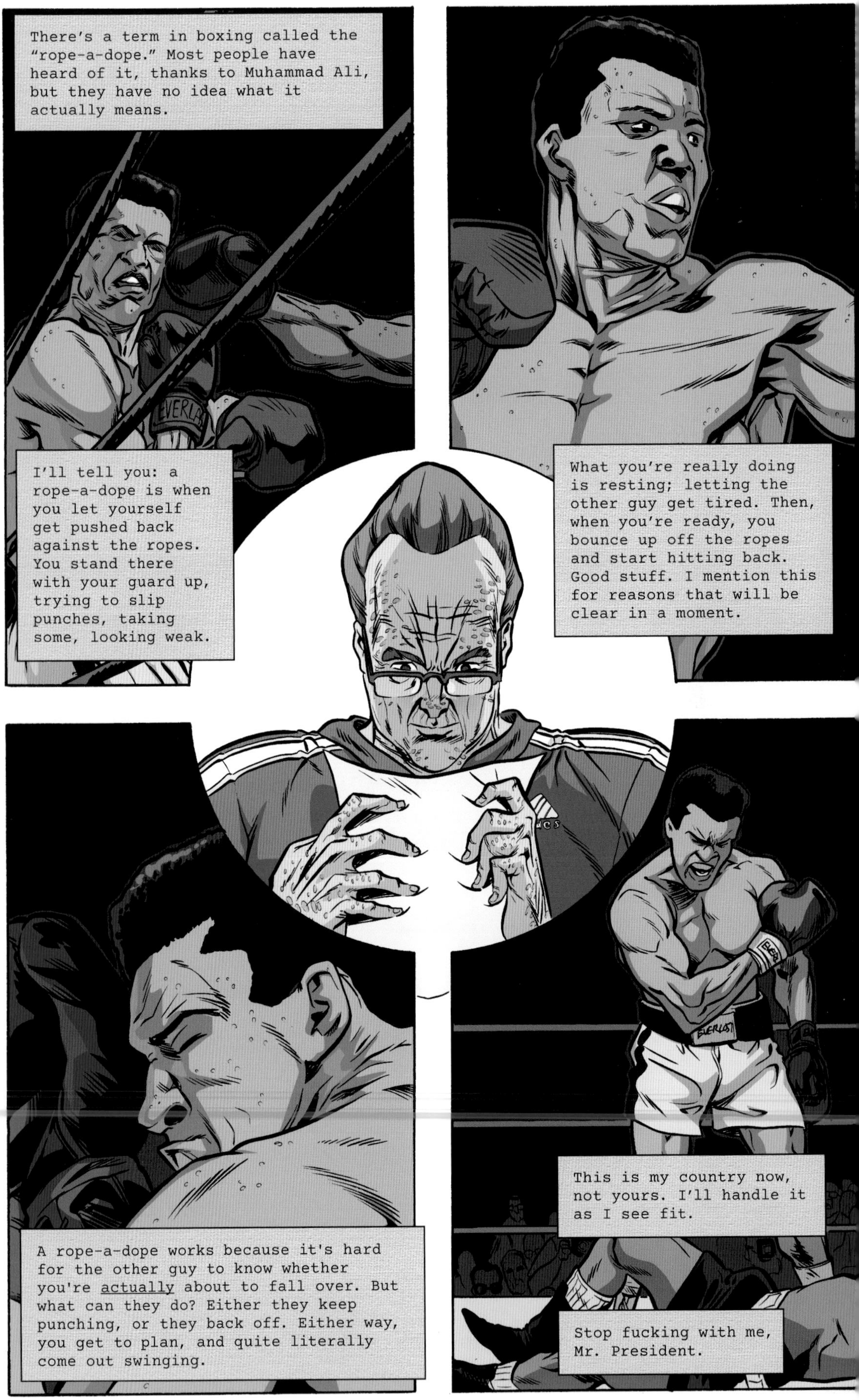
There's a term in boxing called the "rope-a-dope." Most people have heard of it, thanks to Muhammad Ali, but they have no idea what it actually means.
EVERLAST
I'll tell you: a rope-a-dope is when you let yourself get pushed back against the ropes. You stand there with your guard up, trying to slip punches, taking some, looking weak.
What you're really doing is resting; letting the other guy get tired. Then, when you're ready, you bounce up off the ropes and start hitting back. Good stuff. I mention this for reasons that will be clear in a moment.
A rope-a-dope works because it's hard for the other guy to know whether you're actually about to fall over. But what can they do? Either they keep punching, or they back off. Either way, you get to plan, and quite literally come out swinging.
EVERLAST
This is my country now, not yours. I'll handle it as I see fit.
Stop fucking with me, Mr. President.

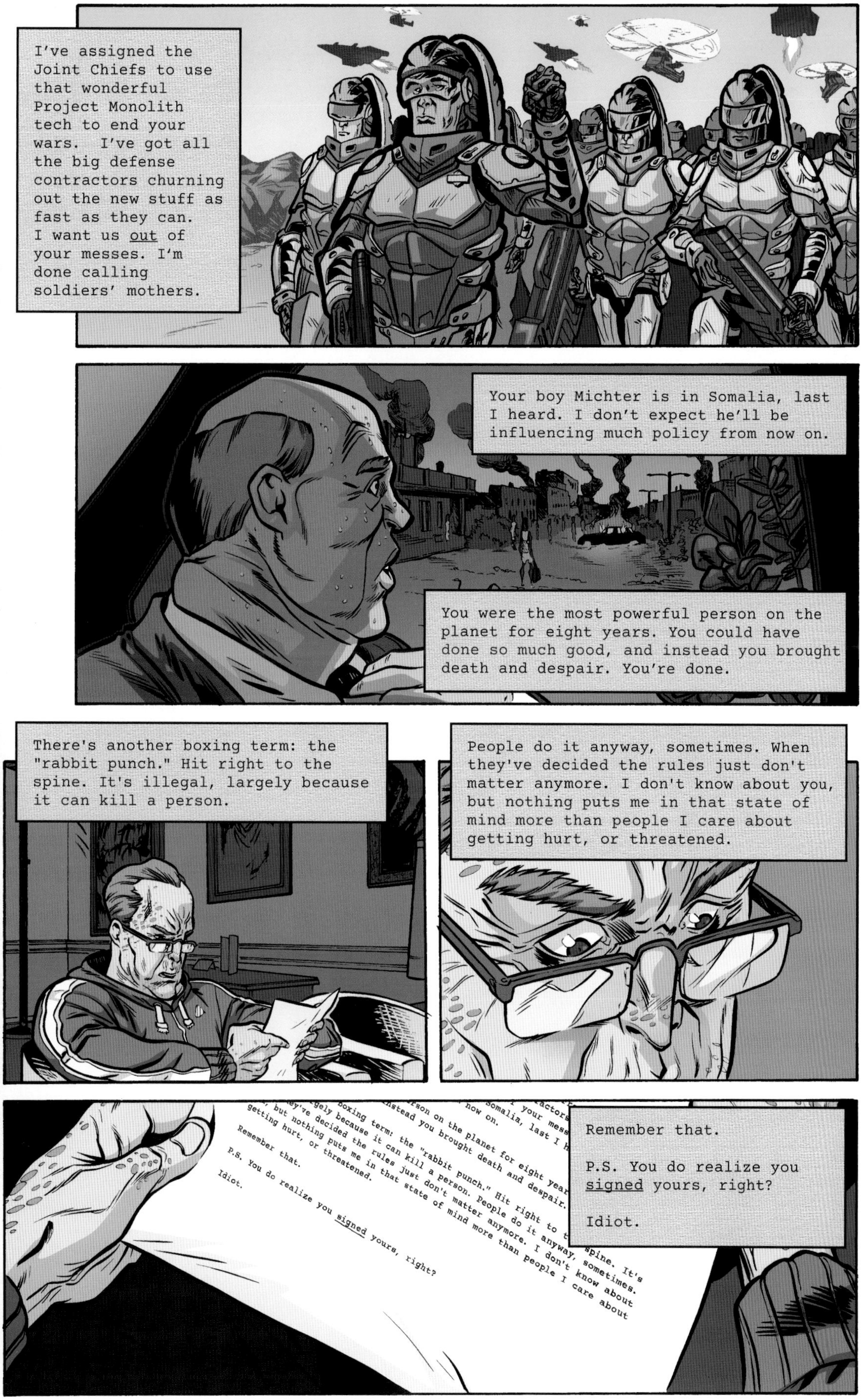

I've assigned the Joint Chiefs to use that wonderful Project Monolith tech to end your wars. I've got all the big defense contractors churning out the new stuff as fast as they can. I want us out of your messes. I'm done calling soldiers' mothers.
Your boy Michter is in Somalia, last I heard. I don't expect he'll be influencing much policy from now on.
You were the most powerful person on the planet for eight years. You could have done so much good, and instead you brought death and despair. You're done.
There's another boxing term: the "rabbit punch." Hit right to the spine. It's illegal, largely because it can kill a person.
People do it anyway, sometimes. When they've decided the rules just don't matter anymore. I don't know about you, but nothing puts me in that state of mind more than people I care about getting hurt, or threatened.
Remember that.
P.S. You do realize you signed yours, right?
Idiot.

I don't know if they just don't think the way we do about security and encryption, but it's all right there--I barely had to try.

The pattern was obvious immediately.

What do you mean, Manesh?

Pritchard, you said they're fractal, right? The whole organism--every piece is a copy of the bigger whole.

That's right.

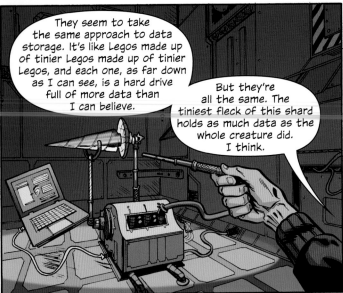

They seem to take the same approach to data storage. It's like Legos made up of tinier Legos made up of tinier Legos, and each one, as far down as I can see, is a hard drive full of more data than I can believe.

But they're all the same. The tiniest fleck of this shard holds as much data as the whole creature did. I think.

It's beautiful.

[142]

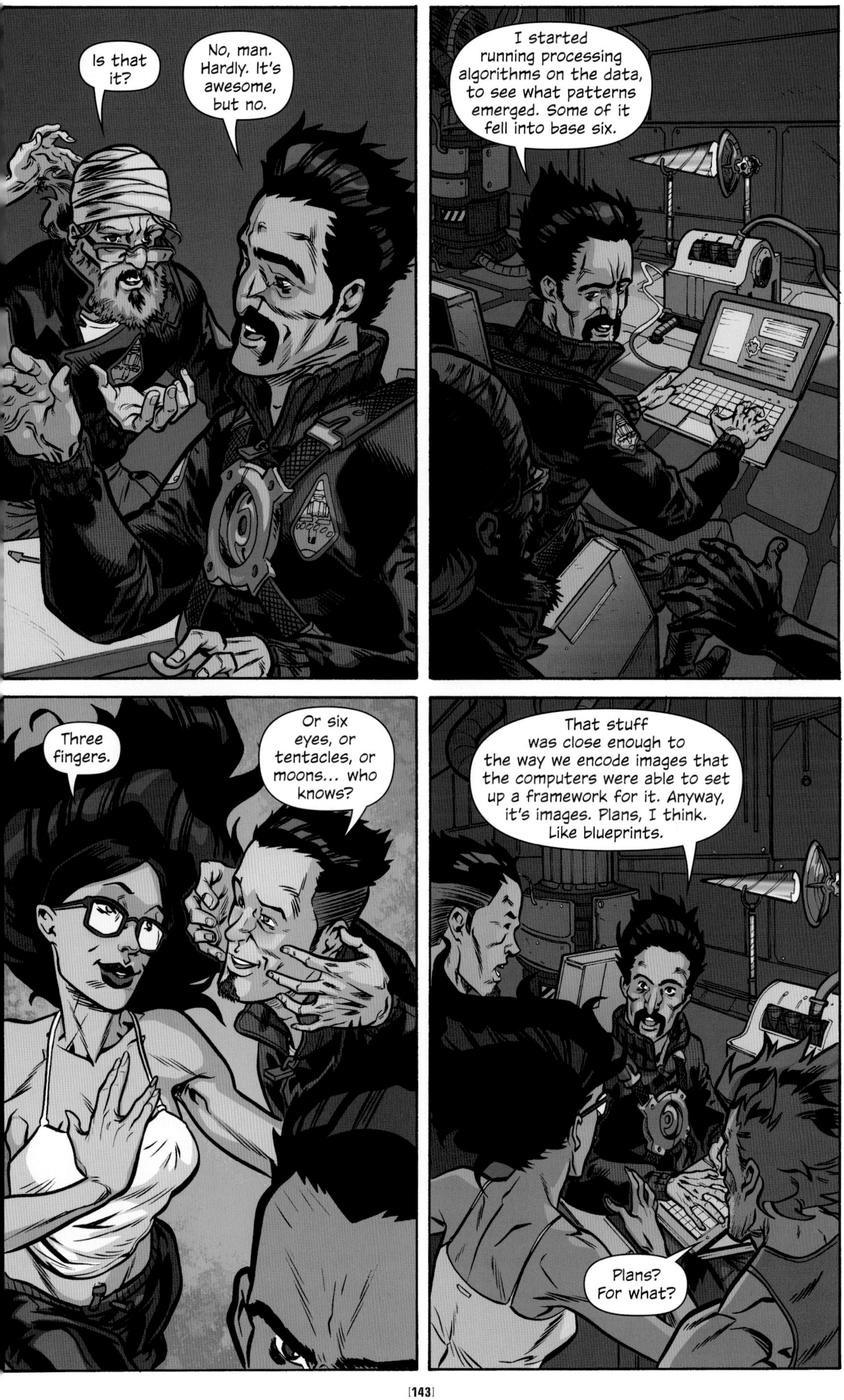
Is that it?
No, man. Hardly. It's awesome, but no.
I started running processing algorithms on the data, to see what patterns emerged. Some of it fell into base six.
Three fingers.
Or six eyes, or tentacles, or moons... who knows?
That stuff was close enough to the way we encode images that the computers were able to set up a framework for it. Anyway, it's images. Plans, I think. Like blueprints.
Plans? For what?

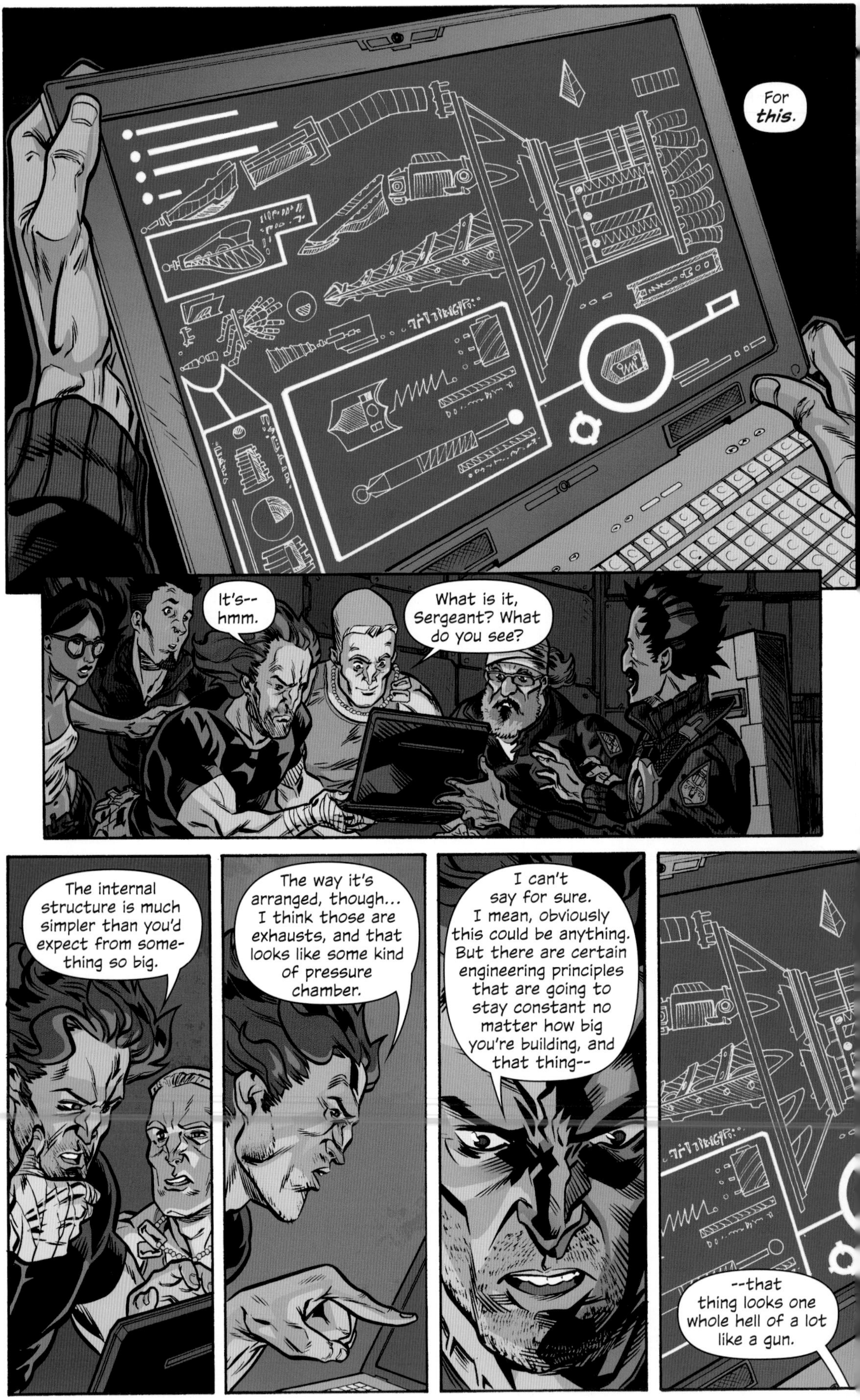

For this.
It's-- hmm.
What is it, Sergeant? What do you see?
The internal structure is much simpler than you'd expect from something so big.
The way it's arranged, though... I think those are exhausts, and that looks like some kind of pressure chamber.
I can't say for sure. I mean, obviously this could be anything. But there are certain engineering principles that are going to stay constant no matter how big you're building, and that thing--
--that thing looks one whole hell of a lot like a gun.

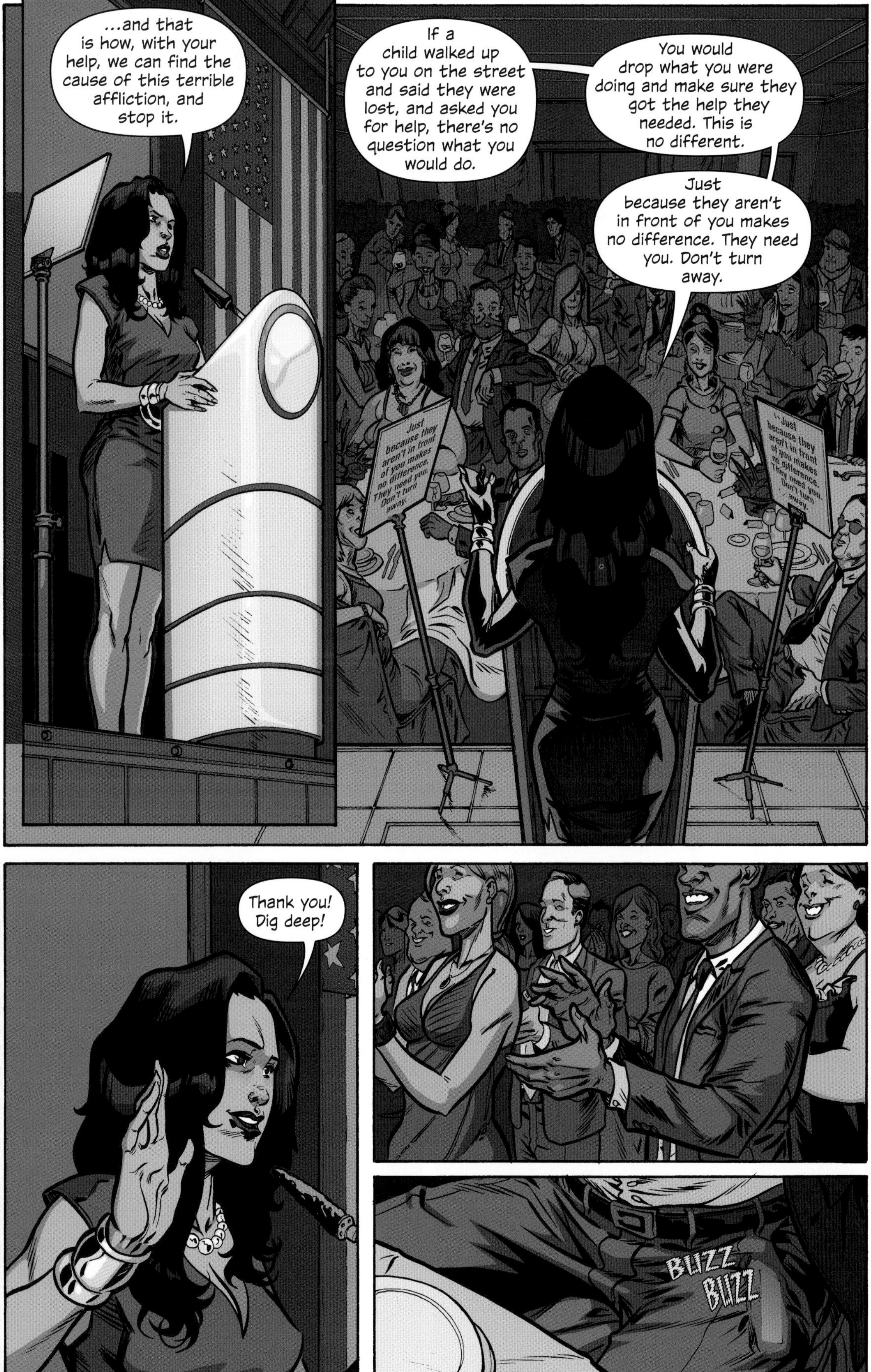

...and that is how, with your help, we can find the cause of this terrible affliction, and stop it.
If a child walked up to you on the street and said they were lost, and asked you for help, there's no question what you would do.
You would drop what you were doing and make sure they got the help they needed. This is no different.
Just because they aren't in front of you makes no difference. They need you. Don't turn away.
Just because they aren't in front of you makes no difference. They need you. Don't turn away.
Just because they aren't in front of you makes no difference. They need you. Don't turn away.
Thank you! Dig deep!
BUZZ BUZZ

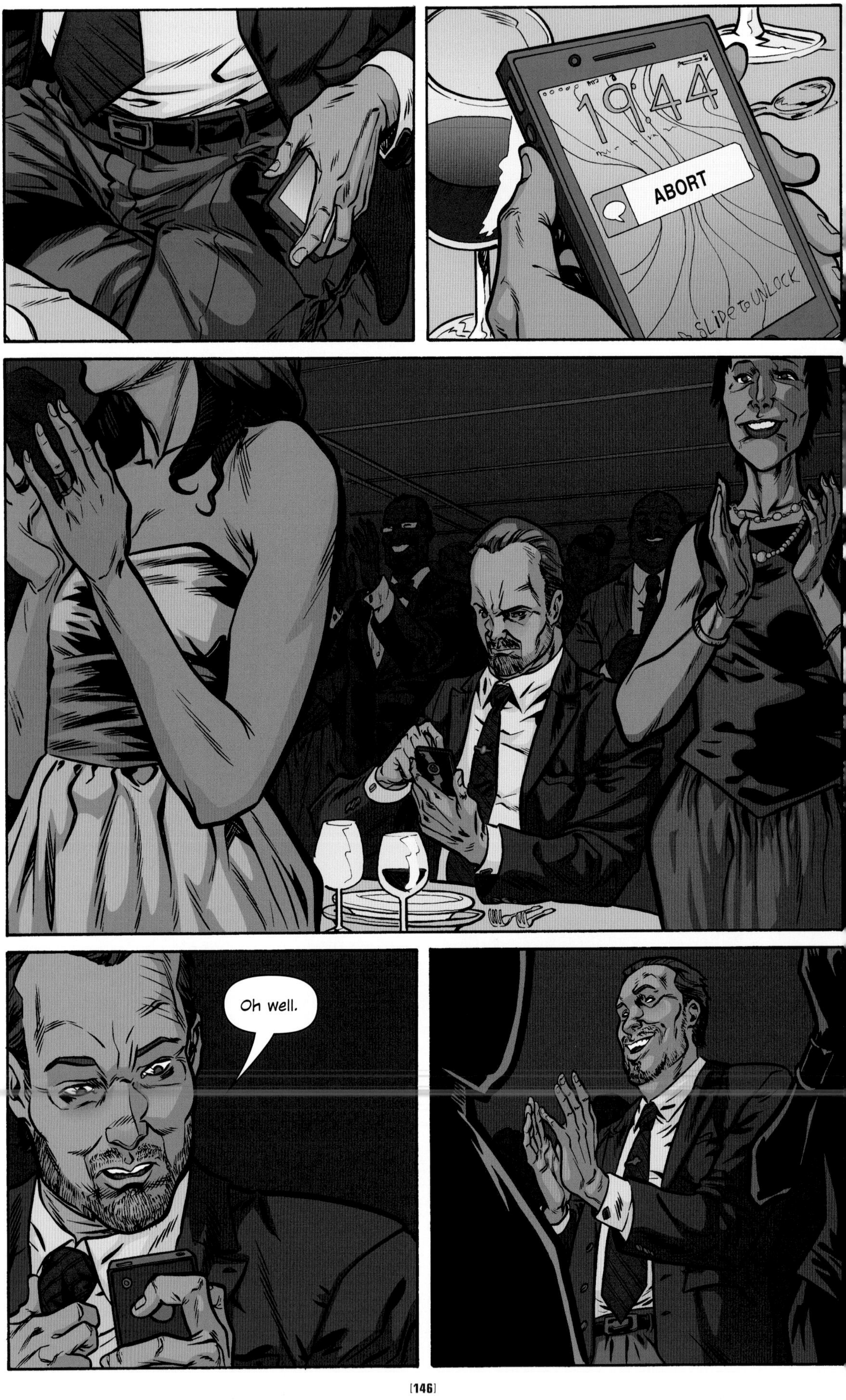
19.44
ABORT
SLIDE to UNLOCK
Oh well.

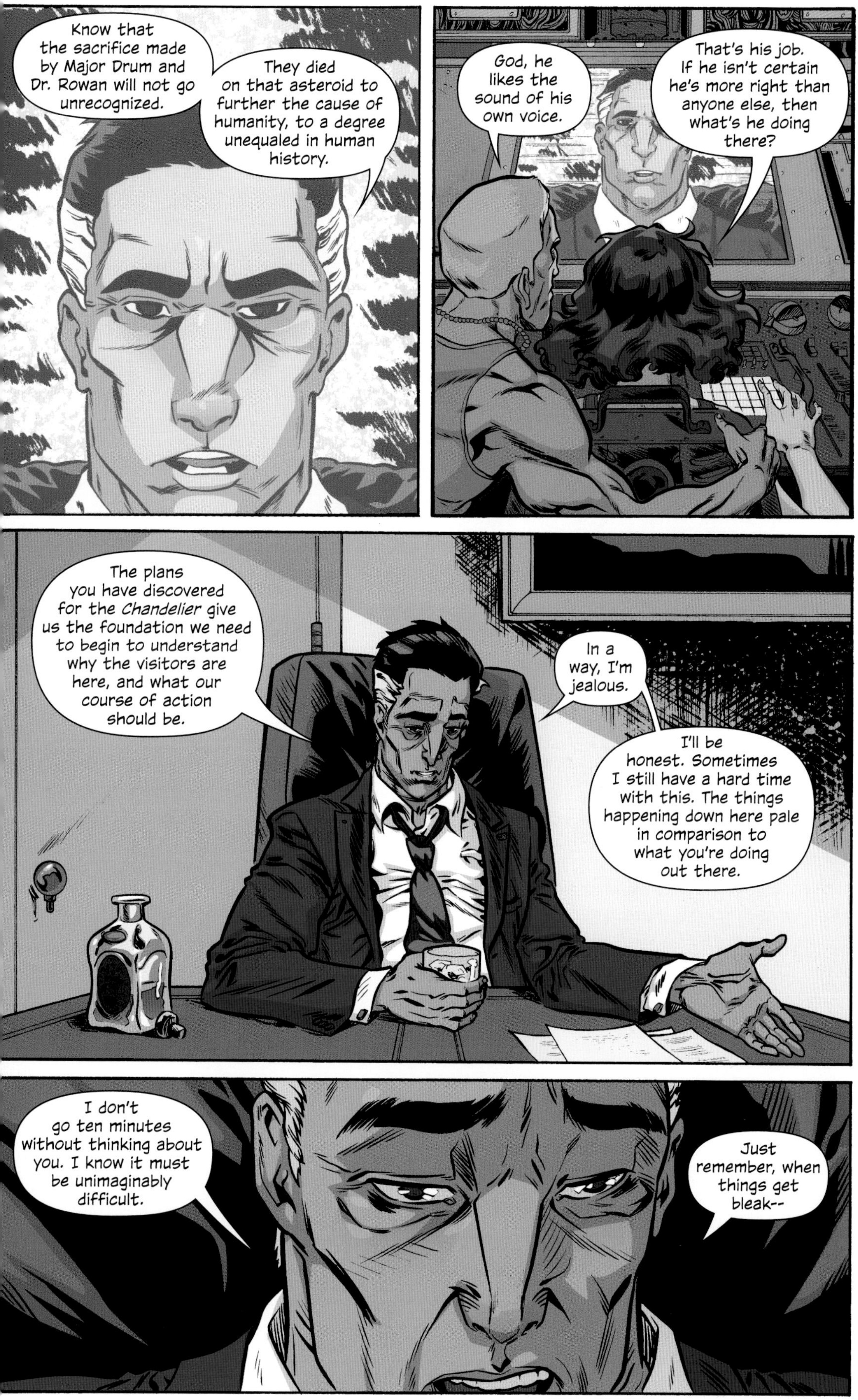

Know that the sacrifice made by Major Drum and Dr. Rowan will not go unrecognized.
They died on that asteroid to further the cause of humanity, to a degree unequaled in human history.
God, he likes the sound of his own voice.
That's his job. If he isn't certain he's more right than anyone else, then what's he doing there?
The plans you have discovered for the *Chandelier* give us the foundation we need to begin to understand why the visitors are here, and what our course of action should be.
In a way, I'm jealous.
I'll be honest. Sometimes I still have a hard time with this. The things happening down here pale in comparison to what you're doing out there.
I don't go ten minutes without thinking about you. I know it must be unimaginably difficult.
Just remember, when things get bleak--

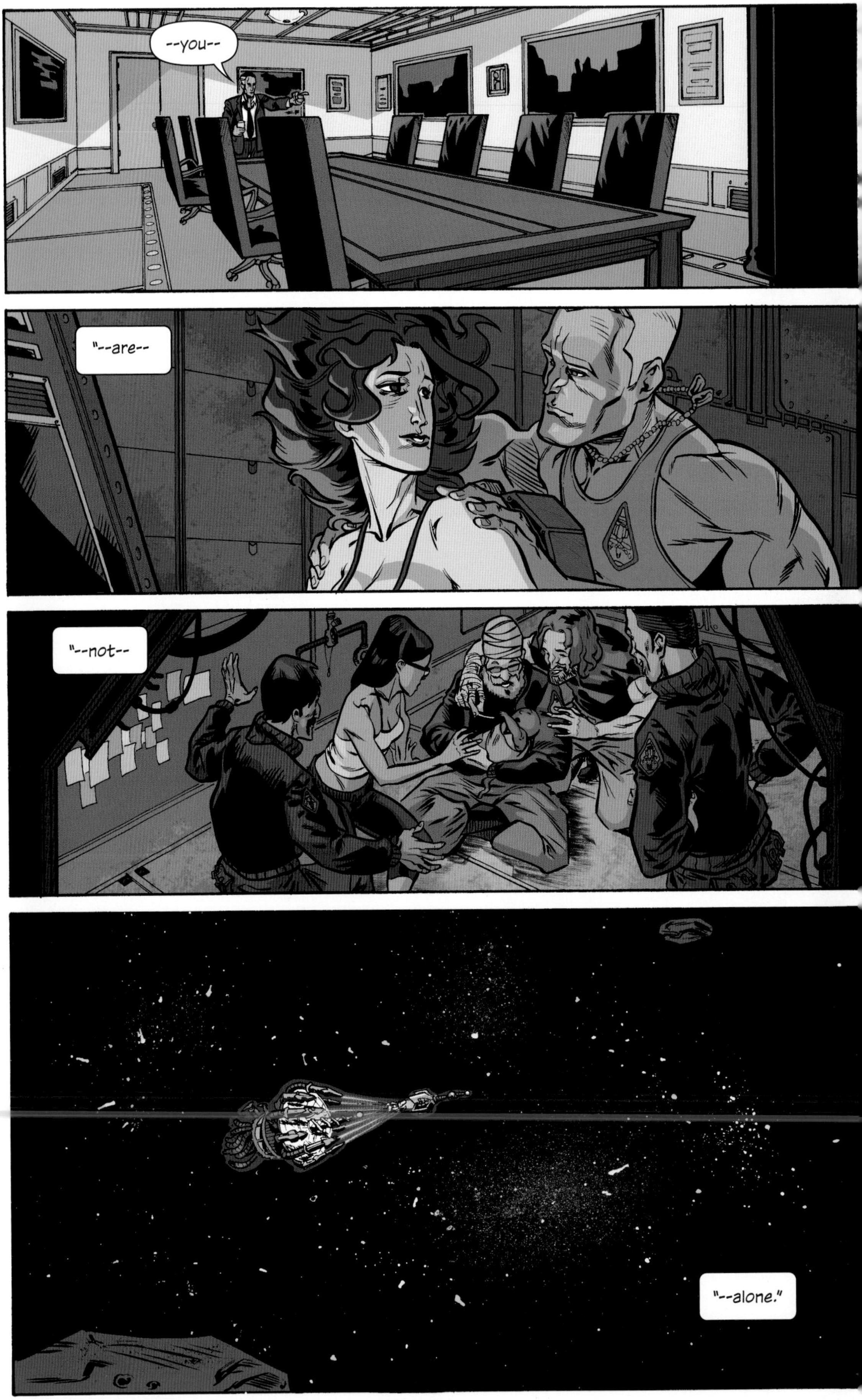
--you--
"--are--
"--not--
"--alone."

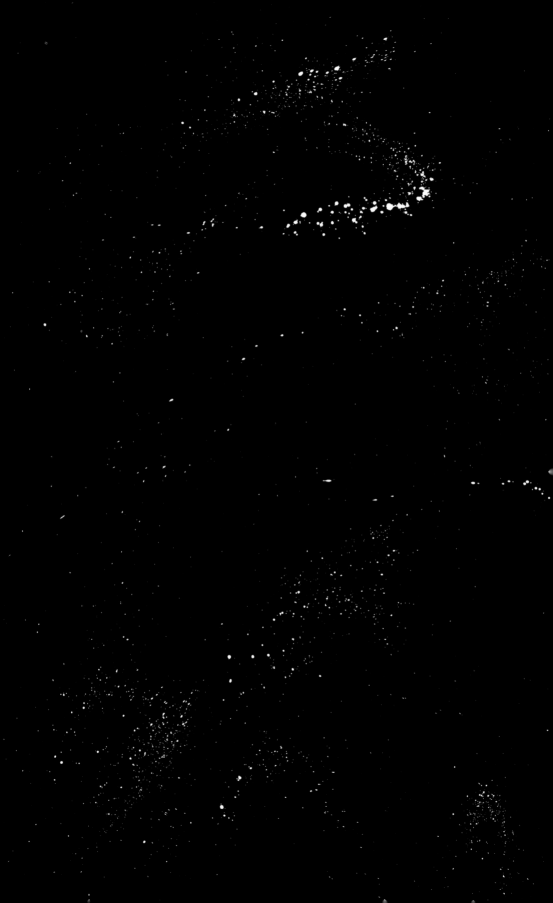

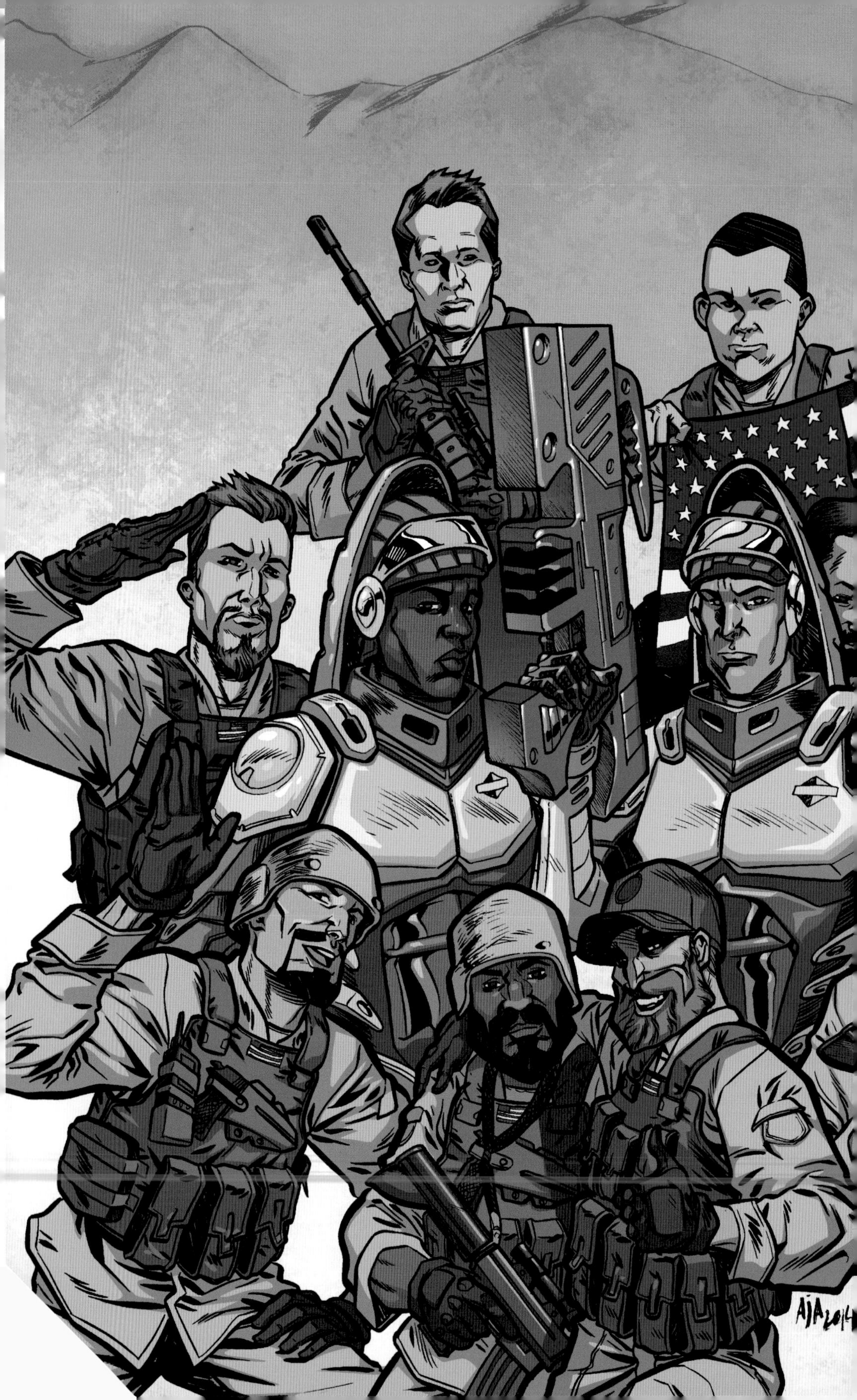
AJA 2014

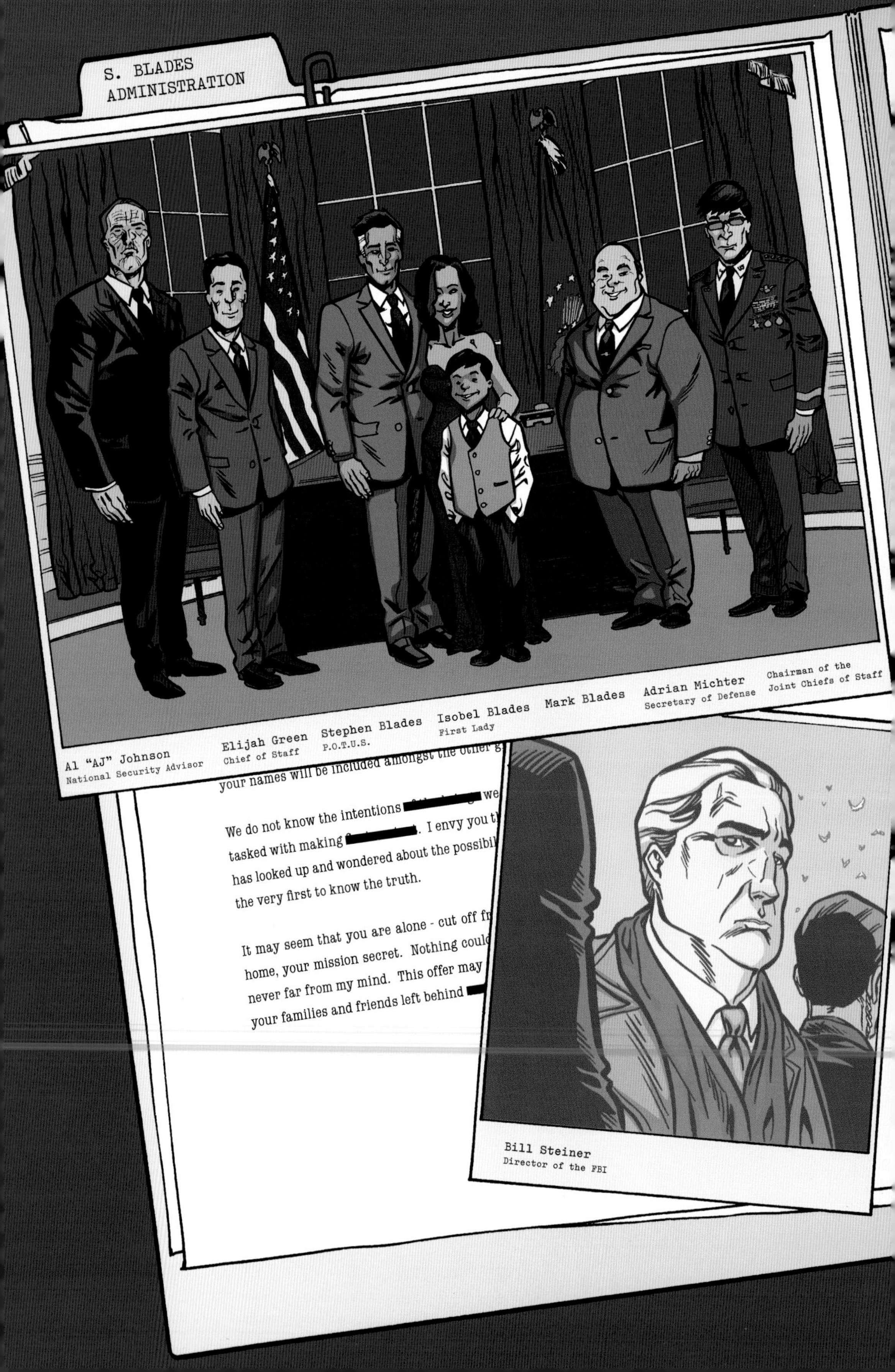

S. BLADES
ADMINISTRATION
Al "AJ" Johnson
National Security Advisor
Elijah Green
Chief of Staff
Stephen Blades
P.O.T.U.S.
Isobel Blades
First Lady
Mark Blades
Adrian Michter
Secretary of Defense
Chairman of the
Joint Chiefs of Staff
your names will be included amongst the other g
We do not know the intentions [redacted] we
tasked with making [redacted]. I envy you th
has looked up and wondered about the possibil
the very first to know the truth.
It may seem that you are alone - cut off fr
home, your mission secret. Nothing could
never far from my mind. This offer may
your families and friends left behind [redacted]
Bill Steiner
Director of the FBI

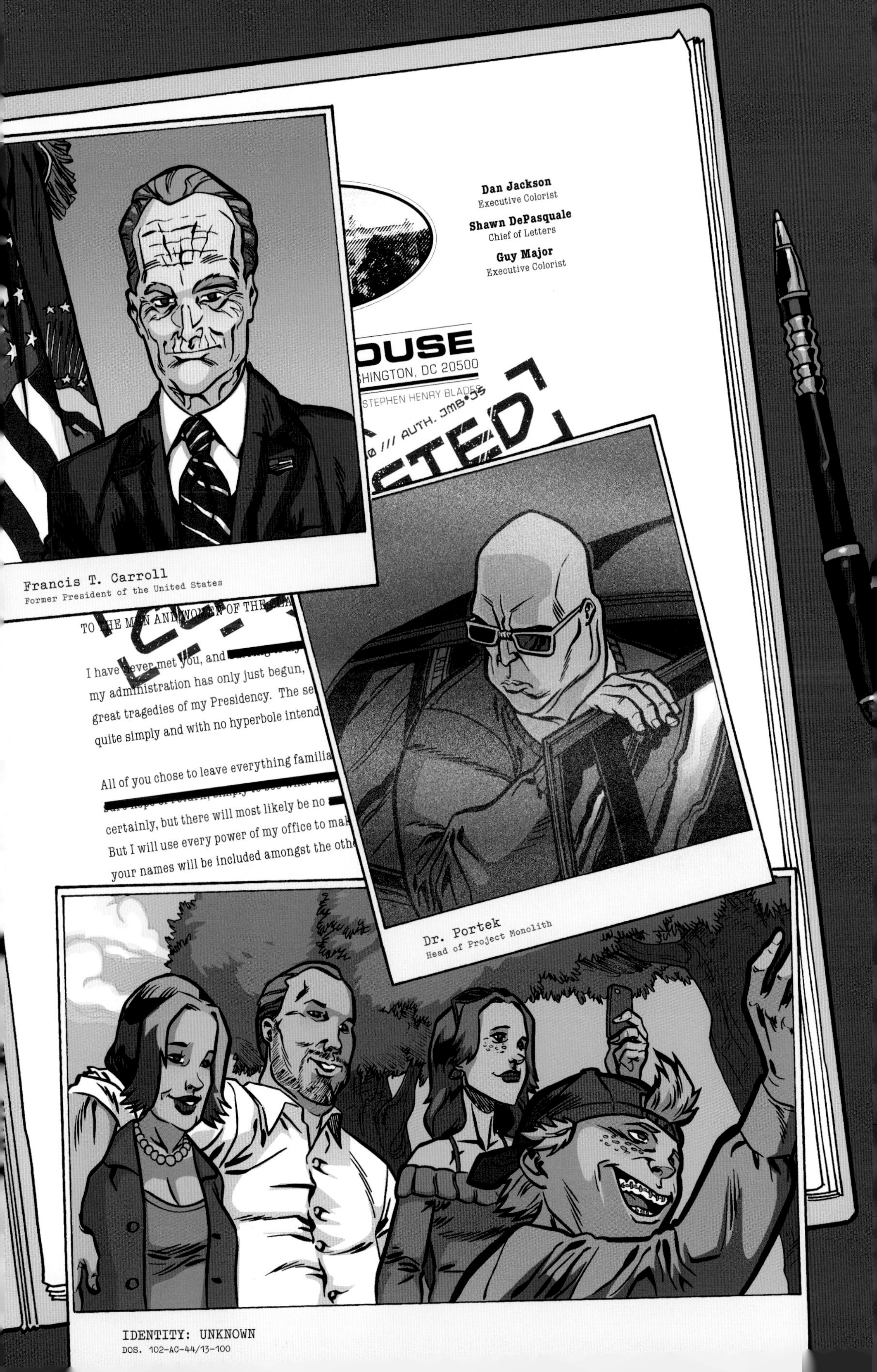
Dan Jackson
Executive Colorist
Shawn DePasquale
Chief of Letters
Guy Major
Executive Colorist
OUSE
SHINGTON, DC 20500
STEPHEN HENRY BLADES
0 /// AUTH. JMB*JS
CTED
Francis T. Carroll
Former President of the United States
TO THE MEN AND WOMEN OF THE
I have never met you, and [redacted]
my administration has only just begun,
great tragedies of my Presidency. The se
quite simply and with no hyperbole intend
All of you chose to leave everything familia
[redacted]
certainly, but there will most likely be no [redacted]
But I will use every power of my office to mak
your names will be included amongst the othe
Dr. Portek
Head of Project Monolith
IDENTITY: UNKNOWN
DOS. 102-AC-44/13-100

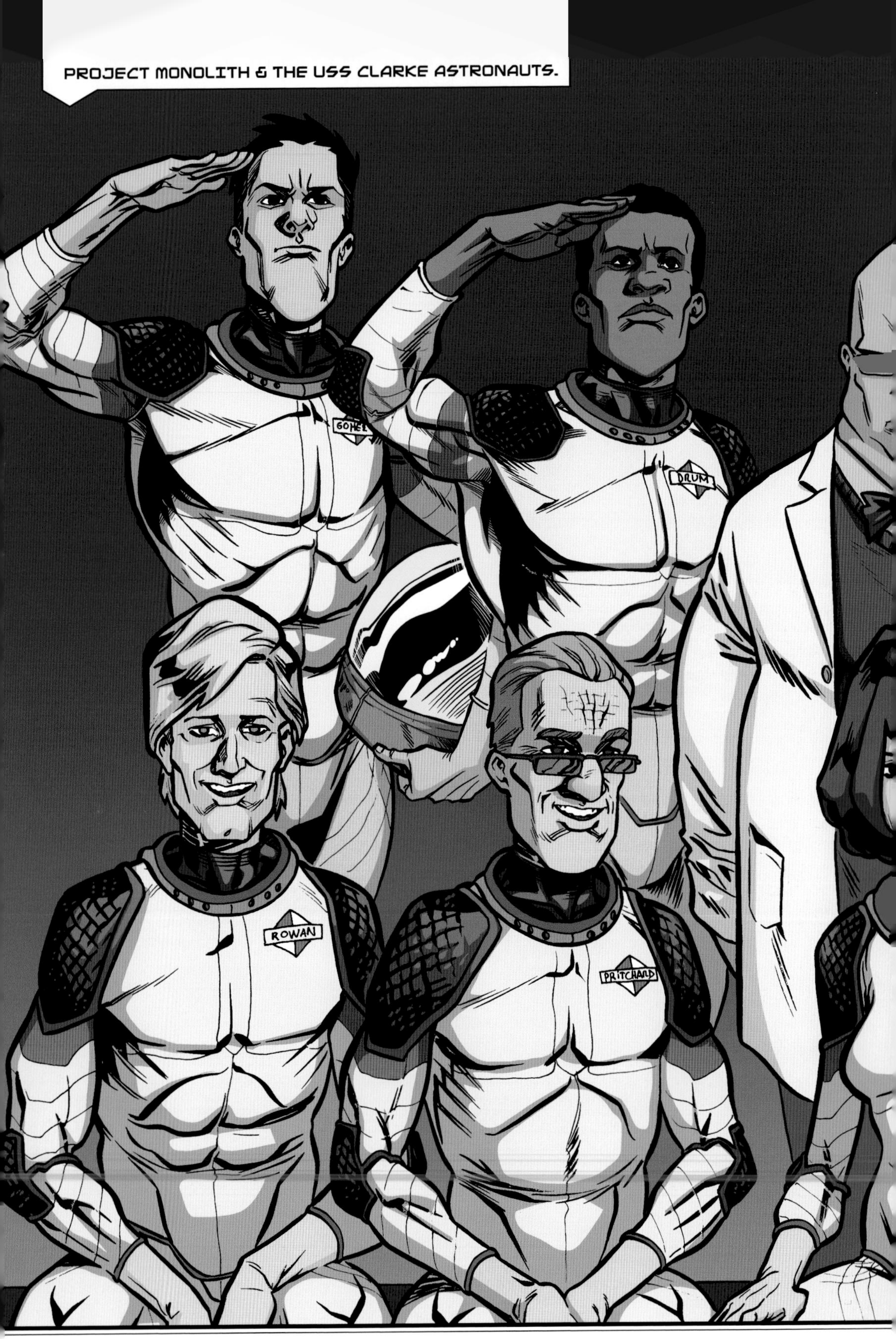
PROJECT MONOLITH & THE USS CLARKE ASTRONAUTS.
GOMEZ
DRUM
ROWAN
PRITCHARD

TOP ROW (FROM LEFT TO RIGHT):

LIEUTENANT ALBERTO GOMEZ, MAJOR GABRIEL DRUM, DR. PORTEK (HEAD OF PROJECT MONOLITH), **COLONEL JACK OVERHOLT, SERGEANT JOHN WILLET**

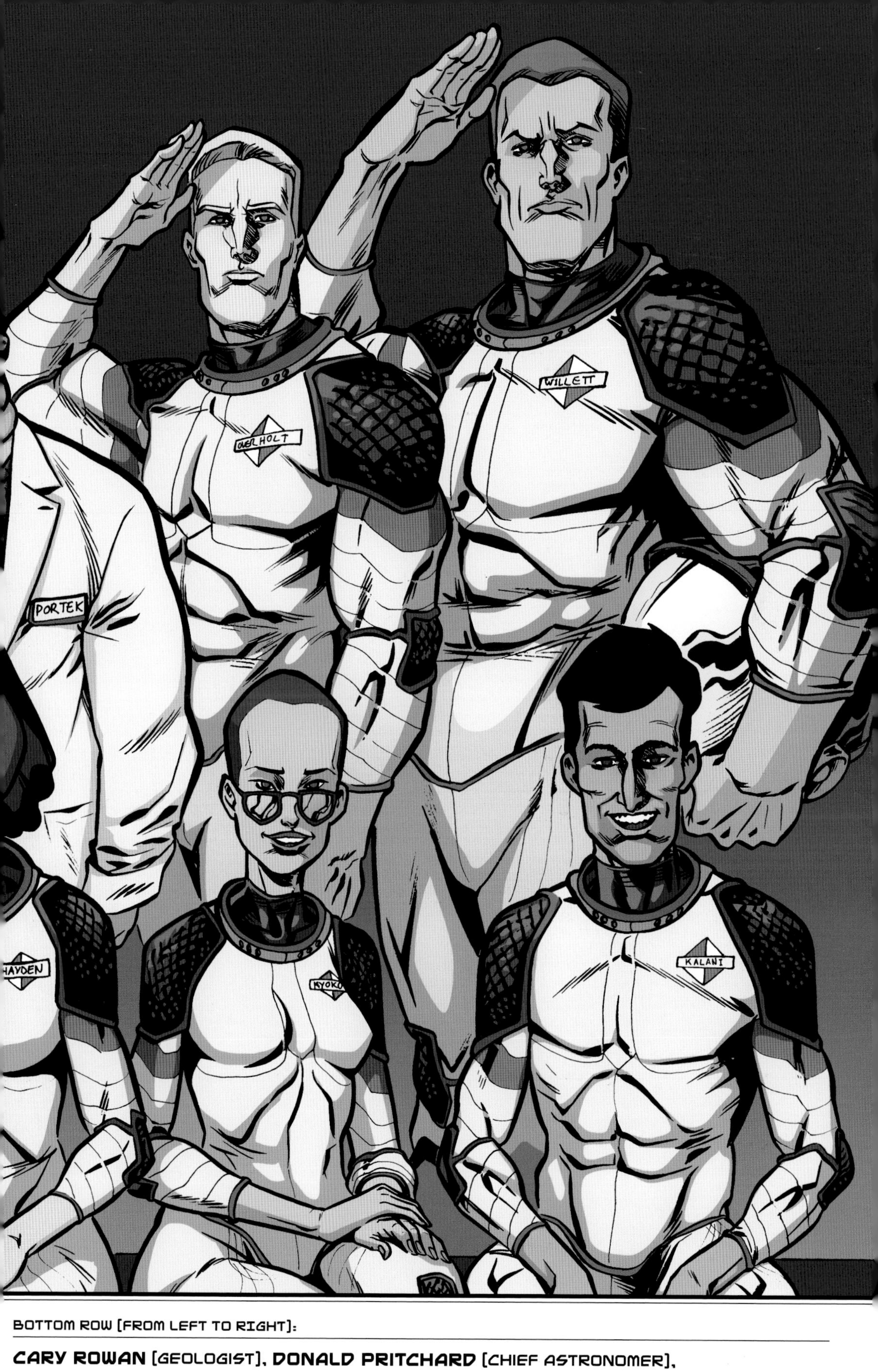

OVERHOLT
WILLETT
PORTEK
HAYDEN
KYOKO
KALANI

BOTTOM ROW [FROM LEFT TO RIGHT]:

CARY ROWAN [GEOLOGIST], **DONALD PRITCHARD** [CHIEF ASTRONOMER], **CHARLOTTE HAYDEN** [SENIOR MISSION COMMANDER], **KYOKO TAKAMURA** [DOCTOR], **MANESH KALANI** [LINGUIST AND COMPUTER SPECIALIST]

Charles Soule
Writer-In-Chief

Alberto J. Alburquerque
Executive Artist

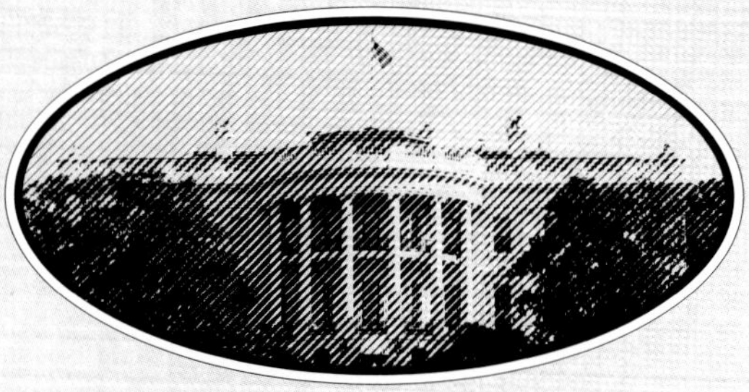

Dan Jackson
Executive Colorist

Shawn DePasquale
Chief of Letters

Guy Major
Executive Colorist

THE WHITE HOUSE

1600 PENNSYLVANIA AVE NW, WASHINGTON, DC 20500

FROM THE DESK OF THE 44TH PRESIDENT, STEPHEN HENRY BLADES

NAME:

Charles Soule

LOCATION:

Brooklyn, NY, United States of America

BIO:

CLASSIFIED

Charles Soule was born in the Midwest but often wishes he had been born in space. He lives in Brooklyn, and has written a wide variety of titles for a variety of publishers, including others' characters (*Swamp Thing, Superman/Wonder Woman, Red Lanterns* (DC); *Thunderbolts, She-Hulk, Inhuman* (Marvel)); and his own: *27* (Image); *Strongman* (SLG) and *Strange Attractors* (Archaia). When not writing –which is rare–he runs a law practice and works, writes and performs as a musician.

One of his biggest regrets is never personally witnessing a Space Shuttle launch.

Charles Soule
Writer-In-Chief

Alberto J. Alburquerque
Executive Artist

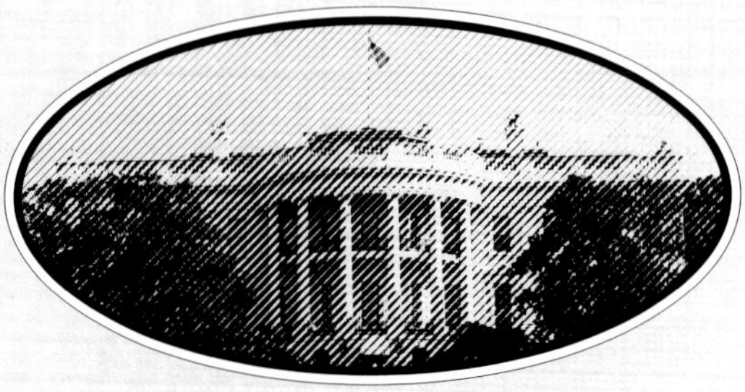

Dan Jackson
Executive Colorist

Shawn DePasquale
Chief of Letters

Guy Major
Executive Colorist

THE WHITE HOUSE

1600 PENNSYLVANIA AVE NW, WASHINGTON, DC 20500

FROM THE DESK OF THE 44TH PRESIDENT, STEPHEN HENRY BLADES

NAME:

Alberto Jiménez Alburquerque

LOCATION:

Madrid, Spain

BIO:

CLASSIFIED

Alberto Jiménez Alburquerque (AJA) is an artist born, raised and currently living in Madrid, Spain. He has put lines in French comic-books (BD's) for almost a decade now, working for Paquet Ed. and Soleil Ed. Some of his titles are: *Fugitifs de l'Ombre* (Paquet), *Le Dieu des Cendres* (Soleil), and *Elle* (Soleil). He has also drawn some short stories for the American comics *Skull Kickers* (Image) and *Pathfinder's Goblins* (Dynamite). He's currently the regular artist in the new series *Letter 44* (Oni Press) with writer Charles Soule and is starting a new project for the French market with Glènat Ed.

Charles Soule
Writer-In-Chief

Alberto J. Alburquerque
Executive Artist

Dan Jackson
Executive Colorist

Shawn DePasquale
Chief of Letters

Guy Major
Executive Colorist

THE
WHITE HOUSE
1600 PENNSYLVANIA AVE NW, WASHINGTON, DC 20500

FROM THE DESK OF THE 44TH PRESIDENT, STEPHEN HENRY BLADES

NAME:

Dan Jackson

LOCATION:

Portland, Oregon, United States of America

BIO:

What is the most unfair thing you can think of? Got it in your head? Okay, forget that because there's a worse one: There's this guy who gets paid money for coloring comic books. Right. Dan Jackson has been gainfully employed to one degree or another with the coloring of comic books for the better part of 17 years. He's done other Great Big Projects with the fine folks at Oni Press, and he's done a bunch of covers and short projects with them as well. He's a pretty versatile guy. Even writes his own bios.

Mr. Jackson lives in the beautiful Pacific Northwest with his scorching hot wife (see? UN-FAIR!), and two hilarious kids.

MORE BOOKS FROM ONI PRESS

THE
BUNKER

THE BUNKER: VOLUME 1

**BY JOSHUA HALE FIALKOV
AND JOE INFURNARI**

136 PAGES /// SOFTCOVER /// COLOR INTERIORS

ISBN 978-1-62010-164-3

GUERILLAS
VOLUME 1
BRAHM REVEL

GUERILLAS: VOLUME 1

BY BRAHM REVEL

168 PAGES /// SOFTCOVER /// B&W INTERIORS

ISBN 978-1-934964-43-9

GREG RUCKA
QUEEN & COUNTRY
01

QUEEN AND COUNTRY DEFINITIVE EDITION: VOLUME 1

**BY GREG RUCKA, STEVE ROLSTON,
BRIAN HURTT, AND LEANDRO FERNANDEZ**

376 PAGES /// SOFTCOVER /// B&W INTERIORS

ISBN 978-1-932664-87-4

THE SIXTH GUN
BUNN
HURTT

THE SIXTH GUN: VOLUME 1 COLD DEAD FINGERS

**BY CULLEN BUNN, BRIAN HURTT,
AND BILL CRABTREE**

176 PAGES /// SOFTCOVER /// COLOR INTERIORS

ISBN 978-1-934964-60-6

WASTELAND
BOOK 01

WASTELAND: VOLUME 1

**BY ANTONY JOHNSTON
AND CHRISTOPHER MITTEN**

160 PAGES /// SOFTCOVER /// B&W INTERIORS

ISBN 978-1-932664-59-1

STUMPTOWN

STUMPTOWN: VOLUME 1

**BY GREG RUCKA
AND MATTHEW SOUTHWORTH**

160 PAGES /// HARDCOVER /// COLOR INTERIORS

ISBN 978-1-934964-37-8

ONI PRESS
www.onipress.com

FOR MORE INFORMATION ON THESE AND OTHER FINE ONI PRESS COMIC BOOKS AND GRAPHIC NOVELS, VISIT WWW.ONIPRESS.COM. TO FIND A COMIC SPECIALTY STORE IN YOUR AREA, CALL 1-888-COMICBOOK OR VISIT WWW.COMICSHOPS.US.